The
Story
of the
English
Garden

Ambra Edwards

The Story of the English Garden

National Trust

Page 2: The walled rose garden at Mottisfont, Hampshire.
Right: The double border in the Walled Garden at Felbrigg Hall, Norfolk.

First published in the United Kingdom in 2018 by
National Trust Books
43 Great Ormond Street
London
WC1N 3HZ

An imprint of Pavilion Books Company Ltd

ISBN 978-1-91135-825-1

A CIP catalogue record for this book is available from the British Library.

10 9 8 7 6 5 4 3 2 1

Reproduction by Colour Depth, UK
Printed and bound by 1010 Printing
International Ltd, China

This book can be ordered direct from
the publisher at www.pavilionbooks.com

8–9 Baddesley Clinton, Warwickshire. 32–33 Lyveden New Bield, Northamptonshire. 52–53 Ham House and Garden, London. 84–85 Stourhead, Wiltshire. 130–131 Petworth, West Sussex 166–167 Biddulph Grange Garden, Staffordshire. 212–213 Great Dixter House and Gardens, East Sussex. 242–243 Sissinghurst Castle Garden, Kent 264–265 Barrington Court, Somerset. 280–281 Wildside Nursery, Yelverton, Devon

CONTENTS

INTRODUCTION

LIKE many people, I took little interest in gardens until I had one of my own. But finding myself the proud owner of a tablecloth-sized patch of South London, I started visiting gardens, notebook in hand, to try to work out how to turn this scruffy plot into some vision of loveliness. An early part of my garden education were the gardens of the National Trust. I vividly remember my first visit to Sissinghurst, where I devoured not only exciting new plants and plant combinations but the story of the garden's creators, and realised that a garden could be so much more than a pleasing form of exterior decoration. A garden, I saw, could be a powerful medium for personal expression. It could tell a story of love, longing and relationship as vividly as any piece of theatre, and using far more complex elements – not only plants and architecture but water, light, time and season.

And so began my fascination with the stories behind gardens. A garden is a window on a world – it can tell us what the people who made it valued, what they aspired to, what they believed in, what they considered to be cutting-edge or exotic or beautiful. It tells us about politics, economics, religion, taste, fashion – also about changing social and economic structures, the balance of the sexes, education, transport, the history of exploration, or simply what people liked to eat.

Why is one garden formal, clipped and symmetrical, while another is loose and naturalistic? Why does this one reach out to the surrounding countryside, while that one is secret and enclosed? Why do some gardens consist of little other than grass, water and trees, while others are packed with bizarre buildings or exotic plants? What did people want from the gardens they made?

Although this can be no more than the most perfunctory introduction to this most intriguing and wide-ranging of subjects, I hope it will give just an inkling of the variety, artistry and delight of England's gardens. And I hope that by understanding a little more about who made them, and when and why, readers will find their enjoyment deepened when they visit.

In such a brief account, both many gardens and many people deserving of greater attention have been missed out. (Do look up Harriet Luxborough, or Mary, first Duchess of Beaufort.) Most painfully, because my title was The Story of the English Garden, I have made but one fragrant foray over the border, and have had to exclude important gardens in Scotland, Wales and Ireland. My apologies therefore to the likes of Bodnant and Powis Castle, Ilnacullin and Mount Stewart, and especially to Portrack and Little Sparta – two of the most significant gardens of the 20th century. I urge you to visit them too – along with as many as you can of the exciting gardens being made right now. The story of the English garden is long and colourful, and the chapter we are living through now could be the best yet.

The cottage garden at Sissinghurst in Kent.

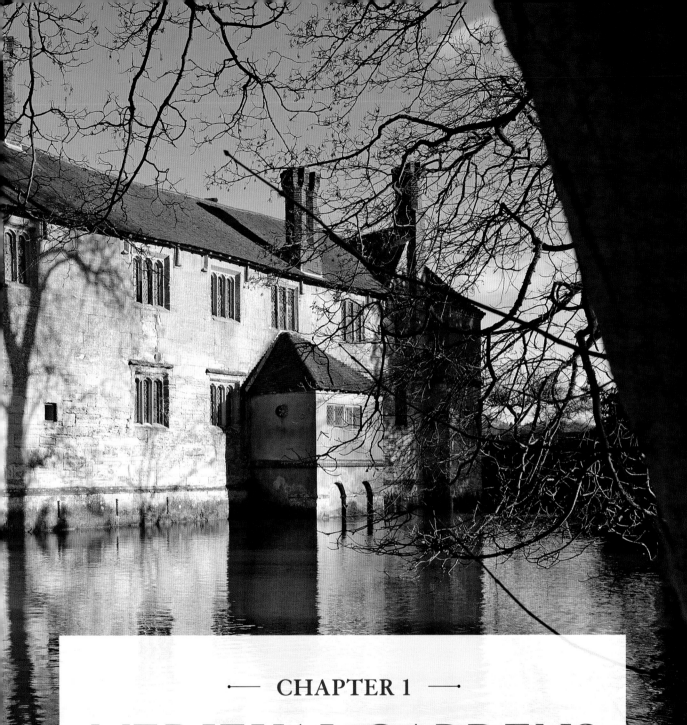

CHAPTER 1

MEDIEVAL GARDENS

A GARDEN ENCLOSED

UP TO 1500

'A garden enclosed is my sister, my spouse ...'

SONG OF SOLOMON

WHERE does the English garden begin? In a silvery glade on a Cumbrian riverbank where the face of a pre-Roman goddess is cut into the rock, still unmistakably a sacred grove? In the mugwort and crab apples planted by the roundhouse door, to keep disease at bay and blend into potent charms? In the old Celtic legends of a garden island of eternal youth, far away across the Western seas?

Britain in 1000BC was not, as we long imagined, a Tolkienish land of ancient forest stretching from Land's End to John o'Groats, but rather a patchwork of scattered farmsteads, intensively managed woodlands and open fields, not so very different from the landscape of 200 years ago. The first gardens we know about in England are the Roman ones, as following the occupation, these small farms gave way to extensive agricultural estates, some owned by British tribal leaders who prospered under Roman rule, some granted to army veterans and some held on behalf of the Emperor. Generally these were orchards and kitchen gardens keeping largely self-sufficient farmsteads supplied with a wide range of foodstuffs entirely new to Britain, but the most prestigious villas also had formal ornamental gardens, as at Chedworth in Gloucestershire and Fishbourne in West Sussex.

This sophisticated manner of gardening did not long survive the fall of Empire: the cultures of the Saxons, Jutes and Danes celebrated the glories of war rather than the fruits of peace. But some small part of this knowledge and plant material lived on, guarded in the monasteries that proliferated from the seventh century, when Christianity, all but driven out by the pagan invaders, made an energetic comeback in Britain. Wealthy and well-defended, the monasteries were oases of stability and civility in warlike times.

Opposite: One of the oldest known depictions of mugwort, from a 13th-century herbal in the British Museum. Mugwort was one of the seven sacred herbs of the Anglo-Saxons.

Right: At Kirklinton in Cumbria, surrounded by ancient woodland, the face of a Romano-British goddess is carved into the cliff above the river, presiding over a still pool where two streams meet. Clearly once a sacred grove, the otherworldly atmosphere is palpable.

10

Ambra ca. e. 7 sic. i secdo. gu. Ambra dr
cee spma crti cete 7 balene. alii dicut ee
alii dicit qd sit dscecudina q emittit post ha
tu hec aut falsu est. Illo aut cu ipuru e
7 sanguinolentu ht colores. Ambra aut est
alba 7 si suediatur crisei coloris melior est
nigru nichil ualet. Sophisticat aut au
pluere ligni aloes 7 storac cal 7 laudano
resoluut i aq. ros. addito mco. 7 appoita
ambra i modica quttitate. Agnoscatur aut
sophisticati qr pot malaxai ut cera. vera
aut no. virtute ht ofortdi 7 diu suai pot.
Cot sincopi fiat pill. ex. z. i. anbre. 7. z. i.
ligni aloes 7 z. ii. ossis deord. cruii. qr trita
resoluat cu aq. ro. fiat pill. dg accipiat duo
ul tres cu uadit dormitu. Cot epilentia
pon ambra ossis deord cui i uase uitreo sup
carbones poat 7 paties recipiat fumu por
7 nares 7 mltu ualet. Cot suffocationem
matricis qn aptimit spualia. ponatur
simlr i uase uitreo cu aliis aromatic ul
sola abra 7 recipiatur p fumus por ul
ue. fetida uo p nares recipiat sic e licitu
ul i olo itictu accensu 7 extitu 7 nariis
appositu. Solu mo liqrio tali olo itictu
accesu 7 extitu 7 nariis appoitu 7 purgat
7 libauit qda nobile. Rota qd ot matri
cis ciis obr por iten fetida uo supi. Arro
matici d suffocaties 7 ouerso.

Artemisia tria sut gna hz maior ye
media 7 minor. d arthmisia maior nuc
dicam. virtute ht ca. 7 sic. i tertio gu.
alio noie dr mater hrbar romani uocant
Regia omani uocat kaniskelli. alii toxo
ter. alii Epesia. alii parthnicii. alii apoli
los Simachi uocit arthmiseo. alii socusa
alii liopias. pseti uocit Entropu. alii se
trese. alii onicatisca. alii leonisis. alii
subaltes. alii ostantopu. alii emeronu
alii Eonostesetus. alii filacterion. alii
serasa. egipti uocit alsabasar. alii toxo
dulus. alii uocit canapaccia. Nasatur
locis sablosis 7 i motibz 7 i fortis. Ht so
lia subalbida 7 loga. asimilat emapa. Ar
thmisia maior folia et 7 flores. so pue rd
petit usu medie. qua radix. viirida mag
qua exiccata exiccata uo p anu possunt
suari. valet dt sterilatio sterilatio q sit
ex humiditate. Satis pot pendi ex splen
one mulieris sisit piguis an macileta d
dbet plueigari. arthmisia cu radice hrte
q dr bistorta 7 cu nuce mscati sifit eade
quttitate. oficiale pluis cu mell simplia rdt
ad modu elli maii 7 sero cu uino doctioi
arthmisie. prost cu macis si bulneet i aq
ubi cocta fuet arthmisia 7 folia lauri
ul si fomentet cytali aq. valet d arthmisia
cocti i olo coi ul olo nucu. Cadmestrua
pucciiu fiat pessarii. exsico ei ul ei toctio
pessariget. Cot tetasmo cefrate paties fumu
colodmie posite sup carbones pani recipiat
drn cuesat arthmisia sup rogula 7 caltsan
poat sup lapizi molarez 7 sup sedoat isir
mus pb e. Cot gladula q nascut inf auru
q uocet atti fiat ipi soirificatio pa puatur
dsup pluis arthmisie 7 marubii. Cot emi
granei 7 cephalei dt aliq aq opiata calida
cu uino doctiois arthmisie. Cot se hrta ar
thmisia quiciq seu portauet i uiatico no
se fatiorus ut diat macro. Jt ualet dt malo
medicamites 7 aduertit oculos dmalo 7
osa dmonia fuguit aduersus eu uiciq ipa
hrba fuet. Cot dol pedu hr arthmisia bn
trita cu axugia 7 suppoista mirabr dol tollit
Cadol ictimor hr arthmisia fac puluee
7 cu mlsa potui dab mir dol tollit. 7 admt
tas alias i firmitates sbuenit hc diat m
mac. Cadmestruis 7 matricis. arthmisia
dety 7 aq 7 potui dab. Jt fumigatio exci
ten receptu ocestrua pucat. Ct uiuu ur
nonis ei sepe bibitu oyulicib no dimittit.

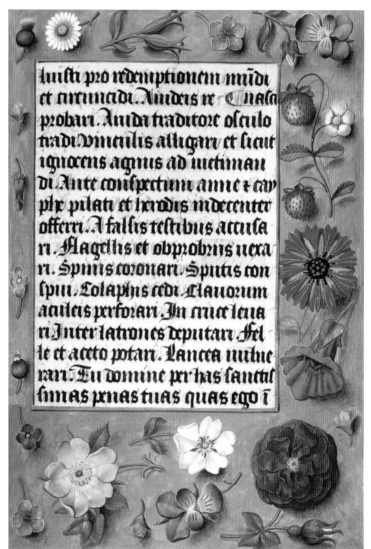

Left: For a saint purporting to be the patron saint of gardeners, St Fiacre's digging technique leaves something to be desired.

Below: Illuminated manuscripts, such as this Book of Hours from 1500, suggest that the monks really knew their plants.

The monastic garden

In AD597, an anxious Pope sent a rescue mission, led by a Benedictine monk, to save our heathen souls. Arriving in Canterbury, St Augustine started work by founding a monastery. From the first, gardening was an essential part of monastic life, not only supplying food for the community but celebrating the unity and humility of the brotherhood, through labouring together. Over time, this pastoral ideal was overtaken by the duty to care for others, and by the twelfth century the requirement to look after the poor and the sick, to offer hospitality to travellers,

and occasionally to entertain grandees with retinues of 300 or more, demanded not so much a garden as full-scale agricultural production. So the monastery developed a complex of gardens, both inside and outside the precinct.

Different monastic traditions developed in different ways. The Carthusians of Mount Grace Priory in North Yorkshire, for example, shunned communal life and lived in isolated compounds, each with its own productive garden. The Cistercians sought spiritual nourishment in remote and beautiful valleys, as at Rievaulx, Fountains and Buckland Abbeys. But it is the Benedictine order that gives us the clearest idea of what most medieval monastic gardens in England would have looked like, through

Fountains Abbey in North Yorkshire. The Cistercians derived profound spiritual nourishment from the beautiful surroundings of their religious houses.

a blueprint for an ideal monastery sent to a Swiss foundation around 820.

This plan shows a cluster of buildings – church, seminary, hostel, domestic and farm buildings – arranged around a series of courtyards or cloisters. At the very heart of the monastery stands an enclosed square garden, the 'cloister garth'. This is divided into quarters with a central basin or fountain, an ancient symbol of Paradise that seems to be common to all religions. There is an infirmary, next to which is a small physic garden with narrow beds, each devoted to a single kind of medicinal plant. Nearby is a cemetery, with 13 fruit trees evenly spaced between the graves, perhaps denoting Christ and his Apostles. And next to this is the vegetable garden, laid out in neat raised beds. The list of suggested crops, however, includes cumin and pomegranates – not readily grown in either Switzerland or Britain. For real-life gardens we must fast-forward three and a half centuries to the Priory of Christ Church, Canterbury, which also includes a private garden for the Prior, plus a large blank space that was the equine equivalent of the car park.

Above: The cloister garth was intended as a space for contemplation.

With so many mouths to feed, much had to be grown beyond the monastery walls. At Christ Church, there was a *pommarium* (apple orchard), *vinea* (vineyard) and *campus* (possibly a cornfield). Flax was grown for linen and hemp for rope. The line between farming and gardening is a fuzzy one: vineyards first planted to produce wine for the sacrament were later enjoyed as gardens, enclosed 'for the solace of the monks and those that had been bled'. Herbs grown for medicine, food or strewing were also delightful to eye and nose. Our twenty-first-century view of life, which separates utility from pleasure, the spiritual from the physical, the life of the intellect from the labour of the hand, would not have been understood in these more holistic times.

The most important of the gardens was the central Cloister Garth – not the romantic enclosure of carefully tended herbs and flowers of popular imagination, but a plain square of turf intended as an aid to spiritual reflection – though the green was also believed to refresh 'encloistered' eyes wearied with copying texts and illuminating manuscripts. Creation, rebirth and eternal life were evoked by the presence of water, intersecting paths or rills made the shape of a cross, and the enclosed garden was itself heavy with symbolism: Eden, the paradise garden of the Song of Solomon, the love of Christ for his new Church, the purity of the Virgin. Who needed plants when there was so much here to stimulate prayer and contemplation?

Opposite: From the ninth to the thirteenth centuries, temperatures in northern Europe were several degrees higher than those today. None the less, the plant list that accompanied this plan, drawn up for Gozbert, the Abbot of St Gall, took no account of the rigours of a Swiss winter.

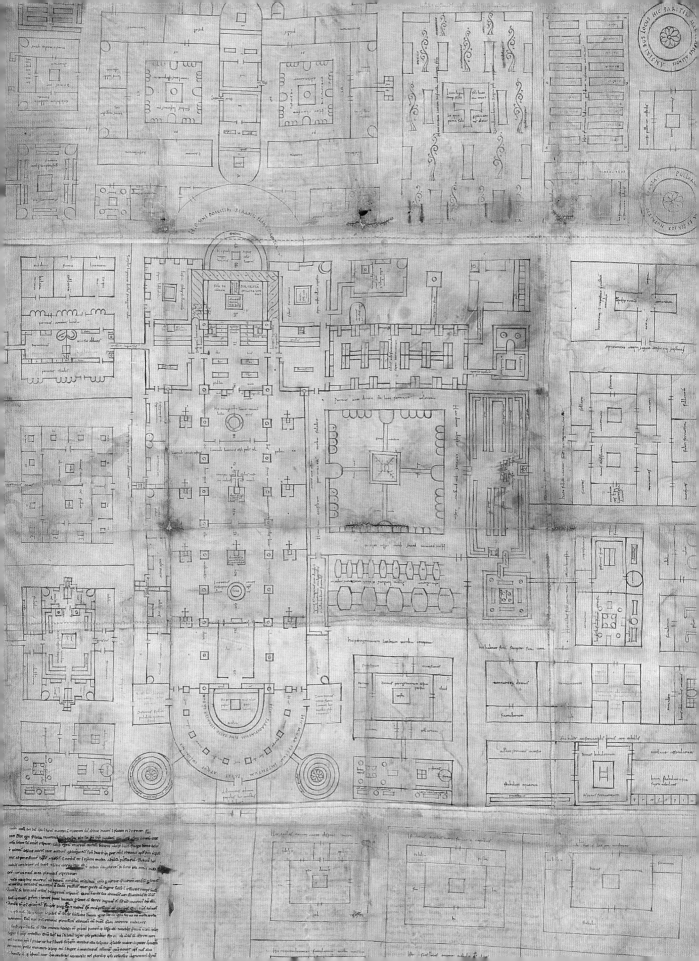

. Eruca 7 nasturtium .

Eruca 7 nasturtium. cplo. ca. 7 buia. in p. Eceto q̃ ſut melioꝛis acũ. uiuãtium. adiut
inſpmate 7 coytu. nocũitum faciũ emigrãeam. Remio cũ ſcariola 7 aceto. Quid grãamẽtis
ſanguinc; acutum, ꝯuenut fris ſcibꝫ byeme 7 ſeptentrionali regiõe.

The cemetery orchard, too, symbolised Paradise – a delightful resting place after a lifetime in the service of God, with fruit trees blossoming between the graves. The trees, often protected from raiders (animal or human) by a moat, provided apples, pears and cherries, medlars and quinces, mulberries, chestnuts and walnuts – all fruits introduced by the Romans. Vines were planted in and between them, as were roses, and the grass was spangled with meadow flowers.

At Christ Church, the cemetery orchard stood close to the infirmary. Here would be found a *herbarium* for the growing of medicinal plants, varying from powerful narcotics like mandrake, hemlock and the opium poppy to familiar herbs such as sage and lavender; from plants we now consider weeds such as plantains, pimpernel and herb robert to flowers valued today for their decorative qualities, such as iris and peony. It would also have contained powerful 'magic' plants, prized by pre-Christian herbalists. *Alchemilla vulgaris*, for example, was cherished for its ability to catch the pure morning dew, which became a key ingredient for alchemy, hence its name meaning 'little alchemist'. Herbs treated everything from the healing of wounds to the soothing of stomachs; marigolds were good for the eyesight; peony seeds were thought to stave off nightmares.

While a locked *herbarium* might contain rare or poisonous plants, more workaday plants would have been grown in the kitchen or cellarer's garden. Here were found not only food plants, but plants for a wide variety of domestic purposes. Coleworts were the most common vegetables (the nearest modern equivalent is kale), followed by leeks, parsley, leaf beets, garlic, onions and root crops – again, all introduced by the Romans. Peas and beans were occasionally grown to be eaten green, but more commonly eaten dried from field crops. There was a huge variety of herbs and salads, including edible flowers such as borage, marigold, poppy and heartsease. Flowers were essential for the bees, which provided both honey and wax for church candles. Fennel was planted not only for feast days but fast days – nibbling on the seeds helped to curb the appetite. Other 'herbs' which made a regular appearance in the pottage pot – dandelions and dead nettle, chickweed and groundsel – may well have self-seeded on fallow ground and perhaps been dug in as green manures. Roses, violets and lavender made fragrant waters, while aromatic herbs such as mint and meadowsweet were mixed with rushes to strew on the floor. Dye plants were needed, for clothes and inks. The iris root made a primitive deodorant.

Opposite: This fourteenth-century Italian illustration appears to show a cut-and-come-again method of harvesting rocket or kale.

Below: Possibly a native plant, borage is mentioned as early as 1265, and was widely cultivated in the belief that it drove away sadness and melancholy.

Plants were also grown for the church, such as bay, holly and ivy for Christmas and yew for Easter 'palms'. Pre-eminent among these were the red rose, *Rosa gallica*, and the showy white Madonna lily, described by the Venerable Bede as the emblem of the Virgin, the white petals representing the purity of her body and the golden anthers the glowing light of her soul. The rose represented divine love, the blood of Christ and of the martyrs, the crown of thorns and, confusingly, could denote the Virgin too. While such flower gardens were not made to please the eye, there is ample evidence that they did so, as did the dovecotes and fishponds (often referred to as stewponds) that provided valuable sources of protein. Fish were eaten on fasting days, of which there were more than full-fat days. Indeed it has been suggested that with so many fasting days, no monastery could have been self-sufficient in fish, and that these ponds were always made mainly for show.

Left: The modern distinction between utilitarian and ornamental planting would have been meaningless to the medieval mind.

Opposite: The medieval stewpond at East Riddlesden Hall, Yorkshire. Most monasteries had at least two ponds – a large *vivarium* or breeding pond and a small *servatorium* or storage pond. One of the more amusing monastic duties was to go out in a boat to net fish from the large pond and transfer them to the smaller ponds where they could be caught from the sides.

A rare survival

Moats were also a handy place to breed some fish, as at Baddesley Clinton in Warwickshire, or at St John's Jerusalem at Sutton-at-Hone in Kent. Here, just off a busy suburban shopping street, is the most astonishing survival – the remains of a commandery established by the Knights Templar in 1199, complete with flowery moat and miniature deer park. The Crusader Knights remained in Kent for three and a half centuries, welcoming travellers and caring for the sick, until forced to flee by the Dissolution of the Monasteries, when their church was converted into a house. While the garden is essentially a twentieth-century creation, it contains many medieval features – a vine-covered tunnel and nut walk, beehives, a dovecote, a quiet grass quadrangle approximating to a cloister garth and borders filled with the kinds of fruit, herbs and flowers that might have grown here 800 years ago. It is interesting because of its powerful 'island' quality, which gives a vivid sense of how the monasteries, with their parks and orchards and fruitful gardens, must have felt in earlier, more turbulent times.

There was plenty of fish at Baddesley Clinton in Warwickshire, with a lake and two stewponds connected to the moat with wooden pipes.

The garden of love

Most of what we know of the ornamental garden or 'herber' comes from illuminations, tapestries and poems. These depict an ideal garden, an Eden concealed by high walls, where fountains play, the grass is thick with flowers and the season is always spring. Reclining on the 'flowery mead', or seated on a bench of turf, is a woman. To the medieval mind, in which Christianity was the very fabric of life, the enclosed garden or *hortus conclusus* meant many things at once. It was a real garden. It was also a symbol either of the Virgin or the Church (the Bride of Christ), drawing on the familiar imagery of the *Song of Solomon*: 'A garden enclosed is my sister, my spouse; A spring shut up, a fountain sealed.' Yet the *Song of Solomon* is one of the world's sexiest poems. So there would be a clear overlap with the garden as depicted in the ballads of the wandering troubadours, as a private paradise of earthly delight.

Painted by an unknown Rhenish artist around 1410, *The Garden of Paradise* presents the garden as a walled *hortus conclusus*, in which the Virgin, saints and angels enjoy reading, music and civilised discourse, while St Dorothy picks cherries from the Tree of Life.

Only the greatest in the land had ornamental gardens, and the castles where they lived were less family homes than working villages, heaving with servants, peasants, men at arms; falcons, horses, dogs. They were noisy, smoky, cramped, crowded, smelly and overwhelmingly male. Imagine, then, the delight of a small, walled, private place, usually built beneath the lady's bedchamber, where she might retreat from the chaos and the din. Imagine the sweetness of unsullied fresh air, the scent of violet and rose; the relief of vine-clad trelliswork and shady bower, shutting out the press of humanity. Here, in blissful seclusion, might be practised the higher arts of civilisation: conversation, poetry, music, flirtation. Here, the elaborate rituals of courtly love could be played out.

The cult of courtly love emerged in the feudal courts of the South of France in the early twelfth century. Its best known expression was the *Roman de la Rose*, a long and immensely complicated poem translated into English by Chaucer around 1370. Here the lover, Amant, travels through an allegorical garden, in quest of the

This Flemish illustration of *Le Roman de la Rose* shows an aristocratic herber divided into two sections – a more productive area with raised beds divided by trelliswork from a flowery mead with fountain and rill.

rose which symbolises his lady's love. A female figure (Lady Idleness) leads him at last through a locked door to an inner garden. The atmosphere is dreamy, almost narcotic. The imagery is clear: the woman holds the key to the garden. To share it is her gift, her power.

The garden, then, became the place for love. Covered walks and arbours, walls and trelliswork kept out prying eyes. Soft turf seats were arranged in a U-shape, embracing a lovers' bed. A tinkling fountain provided soft music. And we know there were features such as mazes and 'Rosamondsbowers', inspired by Henry II, who allegedly hid his beautiful mistress, Rosamund Clifford, in a bower at the centre of a labyrinth, until his queen, Eleanor of Aquitaine, discovered and poisoned her. We can't know exactly what the medieval 'plesaunce' looked like, since none have survived, but an atmospheric recreation has been attempted at Winchester Castle by medieval scholar Sylvia Landsberg and the Hampshire Gardens Trust.

During the second half of the thirteenth century, Winchester Castle was the occasional home first of Eleanor of Provence, wife to Henry III, then

In this fifteenth-century illustration of a tale from Bocaccio's *Decameron,* two knights pine for the lovely Emilia in her garden. She sits on a raised turf seat behind a rose-covered trellis. A tunnel arbour is covered with vines and carnations, pinks and rosemary bloom at her feet.

Eleanor of Castile, wife of Edward I. Both were appalled by the barbarous English court, and turned for solace to gardening. Eleanor of Castile was a renowned gardener, credited with introducing many Mediterranean plants to Britain such as hollyhocks, pot marigolds, wallflowers and lavender.

The central theme of 'Queen Eleanor's Garden' at Winchester is fidelity, symbolised by evergreen plants such as turf, holly, ivy and bay. In the centre is a 'flowery mead' – a carpet of turf bejewelled with flowers. (There are records of Eleanor of Castile paying 3d a night to one of her squires to water a newly laid lawn.) The ancient roses *Rosa gallica* and *Rosa × alba* (later the roses of Lancaster and York) are trained over the trellis panels and tunnel arbour, and additional shade is provided by a tangle of vines and a flowering cherry. The borders mix Eleanor's introductions with plants widely grown at the time – lilies, peonies, flag iris, columbines, wild strawberries. Within a rose-clad inner sanctum, a fountain is surmounted by a falcon, recalling the tale of a lonely young wife who prayed for love, and whose prayers were answered when a falcon flew into her garden. This falcon at once turned into the fairest knight she had ever seen, and they (after some dithering) 'were happy together'. (Within the context of courtly love, fidelity is a bond between aristocratic lovers, and has nothing to do with the property rights of marriage.) Time after time, illustrations depict gardens as places for picnicking, music-making and lovemaking. There is also a good deal of naked mixed bathing – something of a surprise in the age that came up with the chastity belt.

Above: The vine-clad tunnel at Winchester is based on the painting on page 21. Shade was essential to preserve the delicate royal complexion.

Opposite: The Garden of Love as depicted by an unknown fifteenth-century Italian artist, complete with music, feasting, carousing and canoodling in a sumptuous marble fountain.

TRELLIS

TRELLIS, sometimes known by its French name, *treillage*, is one of the oldest of garden features, a structure of interlacing 'threads' of wood (the name comes from the Latin for 'three threads') usually supporting climbing plants. An essential feature in the medieval garden, arches or arbours of trelliswork regularly appear in medieval manuscript illustrations, often wreathed in roses. Other illustrations show panels of trellis dividing or enclosing a garden, just as they do today. The materials used might be a basketwork of willow or hazel, yew saplings or split chestnut.

By the fifteenth century, these constructions were becoming more sophisticated, sometimes elongated into tunnels, and by Tudor times, substantial galleries of 'carpentry work' enclosed shady walks, shade being essential to preserve the pale complexion of the high-born lady. Panels of trellis were used to enclose sections of the garden within the outer walls, and low panels might frame individual beds, as at Kenilworth.

Simple rustic trelliswork grew ever more refined, and sixteenth-century illustrations from France and Italy show some extraordinarily elaborate designs for galleries, pergolas and pavilions, increasingly decorative objects in their own right rather than merely a support for plants. Some look almost like cloisters, and great palaces such as Hampton Court and Theobalds almost certainly had galleries of this type. Less exalted gardeners, however, made do with simpler structures, as depicted in Thomas Hill's *The Gardener's Labyrinth* of 1577.

Trellis constructions, often decoratively painted, were an essential element in the formal gardens of France – a way to bring instant height and structure to a new, flat garden, and some elegant illustrations appear in John James's 1712 translation of Dézallier's *The Theory and Practice of Gardening*. James sadly observed that while 'these Pieces of Architecture … raise and improve the natural Beauty of Gardens extremely', most people 'are out of Conceit with them' as they are annoyingly 'liable to decay'. Nonetheless, two beautiful 'pieces of architecture' of unknown function are depicted in a 1712 engraving of Dyrham Park near Bath.

An account of city gardens in Paris in 1698 tells of the widespread use of green-painted trellis, so useful for hiding 'the ill prospect of the Neighbouring Houses'. While it had no place in the English landscape park, it was no doubt used in town gardens throughout the eighteenth century, and became the distinguishing feature of the fashionable Regency *cottage ornée*. The return to formality in the Victorian garden sparked a revival of fancy trelliswork structures, as in the Italian garden at Belton. E. Adveno Brooke's 1858 picture book *The Gardens of England* records trellis tunnels, arbours and rose arches, while Trentham boasts an especially charming rose-swagged trellis window. At Waddesdon, in 1889, trellis was employed in the grand French manner to construct a magnificent aviary, marking the visit of the Shah of Persia.

Gertrude Jekyll favoured more chunky, rustic pergolas, and rustic arbours and rose tunnels appear in many Edwardian gardens. Cheap, mass-produced trellis has made an invaluable addition to the modern garden, while contemporary designers such as George Carter have shown that trellis can still be used with boldness and flair.

Clockwise from top left: Fanciful trelliswork structures play an essential part in the recreation of the early eighteenth-century formal garden at Hanbury Hall in Worcestershire. A mid-nineteenth-century design for a trellis pavilion by John Adey Repton, son of Humphry. A trelliswork window frames the view of Charles Barry's grand terrace at Trentham. The Bee House at Attingham Park in Shropshire.

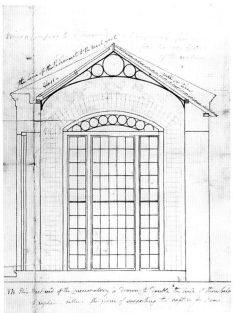

The deer park

If the herber was devoted to love, poetry and music, quite different pleasures
awaited beyond its walls; for the Norman noble, no pastime was more agreeable
than hunting. By 1350, there were at least 2,000 deer parks in England, enclosed
stretches of land, anything between 7½ and 4,000 acres (3 and 1,619ha), made
primarily as preserves for beasts of the chase. A man's social standing was judged by
the amount of land he held, so to own a park was the ultimate status symbol. The
King owned the greatest number of parks, followed by the bishops and abbots; one of
the best-preserved medieval deer parks is at Fountains Abbey in North Yorkshire.

As well as deer, parks often contained wild cattle, sheep and boar, along with
stewponds for fish, dovecotes for pigeons and even cider orchards, all enclosed
within a park pale, a massive fenced or hedged bank often with an internal ditch.
So the park was a vast outdoor larder, but its greatest value lay in being a private
hunting ground, distinct from the vast tracts of 'forest' reserved solely for the King.
This dictated the park's characteristic pattern of woodland for cover and grassland
for grazing which has exerted such a powerful influence on our landscape. Many
survive virtually unchanged: at Knole in Kent and Lyme Park in Cheshire you can
still see the descendants of the fallow deer introduced by the Normans, roaming
just as they did in the twelfth century.

By the time of Henry
II, one quarter of
England had been
designated 'forest',
where only the King
could hunt. So
canny landowners
would establish
their deer parks on
the boundaries of a
well-stocked Royal
Forest – with deer
leaps that would
allow deer to leap in,
but not out again.

Beyond the pale

The Norman elite transformed England, introducing French language and culture and establishing channels of communication with the Arabic world that fed directly into gardens. Influences too would have come from Crusaders returning from the Holy Land after 1096. Magnificent cathedrals rose at Ely, Durham, Lincoln, Winchester and Salisbury; the first colleges were established at Oxford and Cambridge. Manor houses, albeit protected with towers and moats, proliferated. By the thirteenth century, as feudalism went into decline, there arose a new class of yeomen and farmers who leased their own land and lived in their own houses, around which they made small, productive gardens. During the twelfth and thirteenth centuries between 400 and 500 new towns were created. London was by far the biggest, and following a great fire in 1135, the wealthier townsfolk rebuilt their houses in stone, surrounding them with large gardens and vineyards. Holborn was the leafiest of London's suburbs, where 'the Citizens have Gardens and Orchards planted with trees, large, beautiful, and one joining to another.' (By the fourteenth century, the Earl of Lincoln had an immense garden reaching down to the river, with a vineyard, a nursery, and orchards stocked with new varieties from the continent. It survives as Lincoln's Inn.)

The first practical gardening manual in English was probably written about this time, *The Feate of Gardinage* by one Jon the Gardener. He gives recommendations for sowing, planting, pruning and grafting, all in verse. He lists 97 plants, including cowslip, gentian, periwinkle and daffodil; parsley and saffron get whole chapters to themselves. Contemporary images show gardeners at work, using spades, rakes, forks and mattocks that have changed little over the centuries, along with a fearsome range of sickles, scythes, axes and pruning knives. There were wickerwork plant supports and even rudimentary wheelbarrows. It is rather comforting to reflect how little gardening has changed.

But change did come, and it was cataclysmic. Between 1348 and 1350, the Black Death wiped out 25 million people, one third of the population of Europe. Throughout the fifteenth century, the ups and downs (mainly downs) of the Hundred Years War provoked economic crisis and sporadic revolt, followed by the Wars of the Roses, 30 years of intermittent civil war. With the victory of Henry Tudor at Bosworth Field and his marriage in 1486 to Elizabeth of York, the warring factions of Lancaster and York were finally united. The symbol of this union was that flower of multiple meanings – a rose.

The medieval equivalent of the strimmer was the scythe. But the long grass in the orchard still had to be raked up, and the scyther's wife follows behind to tidy up.

THE POWER OF SCENT

TODAY, aromatherapy is regarded by most doctors as a harmless indulgence – pleasant, relaxing, but medically useless. In the Middle Ages, however, scent was an important weapon in the physician's armoury. In 1348–9, the Muslim physician Ibn Khatimah had watched plague rip through Andalucia, and advocated that cities should defend themselves with a green belt stocked with sweet-smelling shrubs. When Adam and Eve were expelled from Eden, among the joys they lost was the perfect health they had enjoyed in that paradisal garden. Heaven was imagined to be sweetly perfumed; Purgatory and Hell, by contrast, stank of sulphur and pitch. So a smell carried with it a whiff of good or evil, but more than that, it could have a direct impact on the 'animal spirits' of living beings.

For 2,000 years, it had been believed that the body was governed by 'humours'. Food, having been 'cooked' in the oven of the stomach, was transmitted to the liver, where it was converted into blood, phlegm, choler and black bile, the relative balance of which gave rise to a sanguine, phlegmatic, choleric or melancholic temperament. Too much of any was harmful, and would cause disease. From the liver, the blood and humoral matter, known as the 'natural spirit', passed into the veins, which carried nourishment to all parts of the body. Some of this blood was warmed by the heart, infused with air from the lungs, and entered the arterial system as a warm, frothy substance known as the 'vital spirit'. This carried heat and life from the heart round the body, just as the natural spirit carried food. On reaching the brain, the vital spirit, now mixed with air from the nostrils, assumed the power to activate both body and mind – hence 'animal' or animating spirit. And it was at this delicate stage that the vital or animal spirit was susceptible to scent. The wrong kind of scent could send the vital spirit screeching back to the heart or brain, leaving the body breathless or fitting or paralysed or dead.

As Bartholomew the Englishman (a thirteenth-century monk who wrote, very beautifully, on gardens) put it: 'if the vapour is malicious, stinking, and corrupt, it corrumptith the spirit that hatte [is called] animalis and often bringith and gendrith pestilence'. Conversely, the delightful smells of cut grass and flowers and trees would have a beneficial and strengthening effect on the animal spirits.

In addition to their pleasing or noisome character, smells were understood to possess characteristics of heat, cold, aridity and moisture that would have a direct effect on the balance of humours in the patient. Violets, for example, were deemed to be moist and cold, and therefore useful for treating 'hot' disorders caused by an excess of choler, such as headaches, fevers and eruptions of the skin. Lemon, mint and oregano, however, were warming smells, good for treating melancholic conditions such as depression and, curiously, bowel problems. Cooling flowers were gathered into nosegays to guard against the plague: hence the 'pocketful of posies' in the old nursery rhyme. So filling your garden with the widest possible range of scented herbs and flowers was as sensible as eating your five a day would be today.

Clockwise from top left: *Rosa gallica* 'Versicolor', one of the earliest and most fragrant of roses. The knot garden at the The Old Manor at Norbury, Derbyshire is sweetened with herbs, no doubt to distract from the catty smell of box. Honeysuckle has long been prized for its evening scent – released to attract moths. The scent of the violet was supposed to aid sleep. Many kinds of mint were grown, for their difference in scent as well as flavour.

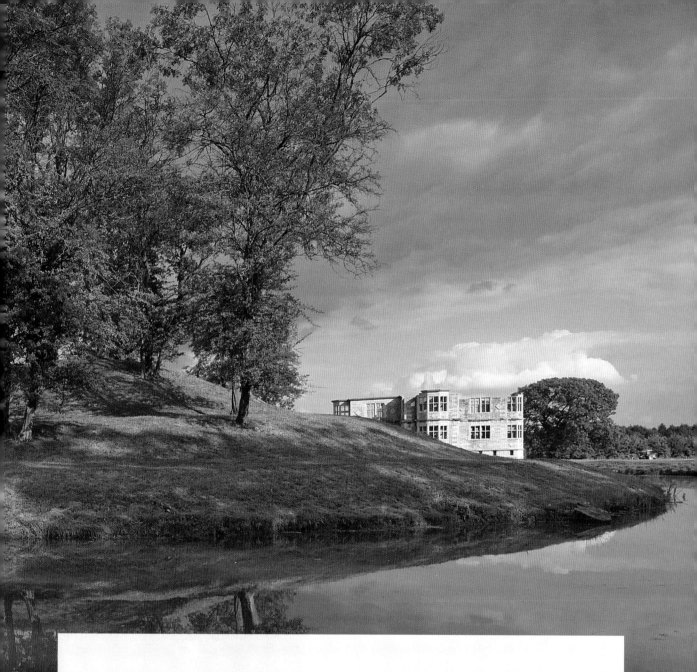

CHAPTER 2

TUDOR GARDENS

GARDENS OF CONCEIT

1486–1604

> '*He brought me to the banqueting house, and his banner over me was love.*'
>
> THE SONG OF SOLOMON

IN 1562, the English physician William Bullein published a self-help guide to keeping healthy, gloriously entitled *Bullein's Bulwarke of Defence againste all Sicknesse*. In it, he suggested that the best defence against disease lay in the partnership between the gardener, Hilarius (meaning Good Cheer), and Health, the physician. In other words, like the medieval physician monks before him, he believed that gardening was good for you. The essentials of a healthy lifestyle, then as now, were plenty of fresh air and exercise – ideally before breakfast. After rising and dressing, you should 'walke in your gardayne or park a thousand pace or two … and before you go to your refection, moderatly exercyse your body with some labour, or playing at the tennys, or castyng a bowle … or some other thynge, to open your poores, and to augment naturall hete'. Nothing is new in gardening: the Tudors had invented the Green Gym.

Densely planted trelliswork tunnels or 'galleries' (as at Alnwick in Northumberland today) offered cover for your thousand paces in less clement weather – though if the weather were really bad, walkers might repair to the Long Gallery, the latest fashionable adjunct to the Tudor house. Generally raised along one side of, or encircling the garden, these also provided a good view of the 'knots', decorative beds that were a distinctive feature of Tudor gardens. There might also be archery buttes (viewers of *Wolf Hall* will have seen these set up at Montacute in Somerset) and a bowling green. Bowls was a game restricted by statute to the landed classes (the lower orders were allowed to play only at Christmas), the greens showing off the fine art of turf maintenance: the perfect lawn was already developing into a national obsession.

That there should be room for all this activity indicates how far the pleasure garden had come from the intimate herbers of the Middle Ages. Henry VII's first act on taking the throne had been to command the tearing down of castle walls,

A modern interpretation of a knot garden at Moseley Old Hall in Staffordshire, showing the intricacy of design, often based on textiles or strapwork, which delighted the Tudors.

and once the danger of attack was no longer an imminent concern, manor houses also did away with fortifications. No longer confined within the perimeter walls, gardens became bigger, spreading out from the house on one or more sides. When Henry VII rebuilt his palace at Richmond in 1497, it was surrounded, for the first time since the Romans, by extensive formal gardens.

Henry VIII certainly enjoyed an action-packed garden: at Whitehall there was a tilt-yard, four tennis courts, a bowling alley and a cockpit. A painting made around 1545, *The Family of Henry VIII*, is believed to show a part of these gardens, glimpsed through arches at the margins of the picture. It reveals a brick-walled Privy Garden divided into neat squares, each edged with a low timber fence painted in the Tudor family colours of green and white, and a thicket of heraldic beasts held aloft on stripy poles. Lions symbolised the crown, the greyhound was a family badge for the Tudors, and dragons denoted Wales, where the Tudors came from – it was a brazen exercise in royal branding, repeated at Henry's palaces at Nonsuch and Hampton Court. Here the beasts were sketched by Anthonis van den Wyngaerde, who came to England in 1550 in the retinue of Philip II of Spain. He is our earliest known garden tourist: his drawings, now in the Ashmolean Museum in Oxford, are the first accurate visual record of English gardens. They depict a jumble of walled gardens (the walls sometimes pierced by windows), containing fishponds, towers and numerous banqueting houses.

Hampton Court had been 'offered' to the King in 1528 by Cardinal Wolsey, in a doomed attempt to save his neck. Henry added a 2,000 acre deer park and

This painting, showing Henry VIII with his children and third wife Jane Seymour, is believed to show the gardens at Whitehall, where an inventory of the garden recorded 34 heraldic beasts arranged round a central fountain.

spent lavishly on the garden. The centrepiece was a colossal spiral mount (see page 38) topped by a palatial two-storey banqueting house – though perhaps not as palatial as the one at Greenwich, reported to be decorated with coral, ruby rocks, pomegranates and roses.

Henry's gardens, then, were no longer just places for serenading his latest lady love or taking vigorous exercise: their primary purpose was to display regal magnificence, just as in the portraits he commissioned, the sumptuous fabrics that he wore, the ritual feasting that was part of court etiquette. That Henry delighted in showing off is clear from the 1520 cockfest of the Field of the Cloth of Gold – two monarchs, Henry and François I of France, vying to outshine each other in glitter and extravagance. (Henry's palace at Nonsuch, the 'pearl of the realm' was conceived to rival François's Fontainebleau.) The desire to show off has always been one of the primary reasons for making a garden. During Henry's reign, however, this was a poor idea: subjects whose gardens threatened to outshine the King's were apt to find them snatched away, along with their heads. The Dissolution of the Monasteries from the 1530s brought even more real estate his way. In 1509 Henry VIII had inherited thirteen properties. By the time of his death, he had more than 60.

In 1520 Cardinal Wolsey arranged a meeting to sign a non-aggression pact between Henry VIII and François I of France that achieved little in political terms, but became famous for its extravagance and splendour, as each king tried to outshine the other with dazzling tents and huge feasts, jousting tournaments, music and games. The site derives its name from the costly fabric so lavishly used, as recorded in a painting now hanging at Hampton Court.

SCULPTING THE EARTH

THE urge to sculpt the land, to carve patterns into hillsides and raise artificial hills over the dead, seems to be eternal and universal. These man-made landforms may be almost indistinguishable from natural forms, but often carry a symbolic significance, as in the barrows, henges and tumuli scattered across Britain.

While the popes and princes of Renaissance Italy were carving their hillsides into panoramic terraces, the English garden remained resolutely enclosed, with dirty, dangerous nature firmly excluded. The artificial hills or mounts that began to appear in the late medieval garden had a spiritual role as meditations on Calvary, but were also a handy way of spying on what might be lurking the other side of the wall.

In the Tudor garden, the mount became an important feature. Henry VIII had a great mount built at Hampton Court Palace in 1532, constructed from 265,000 bricks, planted with 1,200 hawthorns to hold the soil, and crowned with an elaborately glazed banqueting house. Later gardens had multiple mounts, or mounts elongated into bowling greens, or joined together with terraces. In a plan of 1618, garden writer William Lawson proposed a moated garden with a mount at each corner, from where one might 'angle a peckled trout or sleightie eele', or even take a pot-shot at a deer. Just such a plan can still be seen at Lyveden New Bield (1605), which boasts two conical moated mounts ascended by spiral paths, one clockwise and one anti-clockwise. John Leland, antiquary to Henry VIII, described a similar mount in a Yorkshire garden, 'writhen about in degrees like turnings of cokil-shells to cum to the top without payne'. Mounts lasted well into the eighteenth century.

Charles Bridgeman incorporated them into early designs, while his contemporary Stephen Switzer suggested that they could helpfully use up rubble when demolishing an old house. But with the arrival of the Landscape Movement, mounts were superseded by more realistic looking hills, and Bridgeman turned his masterful land-forming skills to ramparts, terraces and great turf amphitheatres, notably the amphitheatre at Claremont in Surrey.

When the Victorians took to making 'Elizabethan' gardens, these did not include mounts – indeed the surviving Tudor mount at Montacute was destroyed. But, from the late twentieth century, inspired by the Land Art movement, earth-sculpting has undergone a revival. The Menagerie in Northamptonshire and RHS Wisley both have spiral mounts, while at Scampston Hall in Yorkshire a grassy truncated pyramid offers pleasing views over the new garden. In 1989 in Dumfries, Maggie Keswick and her husband Charles Jencks shaped the spoil from a lake excavation into a pair of sinuous turf mounds imbued with cosmological meanings. The undisputed master of land sculpture, however, is Kim Wilkie. He made his name at Heveningham Hall, Suffolk in 1995, with a graceful stepped landform that gave the Palladian house room to breathe. In Surrey he created a deep turf amphitheatre to rescue a fine Arts and Crafts garden from the roar of the M25, while at Boughton in Northamptonshire, his 'Orpheus' is an 'inverse mount'. Wilkie maintains there is nothing avant-garde about his creations: rather, they follow a peculiarly British tradition, perfectly adapted to our topography and low Northern light.

Clockwise from top left: Portrack's Double Helix and Snail Mount have inspired garden-makers all over the world. The Tudor mount at Dunham Massey in Cheshire was long thought to be the remains of a medieval motte. Terracing at Dartington Hall at Devon. The snail mount at Lyveden New Bield is intended to invite thoughts of Calvary. Orpheus is a mirror image of a restored pyramidal mount, sinking 23ft (7m) beneath the lawns with a path spiralling down to a square pool.

Gardening for Gloriana

Henry's daughter, Elizabeth, took a very different approach to conspicuous display by the nobility. She actively encouraged it as she moved on her annual Royal Progresses through the land. Courtiers vied with each other to welcome their sovereign with ever more extravagant gardens laden with symbolic features: where gardens had once honoured the Virgin Mary, now they flattered the Virgin Queen. Her right-hand man, William Cecil, Lord Burghley, made a garden of 'immense extent' at Theobalds, famed for its lavish decoration; not to be outdone, Lord Hertford created an entire new landscape with a crescent-shaped lake to stage a re-enactment of the defeat of the Spanish Armada. But no one had more invested in pleasing the Queen than Robert Dudley, Earl of Leicester, Elizabeth's long-time favourite and would-be husband. By 1575, beginning to despair of ever gaining her hand, he invited her to Kenilworth, where he entertained her with 19 days of spectacular pageantry.

The principal site for the party was a magnificent new garden, recreated in 2009, which shows us how very different Elizabethan gardens were from the decorous green knot gardens imagined in the early twentieth century. Kenilworth was pure bling, with obelisks painted to look like porphyry, trellis pavilions draped in roses and a monstrously phallic fountain in shiny white marble, where two musclebound Atlas figures held aloft a spouting globe topped by Dudley's

Elizabeth I had given Kenilworth to Robert Dudley along with his title and she visited several times. This contemporary painting, attributed to Dutch artist Hals Dirck (1591–1656), imagines them there together.

ragged staff. Flowerbeds were filled with eglantine roses, the Queen's most enduring emblem, symbolising her purity and virginity; along with virginal lilies, and heartsease denoting tender thoughts. Above them were fruit trees, laden with apples, pears and ripe cherries. The *pièce de resistance* was a two-storey aviary 'beautified with great diamonds, emeralds, rubies, and sapphires … and garnish'd with gold', loud with singing birds. This was a garden designed to launch a full-scale assault on the senses – but it failed to move the Queen. Dudley was cast aside, suspected of murdering his wife.

As the early years of Elizabeth's reign brought increasing prosperity, old houses were refashioned and surrounded with gardens and orchards. Former monastic buildings became handsome domestic dwellings. And at Hardwick Hall and Montacute, glittering new mansions arose. Montacute, begun in the last years of Elizabeth's reign, was the height of fashion, with its shimmering sheets of glass, its long gallery, its turrets and obelisks and elegant gazebos. The original garden was largely destroyed in the nineteenth century – even the mount was demolished to make way for a more romantically 'Elizabethan' fountain. However, the walls and terraces survive, and the bijou corner pavilions that served as banqueting houses.

The banquet was not a whole meal, as we understand it today, but a gourmet final course of sugary dainties such as cakes, jellies or 'wet suckets'

The reconstruction of the garden at Kenilworth is based on a long letter written by Robert Langham, a member of Dudley's household, in 1575. He describes every detail, from the paths as 'pleasant to walk on, as a seashore when the water is availed', to the fruit trees and flowers, 'the birds flittering, the fountain streaming, the fish swimming, all in such delectable variety …'

Above: These
illustrations from
*The Gardener's
Labyrinth* show
gardeners planting,
tying in roses, and
possibly carrying out
repairs on a shady
wattle arbour for
outdoor dining.

(a form of crystallised fruit in syrup). Once the main meal was finished in the great hall, guests would repair to a banqueting house while the hall was cleared for whatever entertainment was to follow. Banqueting houses came in all shapes and sizes, from the architectural bravura of Lyveden New Bield (see page 46) to simple shelters of willow and fir. At Hardwick Hall there were banqueting houses both in the garden and on the roof. Lacock Abbey, too, has a roof-top banqueting house reached by a vertiginous (balustraded) walk over the leads.

The first gardening books

The invention of printing had changed the world, and classical texts were increasingly available both in the original and in translation. The writers of antiquity had plenty to say on the subject of gardening, as they extolled the virtues of the simple life working the land. The racy tales of the poet Ovid were laced with flowers, while first-century Roman bureaucrat Pliny the Younger sent letters from his two country villas, describing the joys of looking out from the garden to the surrounding countryside. His detailed accounts of terraces, loggias, fountains, topiary and garden buildings would inspire generations of Renaissance architects.

By the middle of the sixteenth century, Britain had a population of about 3 million, of whom probably half a million could read, so books steadily became the medium by which ideas spread. The first books of horticultural advice in English began to appear in the second half of the century. The first plant book was by William Turner in 1551 – a learned book quite unfairly eclipsed by Gerard's *Herball* of 1597. Gerard's work was known to be wildly inaccurate even before it was published, the text plagiarised and riddled with errors, and many of the illustrations muddled up. An altogether better job had been done by Henry Lyte (of Lyte's Cary in Somerset) 30 years earlier, translating the same

Opposite: While high
outer walls were still
essential to keep
Nature at bay, within
the garden they
could be lower and
more decorative,
as at Montacute in
Somerset, where
they are balustraded
and embellished
with obelisks, finials
and elegant corner
banqueting houses.

Flemish source into English and scrupulously marking his own additions. But Gerard was a much better read. He described a curious new plant from Virginia called the potato, and the new-fangled tomato, introduced to Europe in 1544. He also wrote with complete confidence of the barnacle tree, native to the Orkneys, which grows shells rather than fruits, from which hatch geese.

The first book printed in English which concerned itself with gardening as opposed to herbalism was Thomas Hill's *A most brief and pleasant treatise, teaching how to dresse, sow and set a garden*, published in 1558. A second book, *The Gardener's Labyrinth*, was published posthumously in 1577. It advises on 'the choice of seedes, apt times for sowing, setting, planting, and watering [Hill believed in working with the phases of the moon] and the vessels and instrumentes serving to that use and purpose', including the first known metal watering can. There are numerous patterns for 'knots and mazes, cunningly handled for the beautifying of gardens'. 'Knots' were rectangular beds planted with interlacing ribbons of low, evergreen plants such as germander, santolina, hyssop, thrift or rosemary – the more complicated and 'enknotted' the better. (Box, common in Roman times, was not

This section of London's earliest map shows the area around Moorfields, characterised by large gardens behind the houses – some laid out in rectangular compartments, some with long, narrow beds, some with knot gardens and even one with a mount.

reintroduced until the end of the century.) The gaps between the ribbons might be filled with flowers, or, where the knots were more intricate, with coloured sand or gravel, white shells or coal dust. Knots remained popular for over a century, morphing eventually into French-style scrollwork, and making a comeback in olde-worlde nineteenth-century gardens.

Along with Thomas Tusser's *Five Hundredth Points of Good Husbandry* (1573), a practical manual written in catchy doggerel, Hill's chirpy illustrations give us a good idea of what ordinary people's gardens looked like. We can find further evidence in the Copperplate Map, the earliest map of London (*c*.1558), which shows gardens in Bishopsgate containing knots and labyrinths, orchards and banqueting houses, and even a rather grand stepped mount topped by a lofty tree.

Generally only scraps of Tudor gardens remain, in the golden-walled courts at Hardwick Hall or the layouts at Trerice and Godolphin in Cornwall; in a bowling green at Melford Hall in Suffolk, a mount at Dunham Massey in Cheshire. More common are nineteenth- or twentieth-century reimaginings, made to flatter Elizabethan houses, as at Little Moreton Hall in Cheshire or Moseley Old Hall in Staffordshire. There is, however, one astonishing exception – the haunting poetic landscape of Lyveden New Bield.

'The Manner of Watering with a Pumpe in a Tubbe', from Thomas Hill's *The Gardener's Labyrinth*, the inspiration for the Tudor Garden at Trerice in Cornwall, which includes a replica of the pump.

Lyveden New Bield: a garden of faith and treason

When Sir Thomas Tresham died on 11 September 1605, the workmen laid down their tools, and the great garden he was making in the Northamptonshire countryside came abruptly to a halt. Two months later, Tresham's son died in the Tower, implicated in the Gunpowder Plot. The New Bield (or building) at Lyveden had been intended as the focus of a half-mile succession of orchards, terraces, mounts and canals ascending from the family manor house at the foot of the hill. It stands, unfinished, just as the workmen left it, miraculously unsoftened by the passage of time.

Today is not the first time the State has distrusted religious minorities, fearing them as hotbeds of terrorism. Tresham, who was a staunch Catholic, paid dearly for his faith: denied advancement at court, fined some £8,000 (about £1.1 million today) for failing to attend Anglican services, and thrown into prison whenever the activities of Catholics abroad appeared to threaten the stability of the realm. His solace, or revenge, during long years of house arrest and imprisonment was to build a pair of extraordinary garden houses on his two Northamptonshire estates. The first, at nearby Rushton, served as a bizarrely grand (but not very practical) home for the estate rabbit-keeper. The one at Lyveden, however, was intended as a 'secret house': a place to escape to with family or friends, away from the formality of the great house. It was also a spiritual haven, possibly intended for the secret celebration of the Mass – an act of High Treason punishable by death. (From 1585 even harbouring a priest was a capital offence.)

Both buildings were elaborate number puzzles which could be 'read' as statements of his faith. (Twelve years in prison had given Tresham ample time to work them out.) The Triangular Lodge at Rushton was a play on the Holy Trinity, while the New Bield, formed in the shape of a Greek cross and decorated with religious symbols, celebrated the Passion of Christ, strongly associated by the Catholic community with their own persecution

Lyveden New Bield in Northamptonshire, a symbolic landscape made as a statement of faith. Catholics in England would have been acutely aware of how religion was expressed in visual terms, having seen their parish churches stripped of 'idolatry', the walls painted over and the stained glass smashed. Even the roadside crosses and holy wells that once littered the countryside were swept away.

and suffering. With Sudoku-like ingenuity, Tresham devised a building based on the numbers seven and five – five being the number of the Wounds of Christ, while seven refers to the Seven Sorrows of Mary, the Stations of the Cross (the 14 stations did not become current until the eighteenth century) and the Seven Instruments of the Passion.

The garden too, could be enjoyed at two levels – both as a magnificent piece of landscaping and as an aid to spiritual devotion, its journey up through seven terraces recalling both the Way of the Cross and the pilgrim's arduous journey to the Holy Land. In many ways Lyveden anticipates the great landscape gardens of the eighteenth century, the ascent revealing a progression of carefully composed vistas, each rich in association, culminating in the cross-shaped Lodge. A serious devotional building masquerading as a banqueting house, it neatly exemplified the double life of Catholics at the time.

On the sixth terrace stood a large rectangular orchard of some 300 trees, a virtuoso display of fruit-growing, described by Robert Cecil as 'one of the fairest orchards that is in England' and now accurately replanted in the original tree-pits with a central walk of black cherries. To the north was a terrace with a mount at each end in the shape of a truncated pyramid. And then came a surprise – an 'island' garden surrounded by a moat, with two spiral mounts projecting into the water. (In fact, it never quite became an island – the west side of the moat was never completed.) Its purpose remained a mystery until in 2003, a rediscovered

Every element of the landscape could have meaning. The cross-shaped New Bield referred to the Passion of Christ, while Rushton's Triangular Lodge, opposite, denoted the Trinity. The labyrinth, above, showed the difficult path through this earthly life where Ariadne's thread was now the guiding grace of God.

1944 Luftwaffe reconnaissance shot revealed a circular area in the centre, arranged in concentric rings – the pattern recreated today by lines mowed into the turf. This was the site of a labyrinth, planted with cherries and plums, roses and raspberries, the roses representing the purity of the Virgin and the raspberries the blood of Christ. The two spiral mounts reinforced the penitential theme, inviting thoughts of Calvary.

The apex of the garden was the Lodge, set on a mount at the summit of the hill, surrounded by sunken walks and intimate hedged gardens. For 400 years it stood untouched, as the garden slowly vanished under trees and brambles. When recovery began in the 1990s, it revealed an extraordinary survival – clear evidence of the ambition of Tudor gardens, especially in the moving of earth and handling of water. Also remarkable is the sophisticated use, at this early date, of the garden as a vehicle for personal expression. For Tresham, mystery, reverence and awe were at the very heart of his religion. And these are the qualities that endure in the garden he made.

MAZES AND LABYRINTHS

THE ancient concept of the labyrinth, important in Egyptian and Minoan civilisations, was seized on by medieval Christianity as a symbol of man's tortuous journey towards salvation, and labyrinths and mazes became widespread from the twelfth century. Representations of labyrinths often show man in different stages along the journey – in childhood, manhood and old age, concluding, as at Erddig, with a skeleton at the centre. They first appeared as designs worked into church pavements, to be walked as token pilgrimages of penitence. Gradually, these migrated into the churchyard, and eventually into the garden, so that by the sixteenth and seventeenth centuries, the hedge maze had become a popular ornamental feature.

The Tudors, with their love of conceits, delighted in mazes. At Lyveden New Bield, the labyrinth retained its religious function, the pattern of the 'Path to Jerusalem' taken from Chartres Cathedral. But this design was widely copied, and appears in Thomas Hill's *The Gardener's Labyrinth* simply as a delightful garden feature. Henry VIII had a maze at Nonsuch Palace; Lord Burghley had a labyrinth at Theobalds. And there were numerous village mazes cut out of turf in the countryside, most likely for entertainment in the manner of modern maize mazes.

Early hedge mazes were generally only knee-height, composed of hyssop, lavender, cotton lavender or thyme as often as box. They were popular not just for the pleasure of getting 'lost' in them, but as attractive, fragrant features for the winter garden. Head-high mazes did not arrive until the late seventeenth century, when William and Mary, missing their maze at Het Loo, commissioned a new one at Hampton Court. Planted in hornbeam in 1690 (and replanted in yew in the 1960s), it is the oldest surviving example of a puzzle maze, and perhaps the most copied.

The seventeenth-century formal garden often included intricate patterns of paths winding through dense blocks of shrubs, and a maze of this kind at Wrest Park in Bedfordshire, recorded in 1707, has been recently recreated in the kitchen garden. There was no place for such artifice in the English landscape garden, but in the nineteenth century mazes made a comeback: the cherry laurel maze at Glendurgan was planted in 1833, followed by yew mazes at Belton in Lincolnshire in 1890 and Cliveden in Berkshire in 1894 – the last to a design conceived by new owner William Astor.

The decline of the English country house in the twentieth century spelled the end for high-maintenance features such as mazes, but in recent years they have enjoyed a new burst of popularity, notably in maize mazes.

So what is the difference between a maze and a labyrinth? Strictly, a labyrinth only has one path and no dead ends, so you can't get lost, whereas mazes have multiple paths which branch off and do not necessarily lead to the centre. But there are worse fates than being lost in a maze …

Clockwise from top: Resourceful parents Alfred and Sarah Fox planted the maze at Glendurgan in Cornwall as a means of losing their 12 children for a few hours. The pavement maze at Grey's Court in Oxfordshire. The most widely copied pattern was that of the labyrinth at Chartres Cathedral. A modern maze at Hampton Court Castle in Herefordshire. Patterns for mazes appeared in the earliest gardening books.

CHAPTER 3
STUART GARDENS
THE GREATER PERFECTION
1604–1714

'What wondrous life is this I lead!
Ripe apples drop about my head'

ANDREW MARVELL, *THE GARDEN*

WHEN Elizabeth I died in March 1603, she had outlived the myth of Gloriana by an uncomfortable decade. But William Cecil, followed by his no less gifted son Robert, had kept the ship of state afloat, so that for the first time in half a century the succession proceeded without turbulence. Improved relations with continental powers made travel much easier (especially to Italy, effectively out of bounds following the excommunication of Elizabeth I in 1570), and this encouraged a free flow of information that would vastly enhance our knowledge of plants, along with an influx of terracing, embroidered parterres, grottoes and elaborate water features.

James I arrived from Scotland with his consort, Anne of Denmark, but was far too busy chasing either beasts of the field or handsome young men to have much time for gardening. Instead he contented himself with wresting the magnificent palace of Theobalds from the unfortunate Robert Cecil, swapping it for the run-down episcopal seat of Hatfield in Hertfordshire. It fell to the Queen to garden in the grand manner, spending lavishly on Somerset House on the banks of the Thames in London. The high point of her new garden was a monumental fountain – a Mount Parnassus supporting four gushing river gods, with a golden Pegasus prancing on the top. This was the work of polymath Huguenot engineer Salomon de Caus (1576–1626), who had studied the science behind the great Renaissance gardens of Italy, who built the first workable greenhouse in 1619 and is still revered as a pioneer of robotic technology. Inspired by the first-century inventor Hero of Alexandria, he designed all kinds of cunning contrivances such as speaking statues and automated water organs, illustrating some of them in a treatise of 1615 that also included an early version of the steam engine.

When James's daughter was married off, de Caus went with her to Heidelberg. The great garden he had been planning for her brother was abandoned at his death: it was Elizabeth's *Hortus Palatinus* rather than the Prince of Wales's Richmond that now became the most innovative garden in Europe, styled the 'Eighth Wonder of the World', and the giant spouting river god planned for the centre of the Thames was never built.

Before his departure de Caus found time to help out at Hatfield, where Cecil had swiftly pulled down most of the decaying Tudor building and recycled the bricks for a new house by architect Robert Lyminge. (By 1616 Lyminge was at work at Blickling, another red-brick palace with a garden on a massive scale.) Working alongside gardener John Tradescant, de Caus created a dazzling garden packed with extravagant water features. There was nothing to equal it in magnificence till the 1630s, when his younger brother, Isaac, laid out an immense Italianate garden at Wilton House in Wiltshire.

This garden, 1000ft (305m) long and 400ft (122m) wide, was divided into three parts, with a broad, straight walk up the centre. The first section was laid out in 'embroidered' parterres of box in the latest French manner, each adorned with a marble fountain. Next came a densely planted 'wilderness' – not a wild place, but an area intended for solitary meditation – cut through with regular walks and the less regular course of the River Nadder. Beyond lay an oval circus marked out with cherry trees, centred on a copy of the 'Borghese Gladiator', considered by de Caus to be 'the most famous statue of antiquity'. The path terminated at a splendid grotto, full of surprising waterworks.

With their love of trickery, the Elizabethans had been quick to adopt the teasing *giochi d'acqua* so popular in Italian gardens. Elizabeth herself had water jokes at Whitehall that 'plentifully sprinkled' unwary visitors – but at Wilton, de Caus laid on a perfect deluge, with jets up from the floor, showers from the ceiling, statues that spouted water and apparently inoffensive objects that suddenly turned into revolving water pistols. Wilton became famous all over Europe, and was a great favourite with Charles I. It was the grandest of gardens: symmetrical, richly ornamented with statuary, and, above all, designed to be viewed in one seignorial sweep from the principal rooms of the house. It pointed the way the English garden was about to go.

The garden at Wilton House in Wiltshire, designed by Isaac de Caus between 1631 and 1635, introduced a host of Italianate features, with its symmetry, ornament and formal divisions of space.

55

'The purest of human pleasures'

Wilton was a garden for the great. So too was the ideal garden described by the essayist Sir Francis Bacon (1561–1626) in 1625 – probably the most quoted piece of garden literature ever. Compared with Wilton, it seems curiously old-fashioned, with a mount, 'spacious alleys' and shady walks in the Tudor manner, beds edged with 'little low hedges' and fountains embellished with gilded or marble statues. His words were seized on in later centuries because he seemed to favour 'a natural wilderness', dismissed topiary against the fashion of the times as fit only 'for children', and was rude about knots. 'They be but toys,' he scoffed, 'you may see as good sights many times in tarts.' But he also took against pools, declaring that they 'make the garden unwholesome, and full of flies and frogs', a disappointing observation from a man generally regarded as the father of empirical science in Britain.

The garden at Chastleton in Oxfordshire has been replanted several times since the seventeenth century, but is thought to represent the pre-Copernican universe. Bacon's garden at Twickenham, made around 1595, is believed to have been of similar design.

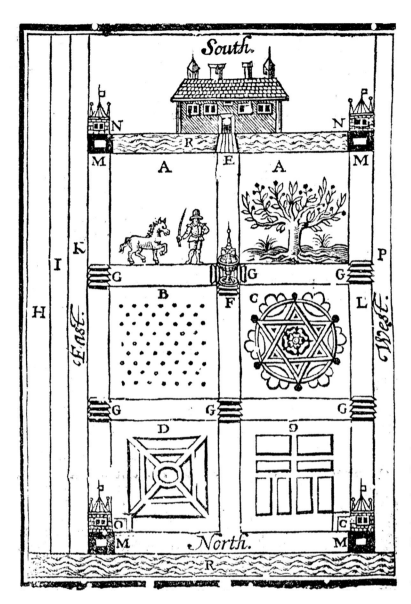

William Lawson's garden plan reflected what was being done in the most fashionable gardens and made these new ideas more widely available.

By the time *On Gardens* was published, Bacon had been making gardens for over 30 years, starting by sprucing up London's Grays Inn with tree-lined walks – arguably the first avenues in Britain. One of his gardens is thought to have resembled the circular layout at Chastleton in Oxfordshire, supposedly representing the pre-Copernican universe, with the orbits of the moon, sun and planets round the Earth marked out in trees. Later he created an idiosyncratic garden in Hertfordshire, but his principal legacy is his essay, which reveres the garden as 'the purest of human pleasures … the greatest refreshment to the sprits of man'.

Rather more affordable than Bacon's 30 'princely' acres was the garden layout proposed by Yorkshire clergyman William Lawson in his 1618 *New Orchard and Garden*. Entered over a moat, with a little pointy house standing on a mount at each corner, the garden is divided into three parts bisected by a central path in a workaday version of Wilton. Each compartment has a different function – a fruit

garden with flowers between the trees, an orchard planted in a quincunx, plus a knot garden, a topiary garden with fanciful figures, and two sections devoted to vegetables. Although Lawson was writing for the country housewife, this was no cottage garden: the distinction between the ornamental and the productive was clear to see.

Some similar features survive at Packwood House in Warwickshire, where John Fetherston II (d.1670) embellished the house his father had built with walled garden courts, garden buildings, fancy gate-piers and numerous sundials. A raised brick terrace runs between jaunty twin gazebos, with a (later) summer-house and banqueting house in the opposite corners. A sketch of 1756 suggests there may even have been a moat. From the terrace, steps led down to orchards and to a spiral mount, set about with yew, which would later spawn its own romantic legend (see page 190). One feature would certainly have met with Lawson's approval – the niches built in the walls for keeping bees.

Packwood's delightful corner banqueting house seems to be just what William Lawson had in mind in his 1618 design.

Flowers of delight

Lawson's plan was a scaled-down version of fashionable gardens such as Hatfield, which Head Gardener John Tradescant was now busily stocking with all manner of new plants. When Tradescant was born, around 1570, the number of known plants was relatively small, and the English gardener's choice was confined to species indigenous to Europe. But political rapprochement with the Ottoman Empire brought plants flooding in from the East, while the voyages of discovery of the maritime nations of Europe opened up new continents to explore, bringing a host of new plants from the Spanish New World and French and Dutch colonies. Writing in 1587, chronicler William Harrison was amazed 'to see how many strange herbs, plants and annual fruits are daily brought unto us from the Indies, Americas … Canary Isles, and all parts of the world'. The most exhaustive European list in 1613 comes to just 3,000 species, compared with 10,000 a century later, and well over 400,000 today.

John Tradescant the Elder is generally acknowledged as the first of the great plant hunters. He started modestly, travelling to Europe in 1610 with a budget of £10 to buy fruit trees for Robert Cecil. A second European trip took him to the court of the 'Gardener King', Henri IV of France, where he met the great plantsman Jean Robin. They became friends, writing and exchanging plants for the next two decades, part of a growing network of plant pioneers across Europe. After Cecil's death, Tradescant journeyed to Russia in 1618 and North Africa in 1620 – ostensibly to fight pirates, but actually to secure an especially desirable apricot.

The tulip tree, *Liriodendron tulipfera*, illustrated here by Caroline Maria Applebee in 1828, was brought from the New World by John Tradescant the Younger.

It was the supremacy of the Tudor navies that had made possible the first plant discoveries of the New World in the sixteenth century. Now, as the colonies were settled, a regular supply of plants made their way to the Tradescants' garden in Lambeth. Both Tradescant and his son, also John, had shares in the English Virginia company, and in 1638, the year of his father's death, John the Younger made the first of three visits to Virginia, bringing back about 200 new plants. Their introductions include Virginia creeper (*Parthenocissus quinquefolia*), the tulip tree (*Liriodendron tulipfera*), the lofty swamp cypress (*Taxodium distichum*), the false acacia (*Robinia pseudoacacia*), the smoke bush (*Cotinus coggygria*) and the trumpet vine (*Campsis radicans*), and by 1634 they were growing over 750 different plants. As well as seeking out plant material, they also collected any curiosities they considered of interest, which they put on display at Lambeth, charging 6d admission – the first public museum in England, later to become (after some lawyerly hanky-panky) the basis of the collection at the Ashmolean in Oxford.

The first botanical gardens had been founded in 1545 at Padua and Pisa, and other European universities soon followed. The purpose of these gardens was to train physicians: to gather an encyclopaedic collection of plants and to learn how to identify them correctly, for mistakes might have unhappy consequences. But with so much exciting new material to explore, it was perhaps inevitable that botany should assume a validity distinct from medicine, and that gardeners both learned and not so learned should begin to take an interest in plants far beyond their therapeutic or culinary potential.

The first book in English to embrace unashamedly the ornamental qualities of plants was by apothecary John Parkinson (1567–1650), who kept what we would now call a plantsman's garden in Long Acre in London. In his 1629 book, *Paradisi in Sole, Paradisus Terrestris* (a laborious pun on his name, meaning 'park in sun') he made his intentions clear:

> *There be divers kinds of Mullein ... all which to distinguish or to describe, is neither to my purpose, nor the intent of this worke, which is to store a garden with flowers of delight and sequester others not worthy of that honour.*

Starting with the Crown Imperial, deserving 'for its stately beautifulness ... the first place in this our Garden of Delight', he described the cultivation of nearly 1,000 different flowers in terms that seem strikingly familiar: 'so delightsome flowers that the sight of them doth enforce an earnest longing desire to be a possessoure of some of them at the leaste'. He acknowledged the skill of fellow plantsmen (and women), shook his head over untrustworthy nurserymen who muddled up the names of plants so he could never be entirely sure what he was buying and moaned about 'knavish Gardiners' who passed off quite ordinary lupins as rarities. While drawing attention to 'outlandish' flowers that would create a tapestry of colour, he also urged the merits of native wild flowers such as Welsh poppy and lady's slipper. He also wrote about fruit and veg, declaring that the very 'choysest' plums were to be had from 'my very good friend Master John Tradescant'. *Paradisi* was just a taster for his compendious *Theatrum Botanicum*, in which he described nearly 4,000 plants and introduced many novelties, including the banana. Parkinson, was, in short, the first great English plantaholic.

Even with 4,000 plants at his disposal, it was still possible, just, to conceive of a garden

Parkinson grew many of the plants he wrote about himself, and picked out those he considered most garden-worthy. Pride of place went to the Crown Imperial, one of the earliest bulbs to be grown in Britain.

In Parkinson's Eden, just above Adam plucking the forbidden fruit, the unfortunate Tartary Lamb dangles on a stalk. One of the exhibits in the Tradescants' Ark claimed to be the skin of such a lamb.

where all known plants could be grown. This, it was believed, had been the case in the Garden of Eden, depicted on the title page of *Paradisi*. Among the tulips, fritillaries, vines and palms that grace the scene is a plant that doesn't get a mention in Genesis – the Vegetable (or Tartary) Lamb. This was supposed to grow on a stalk and graze on the grass around it. Once it had eaten up all it could reach, it starved to death. Not all was happy in Paradise.

The long winter

Nor, as *Theatrum Botanicum* went to press in 1640, was all happy in the state of Britain, as King and Parliament locked horns. By 1642, the country was in the grip of a war that no one wanted, dividing every class, setting region against region and tearing families asunder. Over three in every hundred of the population perished. As the war ended, the country descended into political anarchy, religious extremism and military dictatorship. What could an intelligent, open-minded man do in midst of this maelstrom? Royalists with the means to do so headed off to France. The diarist John Evelyn was one of a group of 'virtuosi' who travelled widely on the Continent during the 1640s, bringing back a host of influential new ideas. John Tradescant the Younger slipped quietly off to Virginia. For countless others the only solution was to keep quiet, work in solitude, outwardly conform, inwardly remain free. Men of both factions kept their heads down and gardened.

Foremost among these was Sir Thomas Hanmer (1612–78), a Royalist who, after a spot of judicious spying, was allowed home from France on payment of a modest fine, and devoted the rest of his life to gardening. His *Garden Book*, completed by 1659 but not published until 1933, gives a detailed account of what he grew and how he grew it, and provides evidence of many new cultivars of plants that had been considered novelties only 20 years earlier. His first love was the tulip, 'the Queene of Bulbous plants' and he introduced many new varieties, including the eponymous 'Agate Hanmer', judged the finest tulip ever grown in Britain.

As well as offering handy advice on how to deal with cats and moles (lie in wait with a spear), or how to catch earwigs with the hooves of sheep, Hanmer also recommended that every garden should have a 'winter house' to shelter evergreens. We cannot underestimate the impact of plentiful new evergreens on a country that until then could rely only on holly, yew and Scots pine for year-round interest. Hanmer describes desirable tender 'exotics' like citrus trees, oleander and the Brazilian coral tree (*Erythrina crista-galli*), spectacular new trees such as Cedar of Lebanon (introduced in 1645) and the strawberry tree, and shrubs we now think of as indispensable, like Pyracantha and bay. 'Greens' would become the keynote plants of the Restoration. For the plant snob, Phillyrea was probably the evergreen of choice: Hanmer's friend John Rea (d.1681), who took care to distinguish between 'trifles adored by country women' and plants esteemed by more expert 'florists', described 12 different kinds, including a striped one. For Rea the Commonwealth years were one 'long winter' during which plants were his only solace.

Thomas Hanmer, above, shared his precious 'rootes' with both royalist friends John Evelyn and John Rea and the famously tulipomaniac Parliamentarian general Sir John Lambert: the love of tulips was far stronger than faction.

Recreating Eden

'And the Lord God planted a garden eastward in Eden; and there he put the man whom he had formed' (Genesis 2, v8). In the seventeenth century, this was a matter of fact. Ever since Adam had been expelled from the Garden of Eden, it was understood that we were pining to return there. So it was eminently reasonable, and pleasurable, and virtuous, to seek to recreate that garden on Earth. This was especially true after the Civil War when, during the Commonwealth, the association of the garden with Eden became part of the drive to build the New Jerusalem. And there was no time to lose – it was widely believed the end of the world was nigh.

The mighty Milton imagined Eden as 'a happy rural seat' with groves of fruit trees and verdant lawns where flowers grew naturally, 'not like art in beds and curious knots'. But if Eden was decorative, that was only in passing; the point of Eden was to be productive. Through hard work and piety (for bad harvests were the result of sinfulness) the soil could be restored to the state of fertility it had enjoyed before the Fall, crops would increase, and the nation would return to its former Edenic state. This certainly was the belief of agricultural reformer Samuel Hartlib (1600–62), who also suggested that all waste ground should be planted with apples, pears, quinces and walnuts 'for the relief of the poor, the benefit of the rich and the delighte of all'. In this way the whole kingdom might become 'The Garden of God'. (When, however, the Levellers sought to put a not dissimilar scheme into action, they found their houses smashed and their crops destroyed.) Similarly, Walter Blith, a captain in the New Model Army, suggested planting the new hedgerows resulting from enclosure with fruit trees to provide food and fuel for the poor.

Prior to the Commonwealth, the growing of fruit had been something of a gentlemanly competitive sport. Now it became a devotional act. Typical was the Oxford divine Ralph Austen, who in his *Treatise of Fruit Trees* (1653), advanced both 'divine' and 'human' reasons for planting fruit – 43 pages of the former, before getting down to the practical business of planting, pruning and grafting. Fruit was the proof of the liberality of God. A well-kept orchard was the mark of an orderly and prospering household, a humble and devout heart and a carefully tended soul. 'The World is a great Library,' wrote Austen, 'and Fruit-trees are some of the Bookes wherein we may read and see plainly the Attributes of God.'

Ralph Austen's fruit manual was the most advanced yet produced in English – yet half was given over to a devotional essay, showing how the Elect would find salvation in God's orchard.

'A Friend, a Booke and a Garden'

Many of Ralph Austen's preoccupations were shared by John Evelyn (1620–1705). Heir to a fortune founded on manufacturing gunpowder for Elizabeth I, he was able to spend most of the Civil War and its aftermath touring France, Italy and the Netherlands. Here he visited nurseries and made a deep study of gardens, along with all he could discover of the latest advances in science and husbandry. Today he is remembered principally as a diarist (he was a friend of the more famous Samuel Pepys); the *Elysium Britannicum*, however, the encyclopaedic work which was still unfinished after 50 years, gives a better idea of the breadth of his learning and interests. He was hugely influential in introducing continental ideas to England, making his own version of an Italian villa garden at his home in Deptford as early as 1652. He championed the planting of avenues, claimed to be the first to use yew for topiary and was famed for his outstandingly well-grown hedges. He was a devotee of the apple (especially in the form of cider) and wrote what is surely the first book on superfoods, advocating a wholesome vegetarian diet. He was also an early ecologist, deeply worried about deforestation. Timber was, in the seventeenth

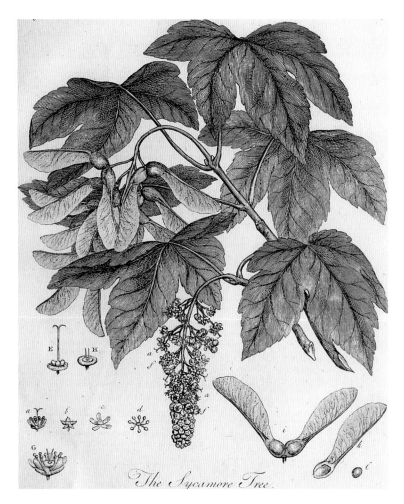

The sycamore, *Acer pseudoplatanus*, pictured in John Evelyn's *Sylva,* in which he argued passionately for the reforestation of Britain.

century, the equivalent of today's fossil fuels, and the prospect of it running out created very similar anxieties.

The year 1660 saw the foundation of the Royal Society, with the aim of 'improving natural knowledge'. It was Evelyn who contributed the Society's first book: *Sylva, or a Discourse of Forest Trees* (1664). 'We had better be without gold than without timber,' insisted Evelyn, 'because without trees there would be no iron and glass industry, no fires to warm houses in winter, nor a navy to protect the shores of England.' He urged landowners to restock as a matter of patriotic duty. Charles II led the way, laying out avenues of elms at Greenwich and St James's Park, and his subjects soon followed suit. *Sylva* became a bestseller (and remained the standard work for the next century), the oak was adopted as a symbol of national pride, and all proceeded splendidly until the Great Storm of 1703, a week-long hurricane that tore through the south of England decimating the new plantings. It was reported that 4,000 oaks were uprooted in the New Forest, and over 17,000 trees in Kent. The Eddystone Lighthouse was swept away, and the chimneys of Wells Palace fell in, killing the bishop and his wife in their bed. It was a disaster, mourned Evelyn, 'not to be paralleled with anything happening in our age or in any history almost'. Evelyn himself lost 2,000 trees.

The avenues planted in St James's Park set a new fashion for tree planting. This coloured engraving made in 1730 shows them well established.

THE BLESSING OF BEES

PLANTING for pollinators has become the latest fashion in our gardens. But bees have been prized in the garden from time immemorial. The Ancient Egyptians, the Romans, even the peasantry in the Dark Ages kept bees, and medieval bee shelters can still be found in British gardens. In Tudor times, all serious books on gardening had at least one chapter on bee-keeping. The first full-length book, by Charles Butler, appeared in 1609. It includes a four-page 'madrigal' – a musical notation of the buzzing of his bees.

Fruit was of first importance to the seventeenth-century garden, and great store was set by its pollinator, the bee. Bees were ideal role models – industrious, clean and well-organised, with an efficient social structure that ensured strict division of labour and property. All this is summed up just in the title of Samuel Hartlib's 1655 bee-keeping manual, *The Reformed Commonwealth of Bees*. Bees, moreover, were believed to reproduce asexually. (They were long thought to spring spontaneously from rotting meat.) They were therefore free from sin – 'living chastely together like so many angels' – and ideal companions in the Garden of Eden.

At this time bees were still kept in skeps, cone-shaped baskets of straw, rope or wickerwork, usually placed in niches in the garden wall. Thirty such niches can be seen in the south side of the terrace wall at Packwood. The longest known beehive wall, with 46 niches, is at the Dolmelynllyn Estate at Ganllwyd near Dolgellau in Wales, discovered during restoration in 2011. (Most gardens would have around five.) William Lawson, however, writing in 1618, preferred a free-standing bee-house in an orchard, 'for bees love Flowers and wood with their hearts'.

The problem with skeps was that there was no way to get to the honey without breaking through the sides, and that could only be done by killing the bees. This quandary was not really resolved until the invention of the moveable cone hive in the mid-nineteenth century. Until then, skeps remained, housed in increasingly elaborate structures such as the beautiful Regency Bee House at Attingham Park in Shropshire (see page 27), a graceful trelliswork pavilion possibly designed by John Nash or Humphry Repton.

The moveable frame hive reached Britain in 1860, and simple, free-standing hives soon became the norm, but at Benthall Hall in Shropshire, bees continued to be kept in the porch of the Restoration church. The stone head of a lion marked the entrance to the colony. Bees flew in though his mouth and crawled up a tube to hives installed beneath window seats in the upper part of the porch.

In 2016, The Hive arrived at Kew. This extraordinary installation, a flickering, lattice-like structure emitting a low humming sound, resembles from a distance a gigantic swarm of bees. The intensity of sound and light changes constantly, triggered by activity in a real beehive at Kew. It is a powerful symbol of the bees' vital role in feeding the planet and the challenges facing them today.

Clockwise from top left: To keep them dry, skeps were often set into purpose-built niches or, bottom left, waterproofed with mud or cow dung and raised on a bench against the wall. The church porch at Benthall Hall in Shropshire provides an unusual beehive. The Hive, an immersive installation by artist Wolfgang Buttress at Kew, draws attention to the plight of bees. Smoking the hives at Hidcote in Gloucestershire. Planting for pollinators was well understood in previous centuries.

Ham House in Surrey, restored to its
splendour in 1671, when its chatelaine
Elizabeth Dysart was a prominent
member of the Restoration court.

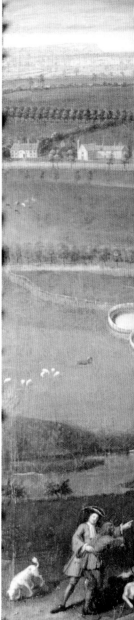

Restoration gardens

During his years of exile, Charles II had sought protection from his cousin Louis
XIV of France. Louis was untroubled by doubt about the proper powers of the
monarchy, and to prove the point, would shortly commandeer the great French
gardener André Le Nôtre to make the most ostentatious and self-glorifying garden
that the world had ever seen.

   As Charles sailed back to England in triumph in 1660, Versailles was still
no more than a humble hunting lodge. Nonetheless the new king came home
with a head full of the ambitious gardening ideas being perfected in France –
patterns of avenues radiating from a single point to roll out for miles on end,
cutting inexorably through field and forest; canals and basins large enough, quite

literally, to float battleships; great scrollwork parterres of embroidered intricacy; water jets that soared to the sky – everything vast, magnificent, the apogee of elegance; monumental in ambition and sheer self-confidence. Designed primarily to be viewed from above from the windows of some sumptuous salon, these were landscapes that proclaimed a proud authority over man and nature alike.

In England many aristocratic gardens, especially royal ones, had been destroyed in the Civil War. The great palaces at Oatlands and Theobalds had been demolished and sold off brick by brick. Greenwich was so degraded that Charles demolished it himself. Countless other properties had been sequestered under the Commonwealth. There had been a few lucky escapes: at Ham House in Surrey, the wily Elizabeth, Countess Dysart, a covert Royalist, had kept her estate intact by holding her nose and getting on intimate terms with Oliver Cromwell. (The

A bird's-eye view of Charlecote Park, Warwickshire in the 1690s – a gentry garden made in the new French-inspired style.

garden had been leased to her Head Gardener with a requirement to maintain the fruit, but also to permit the family to continue to enjoy the garden.) In general, however, royal and Royalist gardening had to make a fresh start, and it was Le Nôtre who provided the inspiration.

Le Nôtre's pupil, André Mollet, had worked in 1640 for Charles's mother, Queen Henrietta Maria. Charles lost no time in summoning him back to London to construct a suitably regal canal in St James's Park and to direct new projects at Whitehall and Hampton Court. Here an even grander canal, flanked by avenues of lime trees stretching to the horizon, was created in honour of Charles II's bride, Catherine of Braganza: the Long Water was designed to be viewed from the new

John Evelyn visited Hampton Court in 1662 and noted with approval 'a flat, naked piece of Ground, now planted with sweete rows of Lime-trees, and the Canale for water now neere perfected.'

Queen's gilded balcony. For the Queen's House at Greenwich, Charles commissioned plans from le Nôtre himself, but his schemes were never realised.

The partnership of engraver Johannes Kip and artist Leonard Knyff provide our best clue today of just how widespread this style became. In 1708 they published *Britannia Illustrata*, a work offering bird's-eye views of '*the Principal seats of the Nobility and Gentry of Great Britain, Curiously Engraven on 80 Copper Plates*'. Time after time we see gardens divided into highly decorated squares, regular blocks of tree planting, *allées* in goosefoot (*patte d'oie*) formation radiating out from the house through the 'wilderness', or wood, beyond. Few traces remain on the ground, but at Dunham Massey in Cheshire there are still faint echoes of the six great avenues that once fanned out from the South Lawn, while at Blickling in Norfolk the paths running through the woods are all that remains of the seventeenth-century layout. A mighty avenue of limes survives at Kingston Lacy in Dorset. At Powis Castle, from the 1660s, formal terraces were carved from the hillside landscape, and a great water garden laid out on the flat land below. Today only the terraces remain.

On Charles's death, his brother James II continued in the Baroque manner, engaging Guillaume Beaumont, who had trained under Le Nôtre at Versailles, as his Head Gardener at Hampton Court. Here Beaumont worked alongside one Colonel Grahame, who acted as supervisor of the Royal gardens. When

This painting by Leonard Knyff, *c.* 1703, shows how Henry VIII's jumble of courtyards at Hampton Court was transformed by successive monarchs into a grand Baroque layout. Charles II introduced the avenues and canal, then William III infilled with intricate box-scrolled parterres, and laid out a Privy Garden on the river side.

the Catholic King James was deposed, both men were dismissed. They retreated to Grahame's home at Levens Hall in Cumbria, where they laid out a topiary garden that was already looking a tad old-fashioned when work began in 1694. Happily Colonel Grahame was indifferent to fashion, as was the Bagot family who followed him to Levens and live there still. For this oversight, every lover of topiary blesses them. Over three centuries Beaumont's yews have grown into mighty trees, clipped into an assortment of gloriously eccentric shapes. There is no other garden quite like Levens – a dizzying step back in time.

Aristocratic gardening, then, prospered, borrowing for the first time a whole coherent look from continental Europe rather than a random hotchpotch of features. But the lower ranks were at it too, laying out geometric gardens that, even if not large, were pleasing to the eye in their regularity. There were many more plants to choose from, and plenty of good advice available, cheaply and in English, from the many who had addressed themselves to husbandry during the Commonwealth period. Among them was John Worlidge, who in his *Systema horti-cultura; or the art of gardening* (1677) could write:

> there is not a Noble or pleasant Seat in England but hath its gardens for pleasure and delight; scarce an ingenious Citizen that by his confinement to a Shop, being denied the priviledge of having a real garden, but hath his boxes. pots or other receptacles for Flowers, Plants, etc ... there is scarce a Cottage in most of the Southern Parts of England but hath its proportionable garden, so great a delight do most men take in it; that they may not only please themselves with the view of the flowers, herbs and trees, as they grow, but furnish themselves and their neighbours ... with the proper produces of their gardens.

The British, in other words, had become a nation of gardeners.

Britain, a fledgling concept at the beginning of the Stuart era, was a very different place by the end of it. Enforced retirement during the Civil War, not only of Royalists, but of parliamentarians who could no longer stomach Cromwell's regime, contributed to a growing conviction, sanctioned by classical models, that country life was inherently superior to urban life. Henceforth, anyone who had a bob to spare would aspire to an estate in the country – a preference that seemed all the more reasonable after the Great Plague and the Great Fire of London.

There were more people – over 5.5 million in 1688 as opposed to 4 million in 1600 – and they were better educated. While classical texts were more widely known, they no

longer commanded unquestioning authority. Instead, observation and enquiry became the foundations of knowledge. This new investigative spirit prompted an appetite for agricultural reform, accelerating enclosure, for only land in private ownership could be improved, or indeed planted with trees, an activity both patriotic and profitable. (Evelyn claimed over 2 million timber trees were planted as a result of his book.)

Most significantly, conspicuous consumption was back on the cards, and it was no longer the preserve of the super-rich: for the first time the middling sort – the merchants, the gentry, a new professional class – had financial clout, and could express their aspirations in gardens.

The topiary garden at Levens Hall in Cumbria, much of which survives from the seventeenth century. The golden yews were added two centuries later.

The future is Orange

On 5 November 1688 William, Prince of Orange turned up in Torbay with 20,000 troops to claim the British crown, and within a few months was ensconced at Hampton Court, revamping Charles II's garden with the garden team from Het Loo.

William and Mary were both keen gardeners. Queen Mary hastened to establish a 'cabinet' of her horticultural treasures; new French-style avenues and a splendid new parterre took shape on the East Front, and work began on the Privy Garden on the South Front under the auspices of Henry Wise. Things did not go well. Or perhaps the Prince, now William III, was less decisive as a gardener than a general. The King had commanded that his new garden be lowered by 8ft (2.4m), so that he could enjoy a clear view of the Thames from the palace. But when he came to inspect his new garden in June 1701, the view was still not to his liking, and the garden was lowered yet again, at a cost of £1,426.4s 4d (about £4.1 million today). No wonder Henry Wise died a very rich man. That garden, immaculately restored in 1995, now shows exactly how it looked in 1702, with its raised terraces and gravelled walks, knife-sharp topiary and *gazon coupé* – a pattern of geometrical designs cut out in the grass.

Ever since the Glorious Revolution had become a twinkle in Whiggish eyes, grandees with an eye to the main chance had been adopting a more Dutch style in the garden: to abjure the Baroque extravagance of Catholic Europe with all its panoplies of fountains and statuary and elaborately patterned parterres in favour of a plainer and more intimate style was not only a discreet statement of political allegiance (and cheaper to maintain), but somehow, with its mistrust of pomp, seemed more closely attuned to the British character.

In reality, it could be hard to distinguish between French and Dutch style, but broadly, the topography of the two countries supplied the clue. In Holland, land was at a premium, so garden spaces tended to be smaller, usually composed of multiple enclosures, both ornamental and productive, set between networks of drainage ditches – translated, in the formal garden, into canals. High hedges kept out the cold winds that blasted across the polders. In France, there were fewer impediments, either topographic or political, to driving immense vistas over hill and down dale. If the French style was all about conspicuous display, the Dutch might be summed up by the splendid Danish concept of *hygge*. Nowhere demonstrates this particular mood more exactly than Westbury Court at Westbury-on-Severn in Gloucestershire.

Here prosperous merchant Maynard Colchester dug out a long straight canal flanked by tall hedges and topiary, in which was reflected an almost frivolously

Opposite: Having secured a top-notch bride, wealthy merchant Maynard Colchester further bolstered his social credentials by doing up his garden at Westbury Court in Gloucestershire in the new, royally sanctioned, Dutch manner.

Left: The Privy Garden at Hampton Court saw Dutch style imported wholesale to the banks of the Thames under the supervision of Henry Wise.

tall summer-house which offered views over the water meadows to the Severn. Further views could be enjoyed through an ironwork *clairvoyée* or grille along an avenue planted in the field across the road. There were yew cones and holly lollies, a neat quincunx of trees and a box parterre, but above all there were flowers: account books show the purchase of hundreds of bulbs, not only wildly popular tulips but irises, crocuses, scillas and hyacinths, double narcissus, anemones and ranunculus, along with scented shrubs and many kinds of fruit growing in the orchard and trained on the walls. A second, T-shaped canal and a small walled garden and gazebo were added by his heir; various other features have been lost. But what has miraculously endured, in spite of the destruction of the house and the loss of much of the garden beneath a housing estate, is an extraordinarily potent atmosphere – calm, intimate, enclosed and nurturing.

There must have been hundreds of these modest gentry gardens in similar style. But other than Castle Bromwich Hall, in the suburbs of Birmingham, Westbury is the only one to survive. On a grander scale, at Dyrham Park, near Bath, William Blathwayt had been busy since 1691 laying out an elaborate garden with flowery courts, a sequence of canals, a mighty cascade and extensive terraces which took advantage of the splendid views out towards Wales. The style had to be Dutch: Blathwayt was effectively William III's chief of staff, in charge of both the army and the diplomatic service, no doubt because he was the only senior official to speak fluent Dutch.

In 2017, the principal flower borders either side of the carriage drive at Dyrham Park near Bath were reinstated in the original Dutch style.

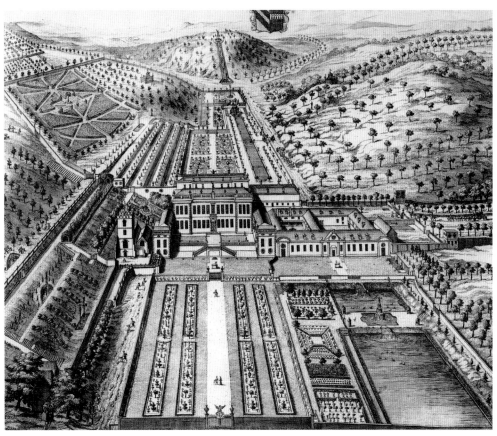

In 1710 Blathwayt commissioned engraver Johannes Kip to record the garden, and today that engraving, supported by extensive garden archaeology, is providing the basis for a major restoration project to bring the garden – arguably the last major Dutch garden in England – back to life. Newly reinstated beds flanking the original approach to the house are bright in spring with tulips and Crown Imperials, with height supplied by topiary and painted white posts. A Victorian rockery has been cleared from Blathwayt's upper canal (though Repton's charming niches overlooking the water remain, perfectly placed to enjoy the morning sun). The terraces are being cleared of centuries of overgrowth, and it is still just possible to discern how plantings of pear and hornbeam, now grown to mighty trees, once made patterns on the steep slopes. Despite its scale and formality, this was a garden devoid of pomposity, bursting with sound and scent and featuring such delightful conceits as 'cabinets' which could be spun to face the sun and wickerwork arbours equipped with bookstands and small desks dotted round the wilderness. Outdoor study was supposed to be refreshing, and the wilderness (which at that time meant a dense but still formal planting) commanded a view that might inspire the dullest brain. Dyrham was also rich in plants – Blathwayt's role as administrator of the American colonies gave him access to seeds that were successfully grown on – Virginian pine, sassafras, tulip tree and many American oaks, while the palatial orangery attached to the house housed many exotic 'greens' which ornamented the forecourt during the summer.

An engraving by Johannes Kip of Dyrham Park, published in 1712, seems to provide an accurate record of how the garden looked, corroborated by the recent discovery of a detailed written description.

London and Wise

The garden at Dyrham was designed by George London, half of a dynamic duo that had a virtual monopoly of upper-crust gardening towards the end of the seventeenth century.

London started out as a junior partner in the legendary Brompton Park nursery, a Gang of Four eminent head gardeners who in 1681 had the wizard wheeze of combining growing with garden design. Their speciality was an Anglicised form of the French Baroque, featuring lengthy tree-lined avenues, neat blocks of 'wilderness' and magnificent parterres delineated in box and

The 'Birdcage', at Melbourne Hall in Derbyshire was made by Robert Bakewell in 1706–8 for £120, bringing him fame but leaving him penniless.

other evergreens. These designs all required prodigious quantities of plants, all grown, often to an advanced and expensive state of maturity, in their nursery in Kensington. This was no small undertaking – it was reputed to cover some 100 acres (40.5ha), covering the site of today's Kensington museums, and in 1702 held a stock of nearly ten million plants (including the eponymous Brompton stock, *Matthiola incana*, still popular in gardens today). They also did a brisk trade in exotics: London had been Head Gardener to the plantaholic Bishop Compton, who continued to help him throughout his career with new seeds and helpful introductions.

In 1689, his erstwhile colleagues having died or retired, London took on a new partner, Henry Wise, and for the next two decades, until London died in 1713, the nursery of London and Wise reigned supreme. Both men were, in turn, appointed royal gardeners, and they worked at all the greatest houses in the land – at Longleat in Wiltshire, at Badminton in Gloucestershire, at Burghley in Lincolnshire and Chatsworth in Derbyshire. Of humble origins themselves, they did not disdain to work for New Money: London's last commission was for Sir Richard Child at Wanstead, which came to be known as 'the English Versailles'. There was a boom of country house building going on at the time, which reached a climax in the 1720s – and of course every new (or palatially refurbished) seat required an appropriately dignified setting.

London was the creative force, riding from one prestigious commission to the next, often covering often 60 miles a day, as Capability Brown would do after him. Wise looked after the money, planning the projects and running the nursery. He does not appear to have ripped off his clients: when the suspicious Sir John Vanbrugh looked into his prices, he found Queen Anne was paying no more for her plants than any other citizen. But he was certainly a supremely able manager: when he died in 1737 he was said to be worth £200,000 (over £600m at today's values). It was Wise, however, who took on the duo's biggest ever project, working with Vanbrugh at Blenheim, where he laid out vast parterres and an 8 acre (3.2ha) kitchen garden which required half a million bricks to build the walls.

London and Wise did not always work on this scale. At Melbourne Hall in Derbyshire, London created a mini-Versailles composed of 'terrasses, sloops, verges and fleets of steps' along with 'reservoirs or bassoons for water', fruit walls, kitchen gardens, orchards and plantations. It is his only remaining garden, significant not just for its rarity, but for the way it leavens a formal French structure with a certain skittishness, such as the 'birdcage' arbour by Robert Bakewell in many ways anticipates the playful Rococo style that would later sweep Europe. There is a similar lightness of spirit at Canons Ashby, in Northamptonshire, restored by the National Trust to its layout in 1710 (albeit with a nineteenth-century overlay), believed to be by Henry Wise and Tilleman Bobart. A sequence of four terraces descends the hill, offering views out over the meadows below. The first is the most formal, but bedded out in cheerful colours, the second plainer and simpler, the lower two devoted to vegetables, fruit and cutting flowers. Especially in spring, when tall purple tulips bob in the beds and the lines of pear trees are wreathed in blossom, it is an Edenic scene that might have gladdened a Puritan heart.

This is why these survivals are so hugely important: looking at the monochrome engravings of these formal gardens that adorn virtually every country house, we might easily conclude that these regular, linear layouts were cold and dull. That is surely the impetus behind the restoration conducted by the National Trust at Dyrham and at Hanbury Hall in Worcestershire, where London's original garden, swept away in 1770, has been lovingly reinstated using original plans and a bird's-eye drawing of 1772. Geometric it may be, but it is anything but dull, with its burgeoning fruit and vegetable plots and shrub-packed wilderness, its brightly painted summer-houses and fanciful gazebos, a liberal scattering of golden balls among the topiary and girly lengths of treillage. The planting of the great sunken parterre is gleaned from lists used by Henry Wise, and from the duo's popular book, *The Retir'd Gardener* (1706) – a translation from a manual by French writer Louis Ligier. It is resolutely formal, with each plant displayed jewel-like against a background of bare earth, but bursting with colour – bright orange marigolds, purple pasqueflowers, and, of course, Brompton stocks – what London and Wise called 'a Cloth of Tissue of divers Colours', set off by glossy topiary forms.

The parterre at Hanbury Hall, restored by the National Trust in the mid-1990s to a framework of mathematical precision in which plants are displayed like jewels in a case.

A similar mood can be gleaned from the Stoke Edith tapestries, a pair of wall hangings made around 1710, now in London's Victoria and Albert Museum. Tradition has it that these were made by the ladies of the family and depict the newly made Herefordshire garden of Paul Foley, Speaker of the House of Commons. But experts at the V&A have suggested that the needlework is too fine to be the work of amateurs, so these may be shop-bought scenes of fashionable garden features rather than a faithful record. What we do know is that the garden was substantially remodelled after a visit from George London in 1692, and very much in his trademark Baroque style. Once again we see a garden of formal compartments, with elaborate fountains and topiary and trees in 'jars'. Tulips and carnations are arranged in double rows in *plate-bandes* – narrow strips of planting bordering the grass parterre. Ladies, children, small dogs, monkeys and a smart black servant stroll the sunny paths, or take tea on them, serenaded by a harpist. Another servant trips and drops his tray. Even the sphinxes look jolly.

But in this garden, completed after Foley's death in 1699, we can see the clues of its approaching destruction. The Italianate orangery and slim cypresses bespeak a growing fascination with that country which was about to revolutionise the English garden. More significantly, here is a garden where we see over the wall, to the woods and villages and hills behind. Nature is no longer excluded but part of the picture. Within 20 years, William Kent will be leaping that wall, discovering that 'all nature is a garden.'

One of a pair of embroidered wall hangings, long thought to depict the 1690s formal garden at Stoke Edith in Herefordshire.

GARDEN VISITING

FOR as long as we have had gardens, other people have come to stare at them, and nearly everything we know about garden history comes from the accounts of garden visitors. The first great English tourist was John Evelyn, who travelled extensively in Europe in the 1640s. It took a certain stoutness of constitution to go garden-visiting in the seventeenth century: roads were appalling, highwaymen legion and accommodation grubby – none of which deterred the redoubtable Celia Fiennes, who in 1697–8 travelled 3,000 miles (4,828km) on horseback, visiting every county in England. Further courage was required when entering the garden, for the most popular features in the fashionable seventeenth-century garden were water jokes: Celia gives a remarkably cheerful account of getting soaked at Wilton.

By the eighteenth century, garden-makers had rather loftier intentions for their visitors, guiding their responses with Latin inscriptions and carefully coded architectural features. All educated persons at the time shared a classical education, and could be relied on to pick up all the references. At Stowe, Lord Cobham wanted to disseminate his political agenda. At The Leasowes, near Halesowen, the agenda was poetical rather than political, but still required visitors to follow a circuit walk. Garden-maker William Shenstone was enraged if people went round the wrong way, and swore visitors from the nearby grand estate at Hagley did so just to tease him. He also had trouble with vandals, pleading with his visitors in verse to 'tread with awe these favour'd bowers,/Nor wound the shrubs nor bruise the flowers' – sentiments familiar to many a head gardener today. But generally Shenstone, a socially clumsy individual, rather enjoyed the society of his visitors. One Sunday in 1749 he counted some 150 people in the garden, and was thrilled that

his humble *ferme ornée* attracted almost as many visitors as aristocratic Stowe.

The key thing about these gardens is that they were designed to be visited, not just for private pleasure. And while the seventeenth-century garden had been open only to the select few, now anyone could enter who was respectably dressed. At Stowe, Stourhead and Castle Howard, inns were provided for garden visitors. It is Rokeby, however, that boasts the first known tea room.

It was during the 1770s that garden visiting really became a national sport, bringing tourists speeding along the new turnpike roads in faster, less bone-shaking carriages, with the writings of the Rev. William Gilpin in hand. He started a craze for 'picturesque' travel, encouraging viewers to seek in the landscape 'that kind of beauty that is agreeable in a picture', and gardens were soon included in these artistic excursions. Jane Austen was a Gilpin fan, and when, in *Pride and Prejudice*, Lizzie Bennett visits Pemberley, Darcy's garden reveals him to the heroine as a man of refined taste. (We also learn how garden-visiting was generally conducted – by applying to the senior servants of the house.) This new appreciation of wild, natural scenery was soon conflated with philosopher Edmund Burke's ideas of the Sublime, sparking a voyeuristic delight in melancholy and terror. By the 1770s, garden tourists were eagerly seeking out scenes that would inspire 'horrid' sensations: the garden visit had metamorphosed from an intellectual game into an emotional rollercoaster.

None of this appealed to Victorian garden guru John Claudius Loudon, who undertook eight lengthy garden tours, writing them up in *The Gardener's Magazine*. Windsor Castle was castigated for its 'shabby, half-starved fuchsias' and Blenheim for its green and slimy lake, while Stowe was pronounced shoddy and old-fashioned. What really interested Loudon was plants, which he desired to see displayed with a 'high and polished neatness'. The point of visiting a garden, for him (as for many of us today), was to pick up tips for your own, and he urged employers to furnish their gardeners with a 'velocipede' and an allowance of 20 shillings, in order to 'see other gardens as frequently and extensively as they possibly can'.

The coming of the railways made garden-visiting an option for a far wider public, and by 1867, Chatsworth was welcoming holiday crowds of 'little pale-faced men and women from the cotton factories of Manchester'. But others took fright at the prospect of such hordes, and by Edwardian times, the gardens of the wealthy were overwhelmingly out of bounds.

It was Miss Elsie Wragg who prised open the garden gate once more. In 1927 she persuaded 609 garden-owners, including the King and Queen, to open their gardens at a shilling a time to raise money for the Queen's Nursing Institute. It was such a success that her National Gardens Scheme is still going strong today.

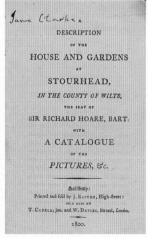

Clockwise from top: Visitors arrive at West Wycombe's Music Temple, only accessible by boat. An illustrated guide to Stourhead in Wiltshire, published in 1800. This painting of a fête in Petworth Park in West Sussex in 1835 records the second of two great feasts laid on by the 3rd Earl Egremont for local people: 54 tables, each 50ft long, were laid out on the lawn and laden with goodies. 4,000 invitations were sent out, but in the event, nearer 6,000 people turned up.

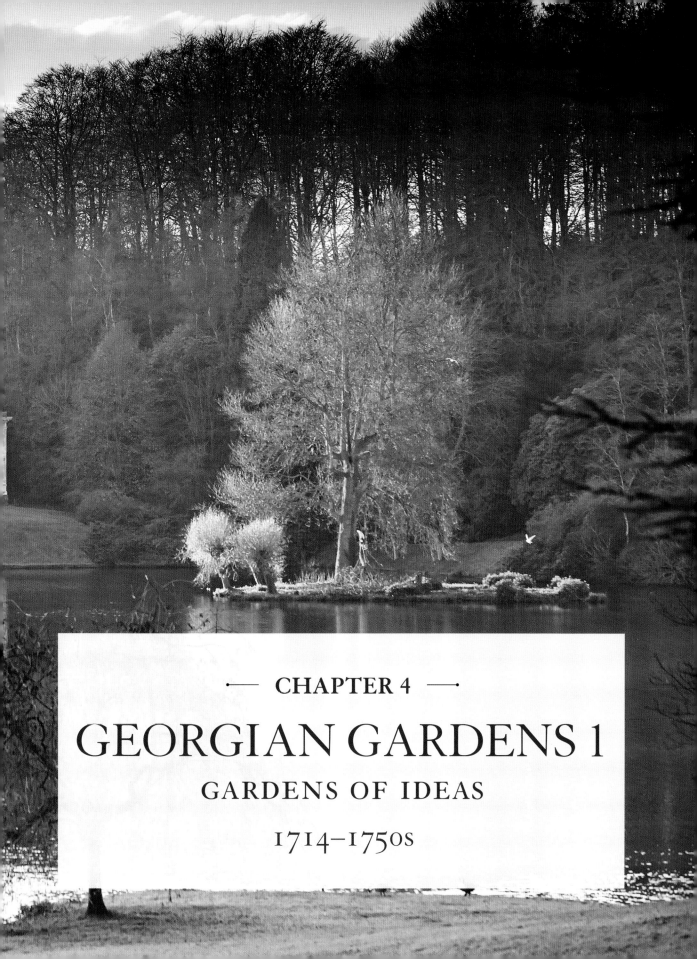

CHAPTER 4

GEORGIAN GARDENS 1

GARDENS OF IDEAS

1714–1750s

'et in Arcadia ego'

FROM VIRGIL'S *ECLOGUES*

THE rise of the English landscape garden has excited strong passions. For some, like Sir Roy Strong, the creation of these gardens was an act of wholesale vandalism, sweeping away in a few short decades the complex, flower-filled gardens we had enjoyed for centuries (and would do again). For others, it is a uniquely British art form, and the greatest contribution to art this country has ever made.

What is undeniable is that the landscape garden, as it emerged from the second decade of the eighteenth century, is the most superlative, the most breathtaking con trick. For looking at the serene expanses of Stowe's Elysian Fields, the lyrical vales of Rousham or the glassy perfection of the moon ponds at Studley Royal, we might easily believe ourselves to be witnessing the ultimate expression of civilised tranquillity, untroubled peace and plenty. Nothing could be further from the truth. Between 1685 and 1750, as this garden style reached maturity, the British mainland was subject to two dynastic and one agricultural revolutions, a financial crash, three rebellions, five invasions (one of which might be deemed successful) and three European wars (not counting those in Ireland); also, for better or worse, the beginnings of party politics as we would now understand it. So although the immediate horrors of the Civil War and the turbulence of the Commonwealth had passed, these were by no means quiet times.

Then, looking at these gardens, you might easily be persuaded that the scene before you was entirely natural. This new style of gardening, enthused Sir Thomas Robinson in 1734, had 'the appearance of beautiful nature, and without

The exquisite balance and tranquillity of the landscape garden at Studley Royal in North Yorkshire was, astonishingly, the product of personal anguish and public humiliation.

being told, one would imagine art had no part in the finishing.' More sleight of hand: to create these pieces of perfected nature took the most colossal effort and expense. Robinson's letter went on to note the teams of labourers hard at work at Claremont, Chiswick and Stowe.

Just one phase of the landscaping of Wrest Park in Bedfordshire (still largely a formal scheme) took over 15 years (1686–1701) and cost £3,348 19s 7½d – which equates to just short of £50 million today. (An item that crops up regularly in the accounts is 'Beer for the Workemen'.) Compare that with another major earth-moving project going on at the same time: the Aire and Calder navigation, which required the construction of 12 locks along the River Aire at the cost of some £10,000. So a landowner might be willing to spend one third of the cost of the nation's most important infrastructure project, just on improving his garden.

Sanderson Miller was a direct contemporary of Capability Brown and shared his skill with water. At Farnborough Hall in Warwickshire, Miller united three fishponds in a boggy valley to create a curving lake that suggested the bend of a great river.

Often the gardens led the way in technology, especially in the handling of water. (Some of the earliest use of steam power, for example, was for pumping engines to fill newly made lakes, adapting pumps more usually used in mining.) Capability Brown, in particular, was to prove a stupendous water engineer, and many innovative techniques ascribed to canal-builders were first employed in gardens.

The fact that the great and the good would invest this amount of time and effort shows the extraordinary imaginative power of this new vision of gardening. More significantly, it soon appeared that everyone wanted to join in. In 1739, *Common Sense* magazine grumbled, 'Every Man Now, be his fortune what it will, is to be *doing something at his Place*, as the fashionable Phrase is; and you hardly meet with any Body, who, after the first Compliments, does not inform you, that he is *in Mortar and moving of Earth*; the modest terms for Building and Gardening'.

Left: The Chinese House at Stowe in Buckinghamshire, probably designed by William Kent around 1738, is believed to be the first garden building in Britain to adopt the new fashion for Chinoiserie (see page 162).

Left: Robert Adam's 1760 design for a hermitage at Kedleston Hall in Derbyshire.

In 1700, most gardens employed a severely geometric style, influenced by Dutch, French and Italian gardens. Within 50 years, formality was fighting a losing battle against harmonious compositions of swelling hills and serpentine waters, adorned with artfully placed clumps and woodlands, with extensive grassy swathes grazed by suitably comely livestock. The outlook was varied by an extraordinary range of garden buildings: not just the ubiquitous classical temples but obelisks, pyramids, dog kennels and baths, hermitages, root-houses, Chinese tea-houses and Turkish tents. In short, the scene on the ground had changed completely. But the biggest change was that these were gardens of ideas.

To some extent that has always been the case. For example, the formal gardens of Le Nôtre, with their lucidity, their rationality, their control, were the perfect expression of the intellectual climate of seventeenth-century France. ('I think therefore I am'). Similarly, the heraldic beasts of Henry VIII expressed some fairly forcible ideas about kingship, and we have noted at Lyveden New Bield that a garden could have a powerful allegorical purpose.

But now gardens began to take on all the big ideas of the eighteenth century – man's relationship with nature, the pursuit of the good life, freedom from tyranny and oppression, social justice, patriotism. They worked by making reference to a body of knowledge shared by all educated men of the time – a process of allusion familiar to us in reading, say, the poetry of Yeats or Eliot, but which no longer (with a few honourable exceptions) pertains in gardens.

A garden, owners found, could say more about you than simply how rich or powerful you were. It could say what you believed in, what you aspired to – even, quite explicitly, what your political allegiances were. It could show you to be a man of honour; above all, a Man of Taste. A garden, in short, could do your talking for you, and that talking could be celebratory or angry or elegiac or deliciously filthy.

A knowledge of the Classics, drummed in at school, supplemented by the experience of art and architecture gleaned as part of the Grand Tour (the early eighteenth-century equivalent of the gap year) provided the language for this discourse. In time, eagerly read books on classical architecture (such as the first English edition of Palladio's *I Quattro Libri dell'Architettura*, published in 1715) would make that language ever more refined. For those who had made it to Italy, memories of the great Renaissance gardens provided both powerful visual imagery and useful lessons in how to harness garden iconography to the message you wished to convey. The garden then, was clearly understood as an art form – on a par with poetry and painting, and drawing inspiration from them both, no less than philosophy, politics and science.

Above right: Merlin's Cave was a thatched rustic folly built by William Kent for Queen Caroline at what is now Kew Gardens. Capability Brown had it sold off for scrap. Right: A dash of exoticism might be added to a garden by a Turkish tent. The example at Painshill in Surrey is a modern reconstruction.

WHIGS AND TORIES

WHEN George I took the throne in 1714, political parties as we know them now were in their infancy. Instead, there were two loose political groupings, rather in the manner of 2016's Brexiteers and Remainers, divided by profoundly opposing visions of where political power should lie. There were no hard and fast rules, but generally, Whigs were modern metropolitan types, more likely to be self-made men (though their leaders were mega-landowners), while Tories tended to come from the long-established country gentry. The Tories had a residual belief in the divine right of kings, and tended towards Jacobite sympathies (although that became treasonous after the Jacobite Rebellion of 1715). The Whigs espoused a constitutional monarchy in which the powers of the Crown were strictly curtailed. The Whigs presented themselves as the party of international trade, religious toleration, personal liberty and even agricultural efficiency; the Tories were High Church and cleaved to traditional values, claiming to preserve what was valuable and decent from the cynical self-interest of the Whigs, and to protect the integrity of what was still (just) a rural land from ignorant townies. Both names were initially terms of abuse: a 'Whiggamore' was a rabid Scots Protestant outlaw, while 'Toraighe' denoted an Irish Catholic bandit.

It was a small band of Whigs who had engineered the 1688 Glorious Revolution. Most were members of the Kit-Cat Club – a powerful group of Whig writers and activists, a curious amalgam of pressure group, drinking club and art appreciation society that met at the Cat and Fiddle in Gray's Inn. Held at a distance during the reign of canny Queen Anne, they kept themselves busy plotting the succession of the House of Hanover. When George I did indeed succeed her, his first act was to sack all the Tories, and the Whigs remained in power for the next 30 years.

Otherwise an unprepossessing dynasty, the Electors of Hanover arrived with some solid cultural capital – championing both the music of Handel and the architecture of Palladio. Antonio Palladio (1508–80) hailed from the Veneto, a region of rather dull farmland around Venice, which he embellished with his graceful reinterpretation of classical Roman architecture. The Hanoverians had been cultivating the Veneto since the 1660s, copying the architecture, holding Venetian-style concerts and masked balls, and even floating gondolas in the royal gardens. For the Kit-Cats, then, to build in Palladian style was an elegant way of signalling their support. The link with Venice struck a chord: it was a wealthy, entrepreneurial mercantile nation, its prosperity based on command of the seas; and it had a successful republican system of government. Palladianism rapidly morphed into the house style of the English Whigs. The first Palladian villa appeared in Wiltshire in 1708. Garden buildings, of course, were a cheaper option, and a rash of Palladian temples soon started popping up in gardens.

Clockwise from top left: The East Front of Stourhead in Wiltshire, by Colen Campbell, one of the first country houses to be built in the new Palladian style. The Ionic Temple at Rievaulx Terrace, North Yorkshire. William Kent's Temple of Ancient Virtue at Stowe, built for disaffected Whig Lord Cobham c.1734. Long-serving Whig prime minister Robert Walpole.

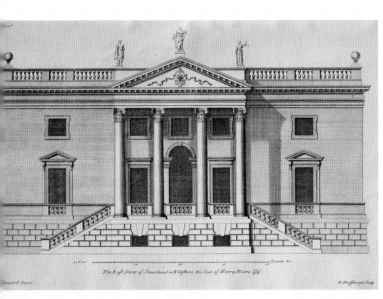

The East front of Stourhead in Wiltshire the Seat of Henry Hoare Esq.

No rush to Revolution

Revolutions rarely happen overnight: design ideas developed by an economic and intellectual elite took time to acquire more general currency. Formal geometric features continued to be made well into the 1740s, and well beyond in gentry gardens less susceptible to changing fashions. Equally, many 'naturalistic' features that took off during the 1720s had had a long gestation. At Wrest Park, for example, during the 1710s, the centrepiece of the scheme was a broad canal-shaped like an immense ice-cream spoon, with blocks of woodland either side, cut through with straight rides and formal glades. But as well as this very formal 'woodwork', a plan of 1715 also shows wiggly walks through woodland. That desire to wiggle had been niggling for a while. George London had admired winding walks he had seen in France, and had started introducing them round the outer reaches of his designs. As early as 1692, Sir William Temple had extolled the virtues of the irregular, informal style employed in Chinese gardens – in which he had never set foot. He named this Chinese style *sharawadgi* – a name that failed to capture the imagination. But the idea of irregularity was taken up by both Stephen Switzer (1682–1745, London's partner after Wise) and the splendidly named garden theorist Batty Langley (1698–1751), who declared that a garden 'should consist of regular irregularities'. He also held that fiddly French parterres were unsuitable for the English climate – far better to stick with a nice piece of lawn.

This is an evolution we can see in a series of watercolours made in 1727 at Forde Abbey in Dorset. There is plenty of impressive topiary, but it rises from broad grass plats; there is no fancy scrollwork swirling around its feet. We can also see how awkwardly the grand French manner sits in the Dorset countryside: the *patte d'oie* that heads off up the hill doesn't march off to infinity in the approved manner, but is foreshortened and awkwardly stumpy – a clue, perhaps, as to why gardens were ripe for change.

It was this kind of infelicity that offended Switzer. He urged landowners to respect the natural contours of the land, to embrace and enhance existing woodland, to make the most of the surrounding views; indeed to think of the whole estate as a form of garden. He described his style as 'rural and extensive gardening', more practical and, crucially, more cost-efficient than the formal French style (though his designs still look formal to twenty-first-century eyes). He was the first to suggest the *ferme ornée* or ornamented farm that was to become fashionable later in the century. Large, simple effects were the thing, but within them he favoured 'Twinings and Windings' that revealed landscape features little by little. There should be woodland walks punctuated with 'little gardens, with Caves [and] little natural Cascades and Grotts of Water' along with statues, seats and fragrant arbours. To us, it all sounds highly artificial, but to Switzer this was a layout in which 'the natural Gardener … has made his Design submit to Nature, and not Nature to his Design'.

Switzer was not alone in his opinions. In June 1712, social and political commentator Joseph Addison had published a series of essays in the *Spectator*, in which he shared a very similar vision of landscape.

… Why may not a whole Estate be thrown into a kind of Garden by frequent Plantations, that may turn as much to the Profit as the Pleasure of the Owner? A Marsh overgrown with Willows, or a mountain shaded with Oaks, are not only more beautiful, but more beneficial, than when they lie bare and unadorned. Fields of corn make a pleasant Prospect, and if the Walks were a little taken care of that lie between them, if the natural Embroidery of the Meadows were helpt and improved by some small Additions of Art, and the several Rows of Hedges set off by Trees and Flowers, … a Man might make a pretty Landskip of his own Possessions.

Addison was a mouthpiece for the Whigs, and if he could suggest a New and Improved form of estate management which combined beauty and utility, that would be certain to annoy the Tory squirearchy who saw themselves as the traditional guardians of the land. It was a subtle point, largely lost – the keenest farm-gardeners proved in the end to be more interested in poetry than politics. But his broader point – a growing impatience with formality and fussiness – did hit home. 'There is generally in Nature,' he opined, 'something more Grand and August, than what we meet with in the Curiosities of Art.' One curiosity he was particularly keen to see the back of was topiary. 'We see the Marks of the Scissars upon every Plant and Bush,' grumbled Addison. He preferred to see a tree 'in all its Luxuriancy and Diffusion of Boughs and Branches' and considered an orchard in flower 'infinitely more delightful than all the little labyrinths of the most finished Parterres'.

This opinion was shared by the other great taste-maker of the time, the poet Alexander Pope (see page 97), who likewise urged a return to the 'amiable simplicity of unadorned Nature.' 'Persons of Genius', he snootily declared, were well aware 'that all Art consists in the Imitation and Study of Nature', and it was only those of lower intelligence who delighted in 'the little Niceties and Fantastical Operation of Art, and constantly think that finest which is least Natural.'

A View of Ford from the North, by Edmund Prideaux, 1727, reveals the shortcomings of French style.

It is probably time to ponder what 'natural' might have meant to garden-makers in the eighteenth century. Clearly something fundamental had changed: Nature was no longer something to be feared, to be shut out behind high walls, but something to be regarded with pleasure. This much had been absorbed from the Renaissance gardens of Italy, which rejoiced in the wider view, while a growing reverence for Nature could be seen in contemporary poetry.

By 1700, enclosure was already well advanced: over 70 per cent of England was owned and managed by someone. Unless you happened to live in the Lake District, nature was no longer synonymous with wilderness. So just as the landscape had been tamed into productive field and pasture ('landscape' or 'landskip' being a new word, coined from the Dutch to refer to a genre of painting), the concept of Nature itself had lost its terror. To the medieval mind, Nature was an anarchic force, unknowable and very likely malign. But in this time of rapid scientific discovery, every new advance seemed to reveal more of God's immensely clever and orderly plan for the universe. As Pope pithily observed in his Epitaph to Newton:

Nature and Nature's laws lay hid in night:
God said, let Newton be! And there was light!

For Pope, the laws of Nature seemed to exhibit the very qualities he and his friends admired in the new Palladian architecture they were importing from Italy – order

and rationality, beauty and harmony, proportion and restraint. These too were the qualities they admired in their classical role models – the emperor Augustus, Cicero, Seneca the Younger.

It is difficult for us now to conceive just how entirely the classical texts furnished the mind of the average educated Englishman: they had become the very bedrock of civilisation. In embracing Nature, he embraced not so much the damp Dorset dell or foggy fen; rather Nature as mediated by Virgil, Horace and Ovid. In this poetic landscape, a shepherd was a rosy boy who sported with nymphs and played the flute rather than a muddy yokel with his hand up a sheep's bottom. So when Pope or Switzer or Addison advocated a 'natural' garden, they were not envisaging a shaggy slice of countryside in the way we would today, but something that might recreate the pastoral images which occupied their imaginations.

In 1719 Pope began work on his garden at Twickenham. As a Catholic, he was not permitted to live in the City of London. But Twickenham was not then tamely suburban: the banks of the Thames between Hampton Court and Kew

were thronged with high-society villas and much frequented by the literati. Pope's modest garden became a kind of test-bed for the associative garden that would soon become fashionable on a larger scale. Glades, groves and mounts, an open-sided shellwork temple, a bowling green, a celebrated grotto, numerous urns, statues and inscriptions – all were stuffed into a scant five acres, including a lugubrious line of cypresses leading to his mother's tomb. Rather than delivering just one big effect, Pope showed how even a small garden could offer a wealth of variety, how it might play with light and shade both physically and emotionally.

Pope's villa on the banks of the Thames, painted c.1760. Congenially rural, yet handy for London (so much easier than travelling by road), with all the pleasing animation of passing barges and pleasure craft, 'Twickenhamshire' was England's answer to Italy's trend-setting Brenta Canal.

His influence was far-reaching. In the days before magazines and websites, new gardening ideas were transmitted through essays, through poems (which we will come to), but principally through networks of friends. Although his very best friend was indubitably his dog, Bounce, Pope was friends with everyone who mattered: with William, 5th Lord Digby at Sherborne (the pleasing irregularity of his Sherborne estate made a deep impression on the poet); with cultural trend-setter Lord Burlington at Chiswick; with both the Princess of Wales (he advised on her new garden at Richmond Lodge) and the erstwhile royal mistress, Henrietta Howard, at nearby Marble Hill. He was a regular guest of both Lord Bathurst at Cirencester Park and the amiable millionaire Ralph Allen at Prior Park, Bath. (Allen took on Pope's gardener, John Searle, after Pope died.) Charles Bridgeman and William Kent, the two leading landscape designers of the day, were also numbered among his friends. It is a letter to yet another friend, Joseph Spence, that spells out Pope's Big Idea: 'In laying out a garden, the first and chief thing to be considered is the genius of the Place'. This is a theme he would develop in a poem addressed to Burlington in 1731 – and identifying and honouring the genius of the place remains the essential principle which guides the management of all National Trust gardens to this day.

In all, let Nature never be forgot.
But treat the goddess like a modest fair
Nor over-dress, nor leave her wholly bare;
Let not each beauty everywhere be spied,
Where half the skill is decently to hide.
He gains all points, who plea singly confounds.
Surprises, varies and conceals the bounds.
   Consult the Genius of the Place in all,
That tells the Waters or to rise, or fall;
Or helps the ambitious Hill the Heav'n's to scale,
Or scoops in circling Theatres the Vale,
Calls in the Country, catches opening Glades,
Joines willing Woods, and varies Shades from Shades,
Now breaks, or now directs, th'intending Lines;
Paints as you plant, and as your work, Designs.

It is all splendidly sensible advice – to blur the boundaries of your plot, not to reveal all at once but to create some sense of journey and surprise, to be led by the natural topography of your site rather than try to bully it into submission. Elsewhere he urges the gardener to avoid ostentatious display, deploring the triumph of design over usefulness – the summer-house without shade, the glade that affords no shelter or the arcade so windy that it causes you to catch cold. In a passage that anticipates the productive landscapes of Capability Brown, he speaks approvingly of 'ample lawns' … 'not ashamed to feed/The milky heifer and deserving steed' and of 'rising forests' planted not 'for pride or show', but to supply future buildings and navies. Yet Nature should not be left 'wholly bare': her charms will appear to best advantage in a little light classical drapery, as in the liberal sprinkling of urns and statues, obelisks

and temples in his own garden and those of his friends. All this was put into action at Prior Park, home of Ralph Allen, who had arrived in Bath at the age of 19 and made a fortune supplying the golden stone for the city's gracious new streets and squares. (Allen is believed to have been the model for Henry Fielding's affable Squire Allworthy, his heart and home always 'open to men of merit' and his house being the only one in the kingdom 'where you were sure to gain a dinner by deserving it.) On a hilly site overlooking the city, Allen and Pope laid out a circuit walk leading down one side of the valley and back up the other, using the natural contours of the land and dense planting to reveal by turn a sequence of features including a lake, a Palladian bridge and a grotto, final resting place of one of Pope's beloved Great Danes.

The Palladian bridge was built in 1755, the third and last of a trio built in England at that time, the others being at Stowe and Wilton.

Chiswick – a temple of taste

The dedicatee of Pope's poem was Richard Boyle, Earl of Burlington, whom Pope had come to know in 1716. He was an enigmatic man, almost certainly more interested in architecture and music than gardens. (He was a patron of Handel, as well as sundry musicians, artists and playwrights.) It has also been alleged that he was a covert Jacobite, which rather scuppers the view of Anglo-Palladianism as a badge of Whig allegiance. Whatever the truth of it, he remodelled his garden at Chiswick three times during the first half of the century, and is credited, not quite accurately, with introducing Palladian style to Britain.

From about the 1660s, the Grand Tour had become an established rite of passage for the sons of the upper classes. (The daughters had no such luck.) While a young man might travel through France, Germany, Switzerland and the Netherlands, the ultimate goal was Italy, and especially Rome. Here, studying the art and architecture around him would round off his classical education, investing the young *milord* with a desirable cultural breadth, a certain polish and a newly refined taste, which he would exercise in buying art. There appeared to be an inexhaustible supply of Old Masters – often copied, sometimes faked, but all good for his social standing.

The acquisition of Taste was important. For these few brief decades in the eighteenth century it became fashionable for country gentlemen to busy themselves with intellectual and artistic pursuits rather than just hunting, shooting and fishing. The appreciation of beauty became conflated with morality: having good taste made you a better human being. But more than that, to be able to make informed judgements about beautiful objects became the most distinctive signal of gentility – a means of establishing your social credentials over your neighbour in an increasingly fluid society. And no one was more of a connoisseur than the determinedly cultured and colossally wealthy Lord Burlington.

Trees were felled and a maze cleared away to create a more open and natural setting for Burlington's Chiswick House.

The 20-year-old Burlington set off on a year-long tour in May 1714, returning home with a collection of porphyry vases, a sculptor and an Italian violinist. In 1719 he was off again, but this time with a particular project in mind. For in the interim he had discovered the Italian architect Antonio Palladio, through the first English edition of his works in 1715, and through *Vitruvius Britannicus*, a compendium of the best of British classical architecture assembled by Scottish architect Colen Campbell. These books hailed Palladio as the purest interpreter of classical style, returning as it were to the source of inspiration which had become debased during the intervening centuries. The young Earl hastened to the Veneto to see for himself. Among the treasures he brought home this time, among his 878 crates of shopping, was a chubby, voluble, drunken Yorkshireman who had failed to live up to his early promise as a second Raphael. His name was William Kent.

By 1719, the old formal garden that surrounded Burlington's Jacobean house at Chiswick had already undergone substantial renovation at the hands of Charles Bridgeman, aimed at creating a suitably Roman setting for a series of garden buildings designed by Burlington in classical style. Around 1725 he embarked on a more ambitious project, to design the perfect Palladian villa, which survives today as Chiswick House. While beautifully proportioned and rich in symbolic associations, it was certainly not a practical home, derided by one visitor, Lord Hervey, as 'too little to live in, and too large to hang to one's watch'. There was no kitchen – meals had to be taken in the old house next door. But there was a wine cellar, and beds – so perhaps it was intended simply as a place to drink and be merry (carefully) among Lord Burlington's exquisite art collections.

Kent, meanwhile, got to work in the garden. An exedra housing classical statues struck a formal note, but elsewhere came his first attempts at what would become his defining skill – at 'loosening Nature's tresses'. The canal was naturalised into a 'river'; twisting paths ran through somewhat skimpy groves; a maze was cleared away to leave just open lawn between house and river; there was even a cascade, though it never worked properly. It was here that Horace Walpole declared that Kent 'leapt the fence and saw all nature was a garden', but in truth Chiswick was just the run-up: he would do better at Claremont, at Stowe and, supremely, at Rousham.

The dawn of modern taste

Horace Walpole (son of Robert), who gives a detailed account of the rise of the landscape garden in his *History of the Modern Taste in Gardening* (1771), credits Kent with the invention of the style. But you could equally well argue that Kent is only part of a double act – that in all his best work, Charles Bridgeman (1690–1738) got there before him. That it was Bridgeman who did all the donkey work, establishing the 'capabilities' of the site as Lancelot Brown would do after him, moulding the topography and marking out the outlines, while Kent followed behind with inspired colouring in. Bridgeman had been, like Switzer, a pupil of London and Wise, and worked with Wise and the multi-talented John Vanbrugh at Blenheim. He continued in a semi-formal manner, creating bold, straight vistas that skilfully exploited the lie of the land to connect the main features of the garden; but he eschewed fussy parterres, was an early adopter of serpentine walks, and was credited by Walpole with the invention of the ha-ha (a sunken wall designed to keep animals out) – though in fact it had been in use for decades, if not for centuries (see page 104).

No one, however, had used the ha-ha quite like Bridgeman. Called to Stowe in 1711, he created a vast five-sided ha-ha which bounded the entire site, and when the garden was greatly enlarged in 1720, it was Bridgeman who pulled all the scattered elements into a coherent whole. At Rousham, a craftily placed ha-ha allowed cattle to graze charmingly right in the heart of the garden. Here too, Bridgeman made sense of an awkward piece of land, jammed between river and road, before Kent worked his magic on it. The awe-inspiring water garden at Stanway in Gloucestershire is probably also his work, with its 500ft (152m) long canal sited, unusually, on a terrace above the house, fed by two immense cascades. The restoration of this garden towards the end of the twentieth century, culminating with the installation of a towering single jet fountain, vividly shows the heroic simplicity and grandeur of Bridgeman's vision.

Yet perhaps Bridgeman's masterwork is Claremont in Surrey. Here he created a stupendous turf amphitheatre overlooking a round pond (the Round Basson). Kent turned it into a lake, adding a temple on an island in the middle and a cascade. (This was later turned into a grotto, suggesting it worked no better than Chiswick's.) Bridgeman's mighty earthwork was cloaked in evergreens; it remained hidden until the National Trust's restoration in 1975.

In 1728 Bridgeman was appointed Royal Gardener, creating the famous Serpentine and formal Round Pond in Kensington Gardens. But for Queen Caroline at Richmond, according to Walpole, he 'dared to introduce cultivated fields, and even morsels of a forest appearance' – further evidence of his 'many detached thoughts, that strongly indicate the dawn of modern taste'.

Bridgeman's great amphitheatre at Claremont in Surrey was conceived as a monumental earth sculpture rather than a performance space. A smaller amphitheatre at Cliveden, however, did play host, in 1740, to the first performance of the patriotic song 'Rule Britannia' during a masque about King Alfred – an eighteenth-century icon.

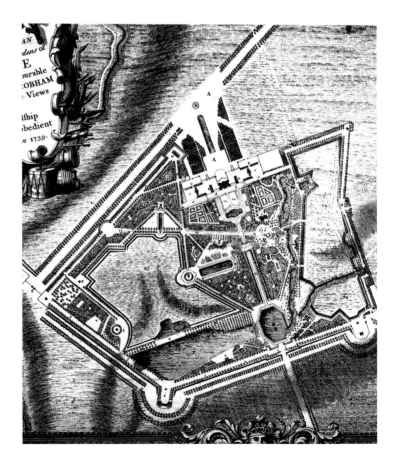

Bridgeman worked at Stowe until 1730, seeking to impose a sense of order on the scattered elements of the garden by making a focal point from Vanbrugh's Rotunda and driving firm axes through the irregularly shaped site.

THE HA-HA

HORACE Walpole gave Charles Bridgeman the credit for inventing the ha-ha – a deep ditch, faced on one side with brick or stone, that formed the boundary between the park and garden, keeping livestock safely at bay. In reality, protective ditches had been common garden features for decades, if not centuries: Dryden's 1697 translation of Virgil's *Georgics* describes a plot 'fenc'd with Hedges and deep Ditches round' to 'Exclude th'incroaching Cattle from the Ground', and medieval monastic orchards had been enclosed by ditches and moats. There was certainly a ha-ha at Althorp as early as 1697, when Bridgeman was still a teenager, and another at Levens Hall, also dating from the 1690s, made by the French gardener Guillaume Beaumont. Known in France as the '*saut de loup*' it was originally a military device; but by 1709 had been adapted for garden use in A. J. Dézallier d'Argenville's book *The Theory and Practice of Gardening* (a treatise on formal gardening translated into English in 1712) – and it is in this form, as a ditch behind a wall which allows gaps to be safely cut in the wall to make viewpoints, that it is used at Levens.

Bridgeman's innovation was hugely to expand the scale of the ha-ha and little by little to dispense with walls altogether (the earlier ones often had low walls) so that the garden appeared to flow into the park without interruption. His first ha-ha, at Stowe in 1719, was no more than a deep ditch bristling with spiked sticks; by 1725, while still walled, it had been enlarged to enclose the park completely; and by 1776 some 400 acres (162ha) of garden and park had merged into a single unit, making Stowe the first landscape park on such a huge scale.

By the 1730s, everyone was playing with ha-has. At Claremont, Kent massaged Bridgeman's military-style bastions into gentle curves; Switzer devised another serpentine 'Ah! Ah! terrass' for Nostell Priory. In 1795 at Moseley Hall in Warwickshire, a ha-ha was built 8¾ft (2.7m) deep, presumably to keep out giraffes. The cost was a staggering £678 a mile. Today the National Trust, which has many miles of ha-ha to maintain, reckons 4ft (1.2m) to be reliably stock-proof.

With the reintroduction of formality in the nineteenth century, the ha-ha gave way to balustrades and railings that clearly signalled the demarcation between park and garden. Some twentieth-century gardens, however, have made creative use of the ha-ha, as at Broughton Grange in Oxfordshire, where a ha-ha allows Tom Stuart-Smith's walled garden to 'call in the country' in authentically eighteenth-century fashion.

But why is it called a ha-ha? The name allegedly derives from the exclamations of those who failed to notice these barriers until too late …

Clockwise from top left: Cannons along the ha-ha at Kingston Lacy in Dorset may be aimed at more determined intruders than cattle and deer. A handsome stone-faced ha-ha at Grey's Court in Oxfordshire. The ha-ha at Rousham, with Gothic seat designed by William Kent. The ha-ha was integral to Capability Brown's landscapes, as at Petworth in West Sussex and Berrington Hall in Herefordshire.

Pope talks the talk but Kent walks the walk

William Kent (1685–1748), born Cant, in Bridlington in Yorkshire, led a charmed life. Starting out as an apprentice coach-painter in Hull, he was talent-spotted by some wealthy patrons who, believing they had found a genius, paid for him to go to Rome in 1710 to study painting. He was never more than a mediocre painter, and during his ten years in Italy barely scratched a living copying Old Masters, but he travelled and took note, and his drawings suggest a playfulness and irreverent wit that no doubt made him excellent company. He clearly delighted the young Lord Burlington, whom he met in Rome. Despite a ten-year age gap, the two became bosom pals, and Kent lived in the Burlington household for the rest of his life. Through Burlington's influence at Court, Kent became designer of choice to a string of Whig grandees, as interior decorator, furniture-maker and architect as well as landscape designer. Blithely apolitical, he worked for both Queen Caroline and her son Frederick, though they hated each other; for Lord Cobham at Stowe and his sworn enemy Robert Walpole at Houghton.

Kent's years in Italy coloured all his work. (The cascade at Rousham, for example, is lifted from the Villa Barbarigo in Valsanzibio.) There is a strong streak of the florid in Italian art which, when given a ceiling or a mantelpiece or even a dog kennel or chair, Kent seemed unable to resist. (His decorations at Kensington Palace are horrible.) His garden drawings, however, reveal a lightness of touch, an element of fantasy, that fed into a new freedom and delicacy on the ground – loose clumps of trees, wings of planting that framed a view, patterns of light and shadow, reflection and silhouette. He had a knack for fantastical buildings, such as the rustic Hermitage and the 'Merlin's Cave' he built for Queen Caroline at Richmond. For Pope he designed a deliciously camp shell temple. But even his most solemn offerings, such as the Temple of Ancient Virtue at Stowe, have a distinctly theatrical quality. Indeed the garden he made for Frederick, Prince of Wales at Carlton House resembles nothing so much as an enormous (12acre/4.9ha) stage, arranged with layers of planting each side, like flats.

'All gardening is landscape painting,' said Pope, and Kent took him at his word. He was a concept man, working entirely from sketches. He famously worked 'without level or line' – or indeed plans or instructions. At Stowe, where he was employed from 1730, it was the conscientious Head Gardener 'Capability' Brown who had to make Kent's schemes work on the ground. His working drawings are adorned with jolly little doodlings – dancing rabbits, frolicking mermaids, a small dog relieving itself on Burlington's aesthetic foot. You can imagine Kent as a bit like Mozart portrayed in Peter Shaffer's play *Amadeus* – frivolous and vulgar, but capable of flights of genius.

By 1737 Kent was at work at Rousham, on both the house and garden which, miraculously, remain almost as he left them. His client here was General James Dormer, a veteran of Blenheim who, after a distinguished military career followed by a botched diplomatic one, sought 'philosophic retirement' in the Oxfordshire countryside. Dormer never recovered from his wounds and was dying as the garden was being made: it is possible to read the garden as a meditation on death, a passage between darkness and light. Green and serene as it is now, it is tempting to see it as the General's own private Elysium, the mythical realm of eternal happiness that awaited the Greek heroes after death. But the patina of age has added to its contemplative quality: letters from Dormer's gardener show it was once full of flowers.

Rousham perfectly embodied Pope's concept of 'calling in' the surrounding countryside to the garden. Mill buildings masquerading as a medieval church pull the eye down to the River Cherwell below, while high on the hillside beyond, another eye-catcher, evoking a ruined castle, claims the surrounding hills as part of the garden scene – a handy trick for a garden of just 25 acres (10.1ha). Within, carefully placed statues lure the walker this way and that, or stop her dead in her tracks.

Kent's vivacious drawing of Pope's garden shows him clapping the diminutive Pope on the shoulder, while gambolling mermaids and mermen spout rainbows over a shell temple, which looks as if it might take off at any moment.

This is a garden that invites exploration: how far we have come from the garden made to be admired from an upstairs window. Dormer's gardener, John MacClary, would meet visitors at a specially built gate and conduct them round a circuit walk to enjoy the proper sequence of views out to the river, leafy tunnels and grassy glades, each springing a new surprise – a pyramid, a temple, Pan playing his pipes or a simple cool, dark pool. The climax of the garden was the Venus Vale, where a garden boy would be sent ahead to turn on the water, so that water spouts shot up in front of the goddess, and tumbled from the cascade above. Water is essential to Rousham – quiet pools, the curve of the river, and, famously, a formal rill that winds its way down through the woods from the Octagon pond.

Rousham is intimate in scale. Stowe, on the other hand, is immense. Rousham has its share of statuary and architectural set pieces, but somehow they seem almost random, as if they have sprouted spontaneously in the woodland. The architecture at Stowe has a very different effect – it is designed to make you think.

Opposite: Within the Temple of Ancient Virtue at Stowe were placed statues of the philosopher Socrates, the poet Homer, the law-giver Lycurgus plus a general, Epaminondas. Latin inscriptions explained their significance: as well as models of civic virtue, they were also all victims of state oppression.

Sounding off at Stowe

Richard Temple, 1st Viscount Cobham, was a distinguished soldier and Whig loyalist devoutly committed to the Hanoverian succession. But during the 1720s, few could fail to observe prime minister Robert Walpole's ever-tightening grip on power, bolstered by open nepotism and corruption. And when Walpole's Excise Bill of 1733 sought to introduce a raft of indirect taxation in order to reduce land tax – a cynical ploy to woo landowners, for only they had votes – Cobham was one of a band of dissidents who voted against. Cobham and six others were sacked from their government posts; various sympathisers, including Lord Burlington, resigned.

A politico in this position today would hasten into print with an incendiary insider memoir. Cobham launched his attack through his garden. Building on a framework created by Bridgeman and Vanbrugh over the previous 20 years (Cobham never stopped tinkering), he began to garden again with ferocious energy, and this time with

Below: Before William Kent, garden water came in canals. But at Rousham, a slender, serpentine rill winds out of the shady woodland, in Kent's most poetic landscape.

an agenda – to expose the corruption at the heart of government, and to publish his own alternative manifesto. He began with a small valley of 40 acres (16.2ha) below the house, which he renamed the Elysian Fields. By the time he had finished, he had created some eight lakes and 36 temples, commissioned about 90 statues and busts, and Stowe had become the focus and symbol of political opposition.

His partner in this enterprise was Kent, who had been working at Stowe since 1730, but on lighter matters such as an erotic Temple of Venus. For Kent, with his innate sense of theatre, to create a visual language for Cobham's propaganda was a gift. They started with classical allusion: in Greek mythology, to get to the Elysian Fields, you must first cross the River Styx. Kent summoned up a narrow, riverine lake, then placed on its bank an elegant Temple of Ancient Virtue, honouring four ancient Greeks who embodied those qualities that Lord Cobham found so painfully wanting in the current administration. Its counterpart, the Temple of Modern Virtue, was built, sarcastically, as a ruin. Within was a statue without head or arms, but sporting the Order of the Garter. Whoever could it be? Walpole was so proud of his Garter that he had Garter stars worked into the decor of his palatial pile at Houghton.

Across the river, the Temple of British Worthies struck a more celebratory note. Cobham peopled it with busts of 16 figures he deemed worthy of respect – philosophers, scientists, writers, men (and one woman) of action. One was Alexander Pope. Also included were William III and King Alfred – in popular political mythology, the founder of a system of civil liberties quashed by the rascally French at the Norman Conquest.

There is much, much more of this. And if we feel we need a guidebook to understand it all, so did visitors at the time. The very first garden guidebook was helpfully published at Stowe in 1744. Decoding these meanings makes it sound as if Stowe was all about righteous indignation. It wasn't: it was also a

For Stowe's Temple of British Worthies Kent developed the notion of a pantheon he had previously used at Queen Caroline's Hermitage at Richmond. Here Caroline, generally acknowledged as the power behind the throne, was doing her own political propaganda in garden form. The figure at the front is Thomas Gresham, founder of Gresham College.

lot of fun. (Kent was involved, after all.)
The longest inscription on the Temple of
British Worthies is still visible on the back
of it – a paean to a favourite dog. There
was a Temple dedicated to Bacchus,
where the god of wine was depicted on
the walls in the likeness of the local vicar.
This same vicar, one Conway Rand, was
later immortalised in verse: while playing
at bowls at Stowe he was so inflamed
by the sight of a young lady on a swing
that he chased her into Dido's Cave, a
rocky 'alcove' ever afterwards known
as the 'Randibus'. More comfortably,
The Temple of Venus was furnished
with a 'pleasuring sopha' and decorated
with some of the raunchier scenes from
Spenser's *Faerie Queene*. Luckily, there
was also a Cold Bath.

A Cold Bath would probably have
come in handy at West Wycombe, where
Cobham's near neighbour Sir Francis
Dashwood (1708–81) inherited an ample
estate at the age of 16. Unlike Cobham, he tried to steer clear of politics, though
he did end up becoming Chancellor of the Exchequer, despite protesting that
he knew nothing whatsoever about finance. (His tenure was short-lived.) His
garden at West Wycombe has been described as a cheeky parody of Stowe, but
there is nothing like the same detailed iconographical programme. Rather it
works by association and theme – and the overriding theme is sex.

As a young man, Dashwood undertook not just one Grand Tour, but six,
spending protracted periods in France and Italy and visiting Russia, Greece and
Asia Minor – beyond the usual tourist circuit. There was, as with most gap years, a
good deal of carousing: the young men's minders abroad were generally known as
'bear-leaders', which gives a clue that not all was conscientious self-improvement.
Dashwood romped through Europe on a joyride of bawdiness, dressing-up and
practical jokes, variously impersonating the King of Sweden and a venerable Roman
cardinal, disrupting a solemn Good Friday service in the Sistine Chapel by running
about with a horse-whip, and attempting to seduce the Tsarina Anna. But his interest
in art was entirely serious, and for 35 years he was the driving force behind the Society
of Dilettanti, generally credited with kick-starting the Greek Revival in British
architecture. Some of the earliest examples were tried out in his park.

Rather more notorious was the club Dashwood founded in 1751, The Knights
of St Francis of Wycombe, later popularly known as the Hellfire Club. To host
their meetings he leased a nearby Cistercian abbey, Medmenham Abbey. He was
the 'abbot' presiding over 12 'monks' or initiates, including the Prince of Wales,

Sir Francis
Dashwood, who
took mischievous
pleasure in his hell-
raising reputation,
founded the Society
of Dilettanti in 1732
to foster wider
appreciation of
classical culture
among those who
had been on the
Grand Tour. The
waspish Horace
Walpole (son of
Robert) sneered
that the chief
qualification for
membership was
being drunk, but
the club did fund
scholarly research
and publications.

activist John Wilkes, the painter Hogarth and gardening supremo (and later prime minister) Lord Bute. There was much dressing up, a live baboon, a library of occult and pornographic books and a series of tongue-in-cheek 'sacred rites', which appeared to involve naked young women in the guise of the goddesses Demeter and Persephone. There was drinking, feasting and whoring aplenty – but there is no evidence at all of the orgiastic devil-worship reputed to have taken place here, or later inside the network of chalk caves Dashwood had excavated while building a new road to the estate.

What is certain is that the presiding deity at West Wycombe is Eros. The imagery could scarcely be more explicit. A Temple of Venus, closely resembling that at Stowe, is set on a hollow grassy mound. Beneath the temple, a narrow oval doorway, finished in rough tufa, allows entrance to a Parlour of Venus inside the hill, with the two curved wings spread, like open legs, each side. (The brick-lined parlour, most appropriately, was later used to store gunpowder.) The glade before it was furnished with 25 erotic lead statues. The swan-shaped lake might represent the respectable symbol of Buckinghamshire – or the rape of Leda by Zeus disguised as a swan. Even the two twin entrance lodges had a whiff of naughtiness. While presenting identical faces to the road, one morphed into a temple dedicated to Daphne, the nymph pursued by Apollo in Ovid's *Metamorphoses*; the other, a dinky cottage known as 'Kitty's Lodge', probably honoured Kitty Fisher, a famous courtesan who was the object of Dashwood's

The Temple of Venus now to be seen at West Wycombe in Buckinghamshire is a reconstruction of the original, made by Quinlan Terry for another Sir Francis Dashwood in 1982. It perches on a mound, with the 'door of life' below.

pursuit. His appetites were legendary: it was said he had 'the staying power of a stallion and the impetuosity of a bull'.

West Wycombe was a playfully iconoclastic landscape, setting out to shock. It was a place to party, with its porticoes reimagined as Bacchic temples and decorated with cheerily sozzled cherubs, its charming island temple for musical entertainments, the golden ball that made a dear little banqueting house, naughtily perched atop the parish church. But above all it was (and remains) superlative garden-making, contrasting its operatic eye-catchers with gentle views of crystal chalk streams and lamb-frisked pasture. Stowe likewise remains a wonderfully calm and confident landscape, serenely absorbing its mass of hectic detail. Stowe may have been an expression of anger, but it was also a landscape of consolation, and in this it has affinities with Rousham and especially with Studley Royal.

Set on an island in the lake, the Music Temple was used as a theatre, and the remains of a stage survive inside it. It is still sometimes used for musical entertainments in the summer.

Divine disgrace

Reckless financial trading by unscrupulous bankers is not a uniquely twenty-first-century phenomenon. The South Sea Bubble was a notorious speculation which, when it burst in 1720, wiped out some of the largest fortunes in England. The man who took the rap was the Chancellor of the Exchequer, John Aislabie. He was briefly imprisoned in the Tower of London, then retired in disgrace to Yorkshire. What should a man do in such circumstances but garden? In 1693 he had inherited a deep wooded valley, some distance from his house, where he had canalised the stream to make some water features. Around 1724, once his assets were unfrozen, he began to garden once more, creating at Studley Royal a breathtaking landscape of grass and water, remote and secluded – a perfect new world of the imagination.

It may be fanciful to call it a landscape of reflection, but Aislabie had more than most to reflect about. He had lost his wife and daughter in a fire at his London house in 1700, so he knew the fragility of happiness. He was not of great

A perfect example of Aislabie's skill in placing statuary to create mood, in front of the Temple of Piety at Studley Royal Water Garden, North Yorkshire.

family, and had reached high office through his own exceptional brilliance: now he had also experienced the vanity of worldly advancement. Looking to his classical antecedents, he could recast this exile as morally superior: for did not the man of learning and moral refinement choose to retire to his country estate, far from the cares and corruption of the city, to lead a simple and a virtuous life? In the Temple of Piety he set a statue of Hercules – routinely used in gardens to illustrate the choice between the primrose path to wickedness and the trickier one to virtue. There were also statues of combat – Roman wrestlers and the Dying Gladiator, which might hint at his personal struggles, or even a sense of being stabbed in the back, in the manner of General Dormer at Rousham. These pleasingly elevated musings end with one of the great set pieces of garden theatre as the climax of the garden is suddenly revealed: the glorious Cistercian ruin of Fountains Abbey. Later gardeners would fill their gardens with fanciful 'Gothick' buildings: Aislabie had the real thing. Or rather the prospect of it, for he never got to own Fountains Abbey: his neighbour refused to sell. His son later secured it, the crowning glory to decades of further development in the garden, much of it in Chinese style. Yet it is hard to be sorry that so few of these distractions survive.

Today the garden entrance is in the wrong place, so that you see Fountains first – which is a bit like watching the final act of a play before the beginning. Happily, just a few miles away you can view the equally spectacular Rievaulx Abbey just as intended, even pausing at each of 13 carefully arranged 'viewing stations'. The Duncombe family, having made a (legal) fortune in banking, built a house near Helmsley, with a wide grassy terrace overlooking the Rye Valley. The

One of four views of the water garden at Studley Royal made by A. Walker in 1758, showing the formality of Aislabie's lakes, before the whole effect was softened by the landscaping of his son.

115

next generation built an even more impressive terrace further along the valley above Rievaulx, commanding a fine prospect of the ruins, and adorned, like the first, with a garden temple at each end. A convenient three-mile drive from Duncombe, the Ionic Temple at Rievaulx was a splendid place to take guests for a stroll, to enjoy the vistas, and to take some refreshment – and not some measly cold collation, but a proper hot meal with spit-roasted meats, prepared in the basement kitchen. Now in the care of the National Trust, the interior of the dining room remains intact, and gives a good impression of how garden buildings were actually used.

The Duncombe family would no doubt have been familiar with Castle Howard, with its great grass terrace providing both a focus for, and a place to admire, the extensive Yorkshire views. (Its grand, uncluttered layout and theatrical way of placing buildings in the landscape have often been described as a quantum leap towards the landscape garden.) And the idea of a hillside walk made expressly to view a historic landscape had already been done with some aplomb by Sanderson Miller (1716–80) at Radway in Warwickshire. In 1739 he constructed a terrace and Gothic tower overlooking the Civil War battlefield of Edgehill, where, in an eighteenth-century version of Warhammer, he marked out the positions of the opposing armies with clumps of trees. At nearby Farnborough Hall, where he advised his neighbour William Holbech on the design of both house and garden, he constructed a vast S-shaped terrace to take advantage of similar views. Carved out on the crest of an escarpment, it curls from the broad lawn behind the house up to an obelisk some three-quarters of a mile away, with huge views out over the broad river valley (now marred by the M40) towards Stratford and the Malvern Hills.

Miller is a really interesting character who has been rather overlooked by garden historians, perhaps because his health failed in later life and he ended his days in an asylum. A scholar, musician, antiquarian and gentleman-architect who never took payment for his work, he was admired in his day for his mock-Gothic castle ruins (page 150). But he was born in the same year as Lancelot Brown and shared a very similar approach to landscape. Like Brown, he was a master with water (demonstrating the same extraordinary skill in the deployment of dams, sluices and drains) and it seems entirely possible that Miller's informal lakes, such as the serpentine 'river' at Farnborough, and his way of arranging trees in clumps and belts, directly influenced Brown's work.

Above: The Ionic Temple at Duncombe in North Yorkshire was originally used as a very superior picnic pavilion, serving fresh hot meals. The scarlet sofas against the wall are by William Kent. By the nineteenth century, it housed the gardener, who mowed the grass and sold tickets to visitors.

Knit your own Arcadia

The Holbechs were gentry rather than super-rich, so Farnborough had to be economically viable: Miller's new lake was used for fish and wild-fowling, the greensward running down to the 'river' (created from three ponds) served as cow pasture, and the dairy doubled as a garden building, dressed up with cut stone. This notion of mixing 'the useful and profitable parts of Gard'ning with the Pleasurable' was taken a stage further by Philip Southcote, who in 1732, aged 34, married the 67-year-old Dowager Duchess of Cleveland. Married life clearly agreed with her, for at a time when average female life expectancy was 41, the lady lived until 80. The happy couple settled near Weybridge in Surrey, where they developed the first English *ferme ornée* – a blend of working farm, flowery circuit walk and prettified farm buildings.

A decade later, poet William Shenstone inherited a farm called the Leasowes, now beneath a golf course on the fringes of Birmingham. He wasn't much of a farmer, and he was a truly terrible poet, as evidenced from the verses he strung about the place. But he did have a powerful literary imagination, and from 1743 set about making a garden that would be the living embodiment of pastoral poetry in the spirit of Virgil. The garden was, in effect, a path, beautified by flowering

Claude Lorrain's *Coast View of Delos with Aeneas,* 1672, is one of six works based on the poetry of Virgil he painted in the last decade of his life. Painters and garden-makers shared the same imaginative sources.

shrubs and trees, which wound round his estate, punctuated by 39 viewing points, each with a seat on which to rest and enjoy the view. Nothing in Shenstone's Arcadia was left to chance: visitors followed a given route, map in hand, and every stopping point was festooned with inscriptions suggesting reflections of an appropriate nature.

At around the same time, work began on what is surely the greatest fantasy landscape of them all, at Stourhead in Wiltshire, where banker Henry Hoare dammed a chalk stream under the downs to create a vast, three-pronged lake. Hoare was a very learned man, and Stourhead has been read, like Stowe, as a garden that tells a story, in this case not a political but a dynastic one. Various scenes in the garden recall episodes in Virgil's *Aenead*, and it has been argued that a painting by Claude Lorrain, *Coast View of Delos with Aeneas*, suggested both the design of the garden buildings and how they were placed in the garden. The picture captures a moment where Aeneas stands with his father and son and prays wearily for a home and lineage for his family. No doubt that is what Hoare longed for at Stourhead: unhappily, he saw two wives and all his children die.

In truth, Hoare cherry-picked the themes that suited him: the unifying idea at Stourhead is not a literary but a visual one. Inspired by the paintings of Claude Lorrain, Nicolas Poussin and his brother-in-law, Gaspard Dughet (all seventeenth-

Stourhead's Pantheon, designed by Henry Flitcroft and completed in 1754, bears an uncanny resemblance to the Temple of Apollo in Claude Lorrain's painting. Both were inspired by the Pantheon in Rome.

century French painters working mainly around Tivoli), Hoare set out to make his own perfect classical landscape in the manner of these painters. He sought to create his own 'charming Gaspard picture' – or rather a whole gallery of pictures, revealed in turn in a series of carefully devised views across the lake.

The collecting of landscape pictures was still relatively new: other genres such as history painting were considered superior prior to the 1740s. But with their honeyed evocations of the Roman *campagna* (complete with sheep and merry swains), their temples and columns and broken porticoes framed by elegantly lacy trees, these paintings – such delightful reminders of happy days on the Grand Tour – became increasingly popular. And being inspired by Virgil and Ovid, just as the garden-makers were, they provided a very exact visual vocabulary for their Arcadian ambitions. That architect Henry Flitcroft's classical buildings should look exactly like Claude's is no great miracle – he was working from the same Roman models. But at Stourhead even the planting was painterly. 'The greens', instructed Hoare, 'should be ranged together in large masses as the shades are in painting: to contrast the dark masses with light ones, and to relieve each dark mass itself with little sprinkling of lighter greens here and there.' Henry Hoare's planting is not as

The view out from Stourhead's grotto, with the lake at eye level, is as spectacular as the view towards it. If anything, the reflections are enhanced.

it was: his grandson Richard Colt planted many more trees, then later generations introduced rhododendrons, which rather undermined the subtlety of Hoare's shadings. And Henry himself got carried away, littering his classical scene with all kinds of unlikely interlopers from a medieval market cross to a 'Chinese Umbrella'. (The more serious-minded Richard did away with most of them.) But centuries on, Stourhead still captures exactly that dreamy, otherworldly feeling of a Claude painting: even on a wet and windy January afternoon there is something about Stourhead that is eternally golden.

A view to the Temple of Apollo, perched on its hilltop, past a noble tulip tree growing on an island in the lake.

The 'ruined abbey' on the lakeside at Painshill in Surrey was the last of Charles Hamilton's follies, reflecting a new delight in romantically decaying garden buildings.

Stourhead is important, not just as art history – for what is Stourhead if not painting in three dimensions? – but because it holds in balance many themes that will take the garden off in new directions. The idea that a landscape should work like a painting will develop into the Picturesque – a codified way of looking that will go so far as to set out rules for how the 'foreground', 'middle ground' and 'background' of a garden scene should be composed. But more significantly, it stands at the cusp of a new way of thinking. Every now and then, a shift occurs that completely realigns our way of looking at things. Today, it is globalisation and the internet: in the eighteenth century, it was the change in focus from the public to the private workings of the mind.

This change in perspective, which has its origins in philosopher John Locke's description of the association of ideas, was expressed, from the very first, through gardens. Writing in *The Spectator* in 1712, Joseph Addison describes how different garden landscapes work on the viewer's imagination. By now garden visitors were used to being active participants in the garden rather than just observers: presented with an inscription or emblematic feature, the educated visitor could be relied on to grasp the allusion and decode the meaning. But what Addison illustrates is very different: the associations prompted by the garden scene not only inform the intellect but colour the emotions.

This opens the door to two important new perceptions. The first is that a garden can manipulate the emotions, creating distinct feelings and sensations in the visitor, a notion that Pope had intuited but not quite realised in his Twickenham garden. The second is that the quality of the experience depends on the viewer as well as what is viewed. The effect of this was to create a new kind of gardening, in which a tour of the garden became a journey through the emotions – something that Kent achieved, seemingly without trying, at Rousham, and that Shenstone was blundering towards at The Leasowes.

You could argue that all good gardens speak to the emotions. But Stourhead signals something new in the eighteenth-century garden. The visitor walking round the lake who picked up the Latin mottoes over the doors and the Virgilian allusions would enjoy an absorbing intellectual entertainment. But if he failed to, it really didn't matter, for the sheer visual power of the garden drew the visitor into Hoare's imaginative universe, appealing directly to a place beyond language. Here was a garden that reached out to everyone.

The emotional journey we experience today at Stourhead is an uplifting one – apart from a little shiver of gloom in the grotto, all is radiance and serenity. But in Hoare's time, it would have been a lot more varied, and more closely resembled another garden that now seems entirely opposite in its effect – the moody, melancholic landscape of Painshill.

Painshill and Stourhead have much in common. Both were created by amateurs, between the 1740s and 1780s, without recourse to a professional landscaper. In neither is there any direct link with a house: each is its own universe, entire and perfect. In both the centrepiece is a natural-looking lake, and reflected in that lake are buildings calculated to delight the imagination,

The restoration of Painshill, begun in 1981, was the first major reinstatement of a historic landscape attempted in the UK. It was hugely ambitious, rescuing a fragmented site, so derelict that it was almost at the point of no return.

and to complete the painterly scene. But if at Stourhead the scene is a Gaspard; at Painshill, by contrast, the landscape evokes the wild, tumultuous paintings of Italian proto-Romantic Salvator Rosa, with brooding dark woods, mysterious ruins, a Gothic tower, and above all the famously 'primitive' grotto (see page 126).

Painshill was the life's work of the Hon. Charles Hamilton, who enjoyed a comfortable income from his position in the household of Prince Frederick, but nothing like Henry Hoare's prodigious wealth. Painshill, on the infertile heathlands of Surrey, was not a promising site: Hamilton's first job in 1733 was to plant turnips and then feed them all to sheep, in a bid to increase fertility. But it was good for growing conifers, for massed dark yews giving a suitably gloomy approach to a Mausoleum or plantings of pines evoking the wildness of mountain slopes. The acid soil was ideal for the new exotics he was collecting, at ruinous expense, from North America – cedars and American oaks, tulip trees and nyssas with their fabulous autumn colour, then a rare sight in Britain. Painshill was, like

Stourhead and Stowe, created to be visited (pages 82–83). It was as artificial as any Disneyland, and was enjoyed in very much the same way. Visitors made their way, on foot or by pony and trap, along twisting paths or carriage drives with hairpin bends tightly enclosed by planting, creating a delicious sense of disorientation so that each new feature was suddenly revealed with the full force of surprise, each entirely different from the last and conjuring up quite distinct emotional responses, of which, of course, 'Ooh-aah' was the most desirable. Buildings – Gothic pavilions or romantic ruins or outlandish exotica like Turkish tents – appeared and disappeared across the lake, doleful scenes like the woodland hermitage (see page 128) contrasted with sunny lawns stocked with cheerful flower beds; within minutes you progressed from China to fairyland to classical Italy. This was no longer Virgil's vision, but resolutely Charles Hamilton's.

The problem was that Hamilton's imagination was deeper than his pockets. He tried various projects to bring in some cash, from making tiles to producing champagne, and even invested heavily in lottery tickets, but eventually had to sell up in 1773. The garden was lost, but a heroic restoration, begun in 1981 and still continuing, has brought the garden back to resplendent life. You can even, once again, sip Painshill champagne.

All good gardens, as we have observed, engage with the emotions. But Painshill is perhaps the earliest example of a garden that would turn this kind of emotional journey into a cult. Painshill also illustrates a distinction that would cause a deal of controversy among garden-makers towards the end of the century – between the 'sublime' and the 'beautiful'. In his essay, *A Philosophic Enquiry into the Origin of our Ideas of the Sublime and the Beautiful*, published in London in 1757, Edmund Burke distinguished between a calm, smooth, harmonious perfection which he styled as 'beautiful' and a more unpredictable and violent form of beauty which he called 'sublime'. Painshill, without a doubt, aspires to the Sublime. But Burke's idea of beauty, which he likened to bowling along in a well-sprung carriage over smooth green turf, is most perfectly exemplified by the landscapes of Capability Brown – landscapes indeed characterised by smooth green turf and gently undulating carriage rides. Perhaps that's what gave Burke the idea.

Charles Hamilton tried many money-making schemes to fund his garden, including planting a vineyard to make champagne. Painshill did not bankrupt him, as is often reported, but when he could no longer service the debt, he was forced to sell up. The sale made him enough to retire to Bath, where he married for the third time, was much in demand as a garden guru, and lived comfortably to the age of 82.

THE GROTTO

GROTTOES first occur in classical poetry, as natural caves with sacred springs. Artificial grottoes or nymphaea were later built by the Greeks and Romans as places to commune with the Muses, and became highly desirable features in the classically inspired gardens of the Renaissance. The sophisticated water tricks of Italian grottoes were brought to England by the de Caus brothers, and at Wilton House in the 1630s, Isaac de Caus created nothing short of magic, with water-powered singing birds and spouting sea monsters, illuminated with rainbows.

The mood of grottoes changed during the eighteenth century. They were now required to demonstrate the marvels of nature rather than the ingenuity of man, and Alexander Pope decorated his grotto with stalactites from Cornwall, basalt columns from the Giant's Causeway, lava from Vesuvius and even gold ore from Peru. Prior Park had a grotto modelled on Pope's, as did Stowe, where it became a favourite place for after-dark entertaining. Lit by flickering lamps and 'furnished with a great number of looking glasses both on the walls and ceiling', the twinkling interior must have been enchanting. Horace Walpole, however, visiting in 1768, complained crossly that it was far too cold and wet.

The grotto of Thomas Goldney, by contrast, drew rapturous responses from visitors. A wealthy banker, he spent 27 years constructing a grotto in his modest Clifton garden, patiently decorating it with 'Bristol diamonds' (actually quartz), fossils, mother-of-pearl, giant tropical shells and over 200 species of coral. It can still be visited today.

Also still surviving is the grotto at Stourhead, intended to inspire gloomy thoughts of the underworld. Owner Henry Hoare, however, enjoyed it as a delectable place for a cool bath on a scorching day. 'A souse in that delicious bath and grot, fill'd with fresh magic,' he wrote in 1765, 'is Asiatick luxury.'

For sheer romance, though, nothing compares with the dazzling 1760s Crystal Grotto at Painshill Park, especially since its magnificent restoration in 2013. A Chinese bridge leads to an island, where a mysterious structure of rocky vaults is ornamented with hundreds of thousands of crystals – calcite, gypsum, quartz and fluorite – all painstakingly stuck to inverted wooden cones in imitation of stalactites, the drama heightened by sheets of water trickling down the walls. This was the work of father-and-son team Joseph and Josiah Lane, who also made grottoes at Bowood and Fonthill. At Hawkestone Park in Shropshire, a hillside grotto offering an 'Awful Precipice' impressed even grumpy Dr Johnson, who generally disdained the grotto as 'an excellent habitation for a toad'. But as landscapes became less poetic, grottoes fell out of fashion, and Josiah Lane ended his days in the workhouse.

A Victorian craze for fern-clad rockwork revived a brief glimmer of the grotto spirit, but generally they were dismissed as damp and unhealthy. There was, though, one last hurrah in the early twentieth century, at Friar Park in Oxfordshire. Here, Sir Frank Crisp created a subterranean ice grotto, with real icicles and distorting mirrors which shrank visitors into dwarfs. More recent attempts at grotto-making include a grumpy-looking Neptune at Woolbeding in West Sussex; a sunken chamber near Edinburgh lined with Brazilian amethyst; and a domed fernery in Herefordshire made from glass bottles and delightfully named the Blotto-Grotto.

Clockwise from top: The magnificently restored Crystal Grotto at Painshill Park. The vertiginous Grotto Hill at Hawkstone Park in Shropshire. The sleeping nymph, Ariadne, at Stourhead.

127

HERMITS

In the eighteenth century, no garden of fashion was complete without a hermitage, preferably with resident hermit. Ideally, it should be located deep in a gloomy wood and be primitive and rough in its construction. Root-houses were particularly admired, but Lord Orrery built a rustic hut of sheep bones, while at Stourhead, Henry Hoare created a vaulted structure of oak stumps plastered with moss. If you really wanted to push the boat out, you could have both a winter and summer hermitage.

Hamilton's attempts to find a suitable tenant for the Painshill hermitage became legendary. Naturally, the ideal hermit should be sober, celibate, silent, solitary and weatherproof: but unaccountably, none seemed to take to the life. Hamilton offered the colossal sum of £700 to a person willing to spend seven years in his 'beautiful retreat'. He would be provided with 'a Bible, optical glasses, a mat for his bed, a hassock for his pillow, and hour-glass for his timepiece, water for his beverage [and] food from the house,' but he was not permitted to leave the grounds or to exchange so much as a single word with the servant who brought his food. The post was taken by a man called Remington, who lasted just three weeks before being discovered in a local hostelry (some say *in flagrante* with a milkmaid). He was promptly dismissed, and ended his days in an asylum.

One John Timbs, of Preston, Lancashire, offered £50 a year for life to anyone who would live for 'seven years underground, without seeing anything human.' He must let his hair, beard and nails grow, but there was at least a cold bath in his 'very commodious' quarters (some employers wanted their hermits 'uncleansed'), he was supplied with books and a 'chamber organ' and might ring a bell for any 'convenience' he wanted. A candidate actually lived in this way for four years.

There are some hair-raising accounts of a hermit of Hawkstone in Shropshire who would charge out of his cave waving two bloody stumps instead of arms. But other accounts recall the more peaceable figure of Father Francis:

The hermit is generally in a sitting posture, with a table before him, on which is a skull, the emblem of mortality, an hour-glass, a book and a pair of spectacles. The venerable bare-footed Father, whose name is Francis, (if awake) always rises up at the approach of strangers. He seems about 90 years of age, yet has all his senses to admiration. He is tolerably conversant …

Father Frances was eventually replaced by an automaton, which could answer questions and recite improving verses in 'a hoarse hollow voice'. 'The gardener,' reported one satisfied visitor in 1801, 'must be the actor, and an admirable one he is.' Other garden-owners simply dressed the hermitage with appropriate props, as if the hermit had just popped out for a moment.

Even those of relatively modest means aspired to a hermitage; the naturalist Gilbert White held melon-eating parties in his, at which his brother Harry obligingly acted the hermit, donning a druidical costume and serving wine. One of White's nieces records an idyllic afternoon in July 1763, when she and her sisters dressed up as shepherdesses and sang songs, and hermit Harry appeared and told their fortunes.

In his 1780 essay *On Modern Gardening*, Horace Walpole was very sniffy about the hermitage, declaring it was 'almost comic to set aside a quarter of one's garden to be melancholic in.' But it is difficult to imagine they were ever taken that seriously. Rather than a pious rejection of the vanities of the world, the horrid uncut toenails of the eighteenth-century hermit had become a fashion statement.

Clockwise from top left: The Hermitage at Stowe. A playful modern version of a rustic hermit's hut at Woolbeding in West Sussex. A human skull was an essential prop for a convincing hermit. Henry White so enjoyed playing the hermit for his brother Gilbert that he commissioned this painting of the scene.

CHAPTER 5

GEORGIAN GARDENS 2

BEAUTIFUL AND SUBLIME

1740–1820s

'... so closely did he copy nature that his works will be mistaken.'

In the 300 years since his birth, Lancelot Brown has been variously lauded as a genius, 'an omnipotent magician' (though that phrase was used in attack) and denounced as a vandal, destroyer both of the formal garden and the early eighteenth-century garden of ideas. What is beyond doubt is that no individual, before or since, has had such a profound effect on the English landscape. Brown's serene compositions of smoothly contoured hills and limpid waters came to express what garden historian Johnny Phibbs terms 'some kind of aboriginal Englishness', so successfully infiltrating our national consciousness that our notion today of what is beautiful in English landscape is an idealisation entirely of Brown's making.

Brown was born a farmer's boy in the village of Kirkharle in Northumberland. He died a gentleman, the wealthy owner of his own country estate, and a celebrity who, according to Pitt the Elder, shared 'the private hours' of the King and dined on familiar terms with 'all of the House of Lords'. On leaving school at 16 (surprisingly late for yeoman stock) he was employed by the local landowner, Sir William Loraine, who had embarked on a major project of estate improvement and enclosure, clearing and draining the land and planting many thousands of trees. Brown seems to have been given considerable responsibility, and once the work was completed in 1738, he headed south, working initially for Loraine's family and friends in Oxfordshire.

In February 1741, Brown was appointed Head Gardener at Stowe, working for Lord Cobham to realise the schemes dreamt up by the notoriously unreliable William Kent. Kent was good at conceptual design, but unlike his predecessor Bridgeman had no practical skills, leaving it to others to sort out the nuts and bolts. It is easy to see how a conscientious head gardener, with well-honed skills in forestry and water management, should soon become invaluable. The Grecian Valley to the north of the Elysian Fields was reputedly planned by Cobham and Brown together, and Brown took charge of removing Bridgeman's terrace, shifting 62,000 cubic feet (17,600 cubic metres) of soil and transplanting

Lord Coventry's monument to Lancelot Brown at Croome in Worcestershire, the landscape that established Brown's reputation.

semi-mature trees from elsewhere on the estate to create the new feature. Before long Brown was acting as Clerk of Works, supervising building as well as landscaping and studying architectural works in Stowe's library, and Cobham had sufficient confidence in him to loan him out to friends. In 1749 Cobham died, and two years later Brown quit Stowe for the Thameside village of Hammersmith, then something of a horticultural hotspot, and set up in business on his own.

Almost straight away, through the good offices of Sanderson Miller, he was invited to Croome Court in Worcestershire, 'as hopeless a spot as any in the island'. Here he remodelled the house, demolished and resited the church and drained the marshy grounds, channelling the water to create a lake, which purported to be the source of the River Severn. His patron, Lord Coventry, was delighted, writing to Miller that 'Mr Brown has done very well by me, and indeed I think has studied both my Place and my Pocket, which are not always conjunctively the Objects of Prospectors'. The two became firm friends, and Brown continued to embellish Croome for the rest of his life, cherishing it as 'his first and favourite child'. When Brown died, Coventry felt moved to erect a monument on the lakeshore, celebrating the man 'who by the powers of his inimitable and creative genius formed this garden scene out of a morass'.

Brown's new church at Croome was dedicated to Mary Magdalene, in memory of Lord Coventry's wife Maria, a famous beauty who died aged just 28, poisoned by her lead-based make-up.

From Croome, Brown went on to work relentlessly for the next 30 years. Some 270 landscapes have now been attributed to him, including some of the most glorious in the land: Bowood and Burghley, Longleat and Harewood, the serene sweep of Petworth, the Golden Valley at Ashridge and the magisterial approach to Blenheim, transformed by 'the most superb piece of water, in which art has any share, in this kingdom'. Here Vanbrugh had erected a majestic bridge to lead to the great palace he had built for the Duke of Marlborough. Unfortunately, the river it spanned was no more than a trickle – a disharmony that moved visitors to ridicule. Brown solved the problem by damming the Glyme to create a vast new lake. Thomas Whately, visiting when the work was just finished, described how the architectural features which had previously seemed scattered round the park without rhyme or reason were now magically united by this noble expanse of water, 'collected into one illustrious scene'. The effect can still be enjoyed today.

Altogether, the industrious Northumbrian probably worked on half a million acres (over 200,000ha) over the course of three decades, usually in England, but occasionally in Scotland and Wales. The story goes that he declined to go to Ireland, on the grounds that he 'had not yet finished England'. Detractors sniped that he made everywhere look the same, but that wasn't necessarily his fault: his clients were buying in to a 'Capability Brown park', just as they might buy into a Tom Stuart-Smith garden today. There was a distinctive Brown look – gently rolling grassland, dotted with clumps of noble specimen trees; a lake in the middle

Left: In 1763, Brown produced a plan for the 1,200 acre (486ha) park at Bowood in Wiltshire, which involved extensive tree planting and the creation of a large lake. He was engaged by the 2nd Earl of Shelburne – one of six prime ministers whom Brown numbered among his clients.

Left: At Blenheim in Oxfordshire, Brown dammed the River Glyme to give purpose to Vanbrugh's mighty bridge. Afterwards he wondered, 'Thames, will you ever forgive me?'

distance, usually made by damming a stream or enlarging an existing canal; an undulating belt of woodland running round the periphery of the park, shutting out the world outside. Serpentine carriage drives meandered in and out of the belt, offering tantalising glimpses of the scene as they made their unhurried way towards the house. If the park were big enough, the perimeter belt was not necessary: the swell of encircling hills might be sufficient to contain the perfected landscape, but the great selling point of the Capability Brown park was that it was sufficiently adaptable to be reproduced on estates both great and small. And copied it certainly was: by the 1780s the last vestiges of formality had crumbled, and everyone who was anyone had a landscape park.

In 1764, after years of hard lobbying, Brown was made Master Gardener to George III – a post which left him sufficient time to work at Chatsworth and Claremont and create the sinuous lakes at Sheffield Park. His last commission was at Berrington Hall in Herefordshire. It gets mixed reviews, but there's no denying the grandeur of the 14 acre (5.7ha) lake, nor the magnificent sequence of views from the house, designed by Brown's son-in-law, Henry Holland.

On 5 February 1783 Brown collapsed in the street on his way home from supper with Lord Coventry. His obituary was prescient: 'Such … was the effect of his genius that when he was the happiest man, he will be least remembered; so closely did he copy nature that his works will be mistaken.'

Above: Having agreed a master plan, Brown would produce further sets of plans to guide the foreman implementing the project. The sketch above is one of six produced for Rothley Lower Lake in Northumberland.

Left: Cattle graze at the water's edge at Croome – a scene we might easily mistake for unadorned nature.

The master planner

Brown was no revolutionary. He was working within established taste, arguably bringing the ideas of Bridgeman and Kent to their logical conclusion and, in so doing, creating a new art form worthy to stand alongside the greatest of literature and art. His uniqueness, modern commentators agree, lay in being so supremely good at his job. Historian Steffie Shields has pointed out his excellence as an engineer, his skill at manipulating water, how cleverly he built on the ideas of Stephen Switzer in combining profit with pleasure. For these were profoundly practical landscapes. The serpentine lake that occupied the mid-ground provided fish as well as a glittering view; tree belts were valuable not only for shelter, but also for timber and game. The acres of grass were fuel for horses, while the sheep that grazed the swards furnished manure for arable land.

Portrait of Lancelot 'Capability' Brown, *c*.1770–75, by Richard Cosway.

So what was the secret of Brown's phenomenal success? For a start, he worked extremely hard, often riding 70 miles in a day between his various appointments. He maintained an enviable contacts book, and was universally liked for his 'wit, learning and great integrity'. And he was a formidable businessman – the front man for a complex network of specialist contractors, working the length and breadth of the land. Between 1761 and 1783 he handled contracts worth a staggering £320,000 – the equivalent of £718 million today.

His landscapes were easy on the eye, offering scale, balance, clarity and animation, their winding carriage drives revealing agreeable vignettes of bosky woods and grazing animals – all the pleasures of country life, but with the everyday filth edited out. They made no intellectual demands. If Brown erected a temple, it was simply as a pleasing structure to be viewed while strolling round the lake; it was no longer intended to inspire lofty thoughts in the viewer. But perhaps because Brown had never made the Grand Tour himself, buildings of this kind were much thinner on the ground. This saved considerable expense, and his landscapes, once established, were to a large extent economically self-sustaining. They were 'politically correct', perceived as embodying liberty, tolerance and democracy (as opposed to wicked French tyranny and autocracy, symbolised by the grandiose formal landscapes of Le Nôtre). It is a fine irony that so many of the fortunes deployed in Brown's improvements were founded on slavery.

At the same time, the belt of trees around the perimeter of the park conveniently shut out all sight of the *hoi polloi*. Gate lodges controlled who could enter; where once a busy roadway had been welcomed as a lively prospect (as at Rousham), now roads and footpaths were diverted to ensure complete privacy. Only a generation ago, the great house had stood hugger-mugger with its neighbours; now it rose in splendid isolation, afloat on a sea of greensward, encircled by a park that in its strong resemblance to a post-medieval deerpark carried all the historic trappings of status. Whether you were of ancient family or an *arriviste*, the landscape park resplendently proclaimed membership of an exclusive social and economic elite.

By the 1770s, Brown had become the victim of his own success. The style which he had created had been so universally admired that it didn't so much trickle as cascade down the social scale, and of course, once a thing becomes popular, the *cognoscenti* move on elsewhere. Poet Richard Owen Cambridge wrote caustically that he hoped to die before Brown so that he could see heaven before it was 'improved'. And William Chambers, the architect of Kew Gardens and a bitter rival of Brown, attacked Brown's designs as differing 'very little from common fields, so closely is nature copied'. Chambers denounced Brown as an ignorant vandal: 'the ax has often, in one day, laid waste the growth of several ages; and thousands of venerable plants, whole woods of them, have been swept away, to make room for a little grass, and a few American weeds.'

There were also practical objections to Brown's practice of bringing the lawn right up to the house. Fanny Burney wrote grumpily in 1786 of being unable to get to the door without getting her feet wet, while Humphry Repton argued for the restoration of the terrace with a delightful 'before and after' picture in which the unimproved site has stags gazing through the salon windows and cattle grazing in the porch. (In reality, unwanted livestock were excluded by a ha-ha.) For the servants, the banishment of the kitchen garden to some distant part of the estate must have been a daily trial. But the most serious objections to Brown's designs were the moral ones. The perfected landscape had no place for the dwellings of the poor, and at Bowood, Audley End, Chatsworth and many others, entire villages were drowned or demolished. The displacement at Nuneham Courtenay moved

Brown's landscapes were not only beautiful, but productive, the woodland offering cover for game, and the grassland pasture for cattle and sheep, and fuel for horses.

Oliver Goldsmith to a furious poem of protest, *The Deserted Village* (1770). It availed nothing. At Milton Abbas, when villagers refused to budge, Lord Milton simply ordered the dam to be opened. Yet such destruction was far from unusual – many villages had been cleared in the course of enclosure, and most of those evicted from parks had disappeared well before 1750. Brown's work has to be set in the context of an insatiable appetite for 'improvement' which saw the first wave of parliamentary enclosures, new roads and canals and wholesale agricultural reform. During Brown's lifetime, arable production increased by 50 per cent without any increase in acreage. He would doubtless have considered better housing stock on drier ground as a change for the better.

Brown's work fell from favour soon after his death, dismissed as dull and insipid as the new fashion for the Picturesque embraced rocky crags, blasted trees and rushing torrents. He was largely ignored by the plant-hungry Victorians,

and really only rehabilitated in the 1950s. Today, his preoccupations seem remarkably like our own – sustainable water use, planting trees for future generations, finding less labour-intensive ways of gardening. Yet barely 40 years ago, at the Victoria & Albert Museum's *The Garden* exhibition of 1979, Brown was acknowledged only by a small and bitter plaque, dismissing his work as 'an aberration lasting only half a century, depriving the English of the sort of complicated flowery gardens that they love'. In reality he did no such thing. In the exalted circles in which he moved, few formal gardens probably remained intact by the 1750s or '60s: walls had already been removed and geometry softened under the influence of Bridgeman and Kent. Far from banishing flowers, he quietly moved them 'out of shot' from the main facade to the side or rear of the house, and was also an eager adopter of the new American shrubs, then just arriving in Britain, that could offer the delights of flowers on a bigger scale. Flowering shrubs were routinely used not only in the pleasure ground round the house (separated from the wider parkland by a ha-ha), but along rides and plantation edges. As well as 'Virginia Shumach' and 'Virginia Raspberry', his plant list for Petworth in 1753 includes lilacs, 'trumpet flowers', honeysuckle, jasmine and a mass of different roses. Croome became famous for its impressive collection of trees and shrubs. And the Cedar of Lebanon, now regarded as the archetypal aristocratic tree, owes its ubiquity largely to Brown. New studies suggest that elements of the formal garden were often integrated into his designs in avenues and 'groves', while research is still required into his walled gardens, which undoubtedly offered flowers as well as produce.

Brown had made a virtue of simplicity, but in the eyes of his critics this was a failure. His designs were considered insufficiently painterly (although Turner painted eagerly at Petworth), with too little evidence of the hand of man. Today, perhaps, we have a better appreciation of the art that conceals art, and the subtlety required in its making. What was needed, said the ever-practical Brown, was 'a good plan', followed by 'good execution, a perfect knowledge of the country and the objects in it, whether natural or artificial, and infinite delicacy in the planting'. Easy …

The Earl of Coventry was an obsessive plant collector and encouraged Brown to include as many trees and shrubs as possible in his design for Croome, the more exotic and unusual the better.

HUNTIN', SHOOTIN', FISHIN'

HUNTING, shooting and fishing have for centuries been the preferred occupations of English gentlemen (and some gentlewomen), so it is no surprise that these activities should have had a huge effect on our parks and gardens.

The Normans identified hunting with chivalry, so hunting became not just a matter of supplying the table, but a noble pursuit. Henry VIII was a keen huntsman, as was James I, and more private deer parks were established in the sixteenth century than ever before. Hunting was very much a spectator sport, and the chase might be watched from the house roof, as at Newark Park in Gloucestershire, or from a 'stand' or 'standing' built within the park. After a serious fall in 1538, or perhaps because he was too fat to sit on a horse, Henry VIII gave up riding to hounds and hunted entirely from stands. Likely quarry would be sniffed out by 'teasers' (small hounds), driven from the coverts by beaters and chased around the park by horsemen and hounds into a 'course', an enclosed area passing the stand where the honoured guest stood ready with a crossbow. Elizabeth I liked to shoot her deer to the accompaniment of a small orchestra. The magnificent stand at Lodge Park in Gloucestershire was built in 1634 by bon viveur and gambler John Crump. As the stag was chased along the course by greyhounds, bets would be placed on which dog would reach it first: only those wagering £20 or more would be eligible for the kill.

The medieval deer park had stood at some distance from the house, but by the eighteenth century, the enclosure and consolidation of land meant that the park now encircled the house and hunting for deer and foxes moved outside to the wider estate. The park now became a private preserve for rearing and shooting small game – hares, or birds like partridges, flushed out by dogs and shot on the ground. But from the 1750s, guns became lighter and more accurate, making it possible to shoot birds in the air. (Indeed, it would be unsporting to do otherwise.) Pheasants became the target of choice. These are birds of the woodland edge, so small copses or thin straggly strips of woodland suited them ideally – hence the clumps and tree belts of the landscape park. They also like a shrub layer, prompting underplanting with bird cherry in the eighteenth century, and rhododendron throughout the nineteenth.

Carcasses from the hunt would need to be hung in a game larder – often highly decorative additions to the garden. At Uppark in West Sussex, Repton decorated the larder floor with the bones of deer, the octagonal larder at Holkham Hall is lined with alabaster, but especially delightful is the game larder at Farnborough Hall, designed by Sanderson Miller.

In the summer, when there was no hunting to be had, landowners could turn to fishing, an activity deemed suitable for ladies and improving for children. In 1618, William Lawson had advocated fishing from a summer-house on your mount. By 1772, at Kedleston Hall in Derbyshire, Robert Adam's elegant Fishing Pavilion was virtually a spa, offering hours of varied entertainment. On the upper floor was a banqueting chamber decorated on a fishy theme, with a large Venetian window from which the ladies of the party might cast their lines without damage to their delicate complexions. Below was a pair of boathouses and a cold bath – considered beneficial to both bodily and mental health. The pavilion still remains – a gently soporific place to while away a summer afternoon.

Clockwise from top left: Fishing in the ornamental canal at Upton House in the early eighteenth century. The hunting stand at Lodge Park, built by the wily John Crump, who contrived to be on both sides at once in the Civil War and wheedled a warrant out of Oliver Cromwell to take deer from nearby Wychwood Forest to stock his new park. The game larder at Farnborough Hall, where a louvred cupola, unglazed and netted against flies, admits a flow of cool air to carcasses hung aloft on a large wooden wheel. Robert Adam's Fishing Pavilion at Kedleston Hall, and one of the murals from the upstairs Fishing Room.

The Picturesque

The Picturesque started with a simple enough idea – that landscape should offer the same satisfactions as paintings. It was something that clearly worked in gardens: Stourhead was a living Claude, while Painshill recalled the thrilling landscapes of Salvator Rosa – all gloomy chasms, storm-blasted trees and ferocious mustachioed *banditti*. But increasingly, the Picturesque appropriated Burke's ideas of the Beautiful and Sublime, and added a weight of emotional baggage. For Burke, 'beautiful' things were smooth, not given to sudden variation, and inspired pleasing emotions. The 'sublime', instead, had the capacity to evoke terror and amazement, and was associated with immensity, darkness and pain. One wasn't better than the other: they were just different. What started as a philosophical distinction soon developed into a matter of fashion, encouraged by such arbiters of taste as the Reverend William Gilpin, a clergyman from Hampshire who toured the land in search of 'picturesque' experience, and published disappointed accounts of scenes that failed to live up to his painterly expectations. Gilpin wanted scenery to be rough and rugged, irregular and dramatic – qualities conspicuously absent from Brown's parks – though he conceded that a park was different from a mountainside

Above left: *Christ in the Wilderness*, circle of Salvator Rosa (1615–73). The jagged rocks and storm-blasted trees favoured by Rosa inspired a new aesthetic in landscaping.

Above: This illustration from *Sketches of Roads, Rivers, Lakes, and Sea-Coasts* by William Gilpin, shows the growing appreciation of mountain scenery, previously considered ugly and threatening.

and a degree of 'neatness' and 'elegance' might be desirable in a domestic environment. No such moderation characterised Uvedale Price and Richard Payne Knight, two garden improvers who, in blazing broadsides published in 1794 (one in verse) lambasted Brown's 'everlasting green', his 'flat, insipid waving plain' and 'never-ending sheets of vapid lawn'. Though they differed in all kinds of niceties, they broadly agreed that all landscape, both natural and man-made, should henceforth be judged by the yardstick of Salvator Rosa.

Now garden visitors were encouraged to become connoisseurs of the sublime, and, increasingly, the 'merely' beautiful was dismissed as boring, and ever more 'terrible' and violent sensations were required — rather as today's theme park visitors demand ever faster and more scary white knuckle rides. They wanted jagged rocks and thundering gorges, mouldering abbeys and mysterious tombs. In garden architecture, the Gothic was progressively preferred to the classical style, the ruined to the whole. Landowners lacking the requisite ruins were obliged to build their own, and numerous pattern books existed for their instruction (see page 150). Thomas Whately, writing in 1771, advised humility in your choice: where a castle or abbey would be too ostentatious, a crumbling cottage or bridge gave an authentic sense of the historical. Or why not a mini Stonehenge? 'It could be done with little trouble and great success;

Sheep made an acceptable addition to the Picturesque landscape. William Gilpin wrote: 'Their colour is just that dingy hue, which contrasts with the verdure of the ground; and the flakiness of their wool is rich, and picturesque. I should wish them however to wear their natural livery; and not be patched with letters and daubed over with red-ochre.'

the material might be brick or even timber plaistered over, if stone could not easily be procured.' (At least three were built – in Somerset, North Wales and on the banks of the Thames.) Above all, no garden of fashion was complete without a hermitage, preferably with resident hermit (see page 128). Grottoes had been popular for a century or more: blissfully cool retreats in sunny Italian gardens, but when transplanted into the dank English climate, nothing could be more mournful. Unless, perhaps, the 'Valley of the Shadow of Death' at Denbies, Surrey, with gateposts of upright coffins, bedecked with human skulls.

Gardens always mirror the fads and fancies of their times. The sensations of danger and gloom sought out in gardens were precisely those which thrilled the readers of Gothic novels such as the best-selling *Mysteries of Udolpho* (1794), so memorably sent up by Jane Austen in *Northanger Abbey*. It was perhaps inevitable that garden-makers should recreate the wild landscapes described in these hugely popular novels.

Newark Park, one of the National Trust's hidden gems, gives something of the flavour: a Gothicised tower teetering on the edge of a precipice with a vast panorama below, lashed by fierce winds, and – what joy! – haunted by the ghosts of dispossessed monks. In the 1790s, a snaking carriage drive was planted with yews and pines to provide the requisite feeling of gloom and doom, and a gatehouse added in the shape of a ruined Gothic castle. Today, a century or so of neglect and ruin has finished the scene to perfection.

Originally intended to view the hunt, the lodge at Newark Park in Gloucestershire perches thrillingly on the very edge of an escarpment.

At Hafod, in Wales, Thomas Johnes planted over 2 million trees to create a suitably spine-tingling landscape around the natural advantages of cascades and mountain streams. At Hackfall, a few miles from Studley Royal, William Aislabie strung buildings along the gorge of the River Ure, including a dining house (Mowbray Point) that opened into heart-lurching nothingness. But most terrifying of all were the 'vast and vertiginous prospects' of Hawkstone in Shropshire. Dr Johnson, visiting in 1774, was appalled:

> *We were always on the brink of a precipice, or at the foot of a lofty rock … Above, is inaccessible altitude, below, is horrible profundity … He that mounts the precipice at Hawkstone, wonders how he came hither, and doubts how he shall return. His walk is an adventure and his departure an escape.*

A peacock surveys the dizzying view from a balustrade at Newark – the epitome of Picturesque chic.

Of course the good Doctor hated it: he was a crusty old rationalist, whereas in the Gothic novel we see a close identification between sublime scenery and the exquisite sensibility of the heroine (who is usually imprisoned, entrapped or in imminent moral danger). It is Jean-Jacques Rousseau (1712–78) who is credited with inventing the cult of Sensibility, the studied cultivation of heightened emotion which paved the way towards Romanticism. He contended that in his natural state, man is both good and happy. To return to that state of grace, we must cast aside the artificial decadence of civilisation, and attend instead to our natural feelings and intuitions, embracing instinct and emotion. In place of intellect, we must develop sensibility, an intuitive capacity for intense feeling.

Rousseau, of course, was trying to say something profound about the corrupting effects of civilisation, but as the cult became fashionable, it became increasingly divorced from real feeling, as artificial as the culture of wit and urbanity it supplanted (which rather proves his point) and with an almost infinite capacity for silliness. Every aspect of this found expression in the garden, from the first delicate flirting with the emotions, as at Painshill, to the cheap thrills of Hawkstone where a blood-soaked 'hermit' would jump out at unsuspecting visitors. The rustic cottage, rough and rude, became the garden ornament of choice. Simplicity, delicious melancholy, rapture and solitude should all be assiduously cultivated. One of Rousseau's favourite hobbies was weeping into Lake Geneva: the garden should provide ample spots for moping.

Hand in hand with all this went a rapturous form of nature worship that vehemently excluded humanity. Man, in Rousseau's view, only spoiled things: it is a curiously twentieth-century notion. In 1793, William Beckford, the richest man in England, began to build a Trumpish 12-foot wall round his property at Fonthill, on Salisbury Plain. Eventually, 'The Barrier' enclosed some 1,900 acres (769ha), where Beckford lived in Rousseauesque solitude (Rousseau became a recluse towards the end of his life) with hares that ate from his hand, tame swans floating on the lake and only a favourite dwarf for company. Beckford tended his flower garden, and planted American conifers – plants plucked from an earthly Eden, where the Noble Savage was pitted against the corrupt forces of civilisation.

Flowers were important too at Nuneham Courtenay, where Rousseau had briefly stayed during his self-imposed exile in England in 1766. In 1771, with the help of poet William Mason, Lord Nuneham (later 2nd Earl Harcourt) made a butterfly-shaped flower garden based on the one described in Rousseau's *La Nouvelle Heloise*, rather beautifully painted by Paul Sandby in 1777. Although they included a Temple of Flora and various busts and inscriptions, artifices of which Rousseau would not have approved, there was also a honeysuckle bower (ideal for solitary weeping), irregular flower-beds haphazardly planted and climbers trailing between the trees, to suggest all was the unaided product of Nature – possibly the first consciously Wild Garden.

The 2nd Earl Harcourt was a friend and admirer of Rousseau, who stayed at Nuneham Courtenay in Oxfordshire in 1766. When Harcourt finally inherited in 1777, he hastened to make his own version of Julie's Nature Garden, and placed a statue of Rousseau among the flower-beds.

The Ladies of Llangollen

It was hard to live the Simple Life when hampered by a mansion. What was needed was a humble cottage, in a suitably Picturesque setting, where you might grow your own vegetables, milk your own cows, wander through the dewy grass on moonlit nights and harbour tender feelings of exquisite delicacy towards your beloved. This was achieved, with a fine disregard for convention, by two Irish noblewomen who came to be known as the 'Ladies of Llangollen'. One night in 1778, 23-year-old Sarah Posonby jumped out of her window in Kilkenny, carrying a pistol and her lapdog Frisk, intending to run off with her dear friend Eleanor Butler. They had urgent reasons for departure: Sarah's guardian had repellent designs on her, while Eleanor, still disgracefully unmarried at 39, was threatened with the nunnery. They were foiled on this occasion, but succeeded at the second attempt, and set up home at Plas Newydd, a cottage above Llangollen. They had no money, and Wales was cheap. But more important, their new home was properly Picturesque. Rocky outcrops, a ruined castle, and below the house a romantic ravine complete with sparkling river – the views could not have been more perfect. The ravine was steadily improved with pools and cascades, and their plain stone cottage was given the full Gothic treatment.

They were not, in reality, ever self-sufficient. And their life of 'simple retirement' required the services of a butler, gardeners and several maids, especially once celebrity visitors started beating a path to their door – Burke, Byron and Shelley, Josiah Wedgwood, Charles Darwin, Sir Walter Scott – all come to admire (and disrupt) this life of idyllic seclusion, devoted to romantic friendship, learning and the arts. Wordsworth wrote them a sonnet when he came to call.

With only four acres, Plas Newydd was laid out like a miniature *ferme ornée*: a circuit walk led through the shrubbery, past the dairy, the chickens, the drying green and glasshouses stocked with peaches and melons. The walk was adorned with flowering shrubs and wild flowers, while in the flower-beds grew dahlias, geraniums, carnations and roses. The ladies gardened on until a ripe old age, attended by their beloved servant 'Molly the Bruiser'. Known in their time as the 'two most celebrated virgins in Europe', they would no doubt have been delighted to learn that they have now been adopted as LGBT icons.

The Ladies of Llangollen favoured Picturesque garden ornaments, including a font purloined from Valle Crucis Abbey, and festooned with mosses and ferns.

ROMANTIC RUINS

FOR two centuries after the Dissolution of the Monasteries, there were plenty of ruins lying about in Britain. Mainly they were robbed for stones or simply left to decay. But in the 1720s the antiquaries Samuel and Nathaniel Buck began to record what was left in a series of engravings, sparking a new interest in abbey ruins. A decade later, John Aislabie extended his garden at Studley Royal to take in a view of Fountains Abbey, prompting the Duncombe family, who were related by marriage, to create their great terrace with views over Rievaulx Abbey. But, obviously, there was not always a ruined abbey conveniently to hand, so at the Leasowes in Shropshire, Shenstone built a sham one using stones raided from Halesowen Abbey, to be viewed from key points of his circuit walk. A 'chapel' followed at Mount Edgecumbe (by 1747) and another 'abbey' at Painshill, hastily built to cover up the site of a tileworks which had gone bust and add value to the property prior to sale. They have never entirely gone out of fashion: a ruined chapel was built at Woolbeding in West Sussex as recently as the 1990s.

So what made ruins so popular? It was Thomas Whately, a widely read commentator on gardens towards the end of the eighteenth century, who put his finger on it in 1771, observing how certain landscape or garden features could 'excite particular ideas and sensations', giving rise to powerful emotions. Ruins, so effective in stimulating 'certain sensations of regret, or veneration, or compassion' were a particularly forceful emotional trigger. And as it was only the emotional impact that counted, it didn't really matter whether they were genuine or not, so long as they were not so obviously fake as to spoil the illusion.

The first sham ruin was probably Alfred's Hall at Cirencester Park, the first known 'Gothick' garden building. It was supposed to evoke a ruined medieval castle, an idea that was seized on by Sanderson Miller, who built up quite a reputation as a designer of ruins. In the 1740s he built a cottage on the escarpment of Edgehill, and next to it a tall octagonal tower with mock-ruined walls, modelled on Guy's Tower at Warwick Castle: together they created a satisfying illusion of a decaying castle, and made an excellent venue for parties. Sanderson's next ruined castle, at nearby Hagley, doubled as house, coal store, henhouse and cowshed. A third, at Wimpole Hall, remained just for show.

In the nineteenth century, the romance of the medieval received a major boost from the novels of Sir Walter Scott. In 1835, Edward Hussey inherited a fourteenth-century castle his grandfather had bought in Kent. Scotney Castle was beautiful, but damp and cramped, so with the help of William Sawray Gilpin (nephew of the first Gilpin), he built a new mock-Elizabethan house and partially demolished the old, making it the focus of a new Picturesque landscape which followed to the letter the principles promulgated by Payne Knight and Uvedale Price. Although the glorious picture he created was severely battered in the storms of 1987, and many fine trees were lost, some judicious short-term planting has helped to restore the scene, so it remains, for many, the most romantic garden in Britain.

Clockwise from top left: Built in the 1830s in the form of a ruined castle, Parson's Folly at Newark Park stands on the site of a former privy. Scotney Castle in Kent. The Gothic Tower at Wimpole Hall, designed by Sanderson Miller in 1749, but only built, in simplified form, by Capability Brown 20 years later. Woolbeding's 'ruined abbey', created from the remains of a Scottish church. Britain's first sham ruin, in Cirencester Park, designed in 1721 by the first Earl Bathurst and Alexander Pope.

Alfred's Hall, Cirencester Park.

The first 'landscape gardener'

While passion and rapture exploded through the garden, Brown's reputation languished. Brown had died in 1783, so the attacks of Price and Knight were directed at his self-appointed successor, Humphry Repton (1752–1818). He made reply in *Sketches and Hints on Landscape Gardening* (1795), mildly observing that landscapes were not just to be looked at, but lived in:

> *… I trust, the good sense and good taste of this country will never be led to despise the comfort of a gravel walk, the delicious fragrance of a shrubbery, the soul expanding delight of a wide extended prospect, or a view down a steep hill, because they are all subjects incapable of being painted.*

Repton, like Brown, held to the classical (and Bauhaus) notion that beauty derives from fitness of purpose. It was Repton who invented the job description 'Landscape Gardener' and had it engraved on his very fetching calling cards. Repton had no practical experience of gardening, and only decided on this career at the age of 36, apparently overnight, having failed as both merchant and farmer. But he did his homework, reading widely in the library of his friend William Wyndham at Felbrigg, was clever and systematic and a shrewd self-promoter, and by the 1790s he overshadowed all Brown's contemporaries, working in more than 50 country estates, among them Holkham, Woburn Abbey, Longleat and Tatton Park. Charging five guineas a day for consultations, although it did not make him rich, soon put him 'in a state of ease and comparative affluence'.

Repton's success was largely attributable to his Red Books. He was an accomplished watercolourist, and turned this skill to advantage in illustrating his proposals with delicate 'before' and 'after' sketches. First was shown the current scene; then with the lifting or sliding of a flap, the new, magnificently improved outlook was revealed. ('Affordable magnificence' became his watchword.) These sketches were accompanied by a somewhat flowery rubric with such headings as Character, Situation, The Approach, Walks and Drives *et al*, larded with whatever verse or flattering observation Repton considered most likely to butter up his client. Handsomely bound in red morocco, these books were often put on display by satisfied customers, and served as excellent advertisements for his work. It was these, rather than the garden, that were the product: Repton was not a contractor, and while he might supervise the work for an additional fee, it was up to the

Repton's business card. According to nineteenth-century writer J. C. Loudon, the idea of becoming a landscape gardener came to Repton in the course of a sleepless night, and he sprang up in the morning and wrote letters to all his friends announcing his new vocation.

client to get it done. A Red Book did not come cheap: the one at Antony House in Cornwall, where Repton advised on the woodlands in 1792, cost a hefty £31. Repton claimed to have made over 400 such books, of which perhaps a quarter survive. The National Trust is fortunate to have nine of them, including Tatton Park, Attingham, Wimpole and Sheringham Park.

Repton's first paid commission, in 1788, was for a well-to-do Norwich merchant with a new villa, and Repton, the consummate PR man, became expert at helping this new class of landowners with less lavish means to bolster their prestige. He was skilled at placing belts and plantations to make a property seem larger than it actually was, or sending off a drive on a circuitous route so that it seemed to go on for miles. But his cleverest trick was 'appropriation' – spreading the signs of his client's ownership beyond the park gates throughout the whole area of his estate. Thus in his Red Book for Tatton Park he wrote, 'The first essential of greatness in a place, is the appearance of united and uninterrupted property …' This might be achieved through introducing the family coat of arms into the churchyard, or inscribing them on local milestones, or, as at Shute Barton in Devon, by erecting gate piers on a public road which had nothing to do with the property at all. Repton appears to have had a relaxed attitude towards public property: a pair of views of his own garden show him improving it by appropriating the village green.

Repton's Red Book for Wimpole Hall in Cambridgeshire shows his plans for new planting, drawing attention to the entrance front and away from the church and stables.

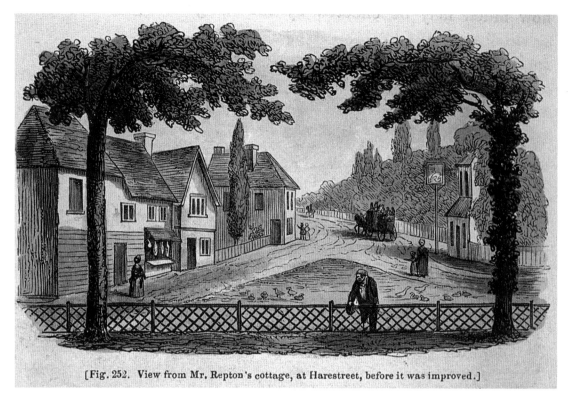

[Fig. 252. View from Mr. Repton's cottage, at Harestreet, before it was improved.]

[Fig. 253. View from Mr. Repton's cottage, at Harestreet, as improved by him.]

154

While still following Brown's lead in the more distant parkland, Repton pushed the grassland away from the house by introducing a formal terrace, as much for practicality as beauty. He also reintroduced gravelled paths and forecourts to keep feet dry when walking or alighting from carriages. The kitchen garden and the laundry yard were rescued from the outer reaches of the estate and returned to a handy distance from the house, albeit behind a concealing thickness of shrubbery. Comfort and convenience were his priority: gardens should be decorative and cheerful.

By 1798 Repton was sufficiently well established for the 2nd Lord Berwick to pay him 100 guineas for just two visits to Attingham Park. The next year he was at work at Plas Newydd in Anglesey (a great James Wyatt mansion on the Menai Strait, not to be confused with the cottage in Llangollen), and in 1800 produced plans for Hatchlands in Surrey. Today the layout remains broadly as he planned. Often Repton was updating grounds that Brown had created 40 or 50 years previously, as at Uppark or Wimpole, humanising, as he saw it, Brown's minimalist design that made 'a country residence as solitary and unconnected as the Prison on Dartmoor'. It wasn't always straightforward. At Wimpole he grumbled, 'There is no part of Mr Brown's system which I have had more difficulty in correcting than the absurd fashion of bringing cattle to the windows of a house'. (Here he proposed to keep them out with railings.)

Repton was a big fan of the flower garden, and his later schemes gave more and more prominence to flowers. He wrote that 'rare plants of every description should be encouraged, and a provision made of soil and aspect for every different class'. One way to do this was to create specialist gardens, and at Ashridge in the Chilterns, a rock garden, a 'Magnolia and American garden' a 'Rosarium' and 'Pomarium' were proposed among a sequence of 15 very disparate gardens. It was all rather random, anticipating the frenzied eclecticism of the century to come.

In 1811 Repton's carriage overturned on the way home from a ball. He sustained spinal injuries and was eventually confined to a bath chair. This did not, however, prevent him pressing on with his 'favourite and darling child in Norfolk': his Red Book for Sheringham Park was produced in 1812. Repton made full use of Sheringham's beautiful coastal setting, reshaping the entrance drive to stage-manage spectacular views of the sea, first closing in the prospect then revealing it on a sudden turn, so that the first view of the house 'burst at once on the sight like some enchanted palace of a fairy tale'. The site of the house had been hotly debated, with the family wanting a view of the sea, but Repton, ever practical, arguing for a more sheltered position. 'The view of the sea at Sheringham is not like that of the Bay of Naples,' he opined. His view prevailed, and his 'favourite child' remains his most complete and best preserved landscape on the ground, less formal and more Brownian than much of his other work, perfectly in tune with 'the genius of the place'.

Unlike his master Brown, who never put his thoughts on paper, Repton was a prolific writer, publishing four major works on landscape design over his 30-year career. These trace the development of his practice, his good-humoured

Opposite: These 'before' and 'after' illustrations of Repton's own garden in Essex appear in his *Fragments on the Theory and Practice of Gardening* (1816). In the 'before' picture, a stagecoach rattles down the street, hams hang from the butcher's shop, geese squawk on the village green and a vagrant peers over the fence. In the 'after' picture, all these nuisances have disappeared, the village green now forms part of the garden, and the vagrant is presumably buried beneath the new flower-bed.

rejection of the excesses of the Picturesque, his growing engagement with the new kind of villa garden that would predominate in the nineteenth century, his journey from Brownian simplicity to complexity and prettiness. There is much that is practical and serviceable; nothing startlingly original, although his thoughts, following his accident, on how gardens could be made more wheelchair-friendly, sound a strikingly modern note.

Perhaps Repton just missed the thing that would have made his imagination take wing. In 1806 he published his *Inquiry Into the Changes of Taste in Landscape Gardening*, in which he predicted that 'we are on the eve of some great change' in both architecture and gardening, 'in consequence of our having lately become acquainted with scenery and buildings in the interior provinces of India'. This was no more improbable than previous fashions for Roman temples or Chinese pagodas, but other than Nash's Brighton Pavilion (which was originally Repton's project), it never took off. There is one glorious exception: Sezincote, a Cotswold garden made for an Indian nabob on an Indian theme. With its Hindu temples and Brahmin bulls, its domes and caverns and elephants and snakes, it is quite unlike any other garden in Britain, and in its powerful fusion of Hindu and Islamic elements, deliberately united as a lesson in cultural integration, it has some powerful messages for today.

Repton undertook more than 400 commissions over 30 years, but Sheringham, he enthused, 'possessed more natural beauty and local advantages than any place I have ever seen.'

The ordinary sort

The history of gardens is inevitably told in terms of the biggest and most avant-garde: the ones people talked about, wrote about or painted. But of course ordinary mortals went on gardening too. We know about a few of them. At Selborne, in Hampshire, the naturalist Gilbert White made eye-catchers out of plywood cut-outs, a summer-house out of a wine barrel and prided himself on growing the plumpest and juiciest melons. In Surrey, the novelist Fanny Burney and her charming but cack-handed husband made rather a hash of their vegetable garden. In Berkeley in Gloucestershire, Edward Jenner inoculated the poor of the neighbourhood with his new smallpox vaccine in his garden shed, reborn as The Temple of Vaccinia.

There are, inevitably, very few accounts of the gardens of agricultural workers, though we know they grew 'kail', both red and green, 'syboes' (spring onions) and herbs for pot and medicine. One rare account occurs in a 1797 pamphlet written by Sir Thomas Barnard, who tells of a Mr Abbot of Poppleton in Yorkshire, a hardworking labourer who had a cottage with two acres of land, common rights and two cows. But when Poppleton was enclosed, Abbot and his six children (with a seventh on the way) were evicted. Abbot considered himself lucky to be given a quarter-acre of roadside land, where he built a house and planted a

The house and conservatory at Sezincote in Gloucestershire, painted by John Martin around 1815. Repton was involved in planning the garden from around 1805, but the extent of his contribution is not known.

garden containing 'fifteen apple trees, one green gage, three winesour plum trees, two apricot-trees, several gooseberry and currant bushes, abundance of common vegetables and three hives of bees'. There is no mention of flowers: the priority was to feed the family. His wife worked at spinning, while at 67, Abbot still went out hoeing turnips and setting hedges to earn a meagre crust. Barnard's object was to highlight the plight of the landless labourer and small farmer, whose livelihoods had been destroyed by enclosure.

Many, of course, migrated to the towns, and in the new industrial heartlands in particular, there grew a tradition of expert working-class flower-growing (page 210). Affluent Bath was laid out by Ralph Allen with both small back gardens and garden squares, and foreign visitors commented on the surprising number of gardens to be seen in London. Towns and villages were growing fast: in Birmingham, for example, the population doubled in the last 40 years of the eighteenth century. The majority of new houses, even quite modest ones, were provided with gardens. But for those that had none, there was always, for the price of a shilling, the prospect of a pleasure garden such as Vauxhall in London, a kind of riotous amalgam of the Tivoli Gardens in Copenhagen, the South Bank and Glastonbury, where all classes mixed to enjoy the latest in art and music, food and flirtation in the magical surroundings of an illuminated garden.

For more than a century Vauxhall Gardens became the essential, slightly naughty, meeting-place for fashionable London. Thomas Rowlandson depicts what we would now call media celebrities, such as the Duchess of Devonshire and the Prince of Wales, rubbing shoulders with the lower orders at an evening concert.

Five continents of plants

The story of the English garden in the eighteenth century tends to be told in terms of ideas and of design, simply because the changes in both were so dramatic. But we cannot finish the chapter without mentioning plants.

The idea has grown up that somehow the eighteenth century turned its back on flowers. Not so. Certainly fussy flower-beds could not sit comfortably with the scale and simplicity of the landscape park, but in smaller spaces flower gardening continued unabated. Typical was Mary Delany, friend and correspondent of many of the century's leading gardeners, who had her own modest patch in London, chock-a-block with blooms. (Her letters vividly recall the misery of the plantaholic who desires a plant but simply has nowhere to put it.) She writes to her sister:

> *You think, Madam, I have no garden, perhaps? But that's a mistake; I have one as big as your parlour in Gloucester, and in it groweth damask-roses, stocks variegated and plain, some purple, some red, pinks, Phillaria, some dead some alive and honeysuckles that never blow.*

At the age of 72, Mrs Delany set down her trowel and began making exquisite, botanically correct paper collages, nearly a thousand in all. The originals she copied so exactly came, in many cases, from the Chelsea Physic Garden, founded in 1673 by the Society of Apothecaries. By 1722 the garden was on its uppers, but was rescued by the philanthropic physician Sir Hans Sloane, who appointed Philip Miller (1691–1771) to run it. Writer, botanist, experimental gardener and overweening ego, Miller dominated English plantsmanship for nigh on a century. His *Gardeners Dictionary*, first published in 1731, was the original gardening encyclopaedia and horticultural Bible. Miller made Chelsea the epicentre of a global network of plant exchange, and the most richly stocked garden in the world.

The history of plant collecting is very much the history of Empire. Victory in the Seven Years' War brought Britain huge new territories including Quebec and Florida in the Americas, new islands in the West Indies and vast tracts of India that had been under French control, including Bengal, Bombay and Madras – all ripe for horticultural exploitation. The Americas had already been a fruitful source for plant-mad Henry Compton (1632–1713), for as Bishop of London, his see extended to Virginia and the West Indies, where he had no hesitation in dispatching ministers to secure plants as well as souls. In the 30 years leading up to the American War of Independence (1775–83), a steady stream of plants came from the North American colonies, many from Philadelphia Quaker John Bartram, who every year sent his friend, Peter

Passionflower, by Mary Delany, 1777, one of 985 life-size botanical studies now held by the British Museum.

Collinson, 20 boxes of plants for five guineas a box. These were distributed both to private collectors like Charles Hamilton and Lord Petre (a fanatical planter of trees) and to a growing tribe of nurserymen.

In 1700 there were just 15 nurseries supplying ornamental plants. By 1760 there were about 100, and by 1800 the number had doubled. For not only were there new sources of plants, but also many more clients to buy them. On the back of developments like the building of the canals in the 1760s, and the invention of the Spinning Jenny and the steam engine (1769 and 1775 respectively), huge fortunes were made. And then, as now, the *nouveaux riches* flocked to display their success in houses and gardens.

Other developments, too, favoured the expansion of the nursery trade. The first was the adoption (from 1753) of the Linnaean system of naming plants, the two-name system

we still use today, which meant that plant descriptions could at last be universally understood. (The influx of new plants had caused nightmares to poor Miller, who had struggled with various naming systems before reluctantly accepting that of Linnaeus.) In addition, there was a growing understanding of hybridisation. In 1717 London nurseryman Thomas Fairchild had brushed the pollen of a carnation on to the stigma of a sweet william to produce a red-flowered 'mule' – a discovery that sent both religious and horticultural shock waves.

The trade was further boosted by the interest of George III, and his installation of Joseph Banks (1743–1820) at the royal garden at Kew. Immensely wealthy and well connected, the youthful Banks bought and blarneyed his way on to the *Endeavour* in 1768, and sailed for Australia with Captain Cook. He brought back 30,000 different specimens of plants, of some 3,500 species – more than half unknown in Europe at that time. (To put it in perspective, Europe's foremost botanist, Linnaeus, could list only 6,000 species.) But Banks's interests were not primarily horticultural: he was looking for plants that might prove of economic benefit to a rapidly expanding Empire.

Banks built Kew into the world's greatest botanic garden, and in his search for profitable plants dispatched botanists to South Africa, the West Indies, North and South America, India, China, Australia and New Zealand. The 60 years of George III's reign saw the introduction of nearly 7,000 plants, most of them at the behest of Banks.

With the end of the Napoleonic wars in 1815, trade rocketed. There were suddenly many more people. (The population increased from 6 to 10 million between 1750 and 1800, and doubled again during the next half-century.) There was more money. And there was a new, prosperous middle class, anxious to expend their wealth on a new kind of house and garden; the suburban villa. All that was needed was a gardening guru to tell them how to do it – amply supplied in the person of John Loudon, founder of the first popular gardening magazine. The scene was set for the great age of the plant hunter.

When the *Endeavour* set sail in 1768, the crew included Joseph Banks (above) and Scottish botanical artist Sydney Parkinson, employed by Banks to paint their plant discoveries, including *Banksia integrifolia* (opposite). Parkinson made nearly 1,000 drawings during the three-year voyage, but died on the journey home.

CHINESE STYLE

THE West has been fascinated with China ever since the thirteenth-century explorer Marco Polo wrote of the wonders of Xanadu, and during the seventeenth and eighteenth centuries, the rare Chinese goods imported by European trading companies became increasingly fashionable. Porcelain was keenly collected by the ladies of the court, and Chinese motifs found their way into the home in 'Chinese Chippendale' furniture and fabulous painted wallpapers.

The first Chinese-style garden building, probably designed by Kent, was built at Stowe in 1738. Around ten years later, Thomas Anson built another Chinese House at Shugborough in Staffordshire, to celebrate the circumnavigation of the globe by his brother George. The design was said to be based on a drawing made in Canton by George's second-in-command, being 'a true pattern of the architecture of that nation, not a mongrel invention of British carpenters'.

One such was William Halfpenny, who in 1750 designed a Chinese bridge for Croome, handsomely recreated in green oak in 2014. This enterprising Yorkshireman published a series of influential pattern books, including temples, pavilions and interior fixtures and fittings, long predating the better known works of Sir William Chambers, designer of the Pagoda at Kew, and furniture-maker Thomas Chippendale. Halfpenny's garden ornaments were clearly sufficiently widespread in 1756 to attract satirical comment in *The Connoisseur Magazine*:

> *The traveller with amazement sees*
> *A Temple Gothic or Chinese*
> *With many a Bell and tawdry rag on,*
> *And crested with the sprawling dragon.*
> *A wooden arch is bent to stride*
> *A ditch of water four feet wide*
> *With angles, curves and zigzag lines,*
> *From Halfpenny's exact designs.*

In 1856 China finally opened its doors to Europe. Chinese style was now available to all, as in the Willow Pattern plates made by Minton – the inspiration for England's most famous Chinese garden at Biddulph Grange. This unusual Staffordshire garden was laid out from 1841 as a kind of virtual world tour, of which the highlight is undoubtedly 'China', an area concealed from the rest of the garden by a rocky 'Wall of China' and high banks and trees. Within is a Chinese Temple overlooking a pool (the Chinese Water), where a red-painted bridge leads to an ornamental landscape of rocks and exotic plants, many collected in the Far East by the plant collector Robert Fortune (1813–80). Another tiny temple, the newly restored Joss House, looks down over a parterre decorated with dazzling red dragons. A gilded water buffalo sits like a garden god above the scene. It is unabashed Technicolor fantasy, besides which the oriental water garden at Cliveden, laid out for William Waldorf Astor in 1900, seems almost self-effacing. Reached by stepping stones across the water, the centrepiece is a six-sided pagoda, originally made for the 1867 Paris *Exposition Universelle*.

From the late nineteenth century, Japan overtook China for Oriental style. But a Peace Pagoda went up in London's Battersea Park in 1985. Soon after, a handsome Chinese bridge was built at Woolbeding, and a regiment of Terracotta Warriors marches over Oxfordshire lawns at Buscot Park.

For most of us, however, the enduring impact of China has been in the many thousands of plants from that country that we now take for granted in our gardens: wistaria and clematis; rhododendrons, camellias and magnolias; as well as showstoppers such as *Lilium regale* or the handkerchief tree *Davidia involucrata* – not to mention a nice cup of tea.

Clockwise from top left: China – not so much a Chinese garden as a world in miniature at Biddulph Grange in Staffordshire. Detail from the Chinese temple at Biddulph Grange. William Halfpenny's Chinese Bridge at Croome in Worcestershire. Chinese wallpaper at Belton House in Lincolnshire.

MENAGERIES

WHAT do you give to the man (or woman) who has everything? What else but an exotic animal?

The first known menagerie was created by Henry I at Woodstock Park, across the lake from Blenheim, housing 'lyons, leopards, strange spotted beasts, porcupines, camells and such like animals' sent to him from 'diverse outlandish Lands'. King John kept beasts at the Tower of London, pitting them against in each other in combat, and lions and leopards were kept at the Tower right up until 1826, when the Duke of Wellington ordered them to be sent to the newly founded Zoological Garden in Regent's Park. It remains a repository for royal gifts to this day.

George III had one of the last quaggas – an animal similar to a zebra, now extinct. His wife, Queen Charlotte, kept an elephant and at least one zebra (scurrilously known as the Queen's Ass) in the stables at Buckingham Palace. At Kew she kept black swans, buffaloes and the first living kangaroos to seen in Britain. When they bred successfully, she gave away the joeys to aristocratic friends with their own menageries, of which there were a surprisingly large number. The Duchess of Portland, it was reported, was 'as eager in collecting animals, as if she foresaw another deluge', and at least 43 menageries are known to have been made in Britain.

Exotic creatures called for exotic buildings – very suitable additions to the landscape park. Princess Augusta accessorised the menagerie at Kew with a Chinese temple standing in the middle of a pond. The frescoed walls and classical urns of the menagerie at Stowe housed flocks of parrots in grand style, while at Horton in Northamptonshire, astronomer Thomas Wright designed a supremely elegant pavilion as the centrepiece of Lord Halifax's private zoo, which held a pair of tigers, 'does from Guadalupe', raccoons, eagles, warthogs 'with

navels on their backs', two 'uncommon martins', and 'many basons of goldfish'.

At Claremont, Clive of India tried to establish table-worthy antelopes in the park, and to cross a zebra with a donkey. The story goes that the zebra's reluctance to mate with so lowly a beast was finally overcome by painting the donkey with stripes, but the resulting foal proved impossible to tame. In the 1890s, however, Walter Rothschild succeeded in driving a carriage drawn by zebras into the forecourt of Buckingham Palace. Queen Victoria declared herself amused.

During the 1810s, an elephant named Sadi lived contentedly at Chiswick House, strolling round the gardens and opening bottles with her trunk during the Duke of Devonshire's many parties. Less fortunate was the giraffe sent to George IV at Windsor. Despite the best efforts of the royal physicians, who declared that her ill health was a sympathetic reaction to gout in the royal toe, she died within weeks. Her portrait still hangs in the royal collection.

Very few menageries have survived. A life-size statue marking the grave of a beloved lioness is the only clue to Goodwood's former riches. At Wimpole, too, the menagerie is only a memory: the local pub is called The Tiger. At Nostell Priory, however, if you follow the winding paths beyond the Middle Lake, you will find the secluded Menagerie Garden, created in 1743, with the Menagerie House designed by Robert Adam. At Tyntesfield there remains a charming cottage-style aviary, strangely modest for a fortune founded on bird poo. But to enjoy the authentic, flamboyant spirit of eighteenth and nineteenth century zoo-keeping, there is nothing to match the magnificent rococo aviary at Waddesdon Manor, Buckinghamshire, built to mark the visit of the Shah of Persia, and every bit as exotic as the endangered birds within.

The Menagerie in the Tower.

Clockwise from top left: There were in fact only three zebras to pull Walter Rothschild's coach: the fourth was a pony painted to look like a zebra. The Menagerie House at Nostell Priory in Yorkshire, where a disused quarry was converted into a menagerie in the late eighteenth century. The Tiger, one of a series of large engravings made by Thomas Bewick in 1799–1800 for Gilbert Pidcock, proprietor of a travelling menagerie. The Aviary at Waddesdon Manor, built to mark the visit of the Shah of Persia in 1889. Lions and leopards were kept at the Tower of London until 1826.

CHAPTER 6

VICTORIAN GARDENS

BECAUSE WE CAN

1820s–1890s

'... scores of unmeaning flower beds in the shape of kidneys and tadpoles and sausages and leeches and commas now disfigure the lawn ...'

T. JAMES, *THE GARDENER'S MAGAZINE*, MAY 1839

It is surprising how many of the ways we think about gardens today have survived intact from the nineteenth century. The first is that a garden is, first and foremost, a place to display plants. In 1958, the no-nonsense landscape architect Sylvia Crowe wrote:

> There are two attitudes to plants in gardens. One is that the purpose of a garden is to grow plants. The other is that plants are one of the materials to be used in the creation of a garden.

In the nineteenth century, as now, there was not the least doubt – a garden was a collection of plants, and the more of them, and the more unusual, the better. Most of the essential features we see in a modern suburban garden were perfectly familiar to the Victorians: a well-kept lawn (a fetish since the 1830s), shrubs and flower beds, perhaps a specimen tree such as a nice magnolia growing in the lawn. A garden should be bright and cheerful, with the longest possible season of colour. Above all, the garden should be neat and tidy – a notion we are only just beginning to question.

Much of this thinking can be traced to just one man. After the death of Repton, gardening became dominated by John Claudius Loudon (1783–1843), a one-armed, workaholic Scot who had opinions on everything and founded the first popular gardening magazine in order to share them with a grateful nation. In doing so, he had 'two grave objects in view; to disseminate new and important information on all topics connected with horticulture, and to raise the intellect and character of those engaged in this art'.

Loudon was a Presbyterian farmer's son from Lanarkshire, whose boundless energy and reforming zeal transformed not only the garden, but the wider urban landscape of the nineteenth century. His range of interests was vast; his capacity for work prodigious. In addition to *The Gardener's Magazine*, which appeared from 1826 until his death in 1843, he founded periodicals on architecture and natural history, wrote treatises on farming, building and universal education and invented a wrought-iron glazing bar that revolutionised the design of glasshouses. In 1822 he published his *Encyclopaedia of Gardening*: it rapidly became the standard reference work of the age. His *Hortus Britannicus* was 'A Catalogue of all the Plants indigenous, cultivated in, or introduced to Britain' and this was followed by the *Arboretum et Fruticetum Britannicum*, an exhaustive study of the trees and shrubs of Britain. Altogether he published over 60 million words and became the most influential gardener in Victorian Britain – and all this in spite of crippling illness, financial ruin and the loss of an arm which made it physically impossible to write. His *Gardener's Magazine* rapidly became a forum for new information

and horticultural debate, aimed less at the great estate than a new readership of middle-class suburban gardeners. As towns became increasingly dirty and overcrowded, those who could escaped to the suburbs, some to newly built terraces, the more prosperous to leafy villas. All were in need of gardens, and Loudon provided the guidance on how to lay them out and manage them, advocating a new style which he called the 'gardenesque', which required individual plants to be placed so that they could grow unencumbered and be admired from all angles, much like pictures in a gallery. He divided the suburban garden into four categories, from the 'fourth rate', built 'principally for the occupation of mechanics' which might be as small as a perch (around 269 square feet/25 square metres), up to the 'first rate', which might cover 50 acres (20.2ha) or more. The larger should include such features as a conservatory, greenhouses, rock garden, shrubbery, fernery and fine specimen trees. But all might aspire to sound horticulture, variety and a high degree of 'polish'.

Island beds at Peckover House in Cambridgeshire, planted in John Loudon's favoured, highly artificial gardenesque style.

Sunnycroft, in Shropshire, falls into the second category, of homes for 'wealthy tradesmen, professional people and gentlemen of good fortune'. Built in 1879 for a prosperous brewer, it has been preserved by the National Trust as a typical creation of Victorian-era suburbia. The five-acre garden (now half its original size) is an exercise in self-sufficiency – Loudon was a great one for 'economy of management' – with henhouses, pigsties, orchard and kitchen garden, even a small area of pasture for two house cows. The formal garden offers herbaceous borders, a rose garden and rockery, and a large, flat lawn suitable for games of croquet or quoits. Everything, from the pre-fabricated glasshouse to the layout of looping paths and the crazy paving is just as might be seen in any late Victorian periodical or manual. Gardening had become commodified.

Whereas the denizen of the landscape park was unlikely to have dirt under his fingernails, Loudon encouraged garden owners to work in their gardens themselves. And as well as digging, he urged them to think about wider economic, social, scientific and cultural issues. Three of his concerns are as topical today as they ever were: the pay and training of gardeners, his insistence on the importance of trees, and the urgent need for green space in towns and cities.

Loudon was not a conservationist in the way we now understand it: he was keen, for example, to see the hills of the Lake District studded with comfortable villas. But he was one of the first to recognise that open space was now a precious and threatened resource, especially in Britain's industrial cities. In 1829, protesting against an attempt to enclose Hampstead Heath for building, he proposed a system of 'breathing spaces' which was eventually to inspire the Green Belts. And he was a tireless campaigner for public parks, which would not only furnish 'green lungs'

Loudon classified suburban houses and their grounds into four grades based on building legislation. Sunnycroft in Shropshire counts as 'second rate'.

for the city (then, as now, air quality was a primary concern, for it was believed that disease was spread by the 'noxious vapours' of the slums), but would bring together people of different classes, resulting in their 'mutual improvement'. Parks would offer opportunities for 'rational recreation', keep workers out of the pub, and provide their families with a valuable educational resource.

At Derby Arboretum, in 1839, he was able to put his ideas into practice, planting a living museum of over 1,000 different trees and shrubs, each one comprehensively labelled. He also erected vases on pedestals, where local horticultural societies were invited to exhibit flowers each week. Within four years a Parliamentary Commission reported that 'The Arboretum … has already produced a perceptible effect in improving the appearance and demeanour of the working classes' and conferred 'an equal benefit upon their health'.

The indefatigable Loudon was aided in his work by his no less energetic wife, Jane (1807–58), at 23 the anonymous author of a sci-fi book (*The Mummy*) which so impressed Loudon that he wrote to request a meeting. Seven months later they were married, and Jane's first job after the wedding was to transcribe the 1,150 pages of his *An Encyclopedia of Cottage, Farm and Villa Architecture and Furniture*. She was, quite literally, his right hand for the rest of his life. Knowing nothing about gardening seemed to her an excellent starting point to write for others in the same position, and she took to her new trade with gusto. Jane Loudon was by no means the first woman writer in the field, but she was the first to reach a mass audience, writing expressly for women and adopting a brisk, practical tone – in marked contrast to the prevailing attitudes of the day, whereby a lower-class woman might slave in a mill or mine or in domestic service, but a lady was unequal to the fatigue of bending down to tend her flowers. Where others commended a little light dead-heading as an antidote to nervous headaches (or a way of acquiring pinkness of cheek and brightness of eye), Jane gave detailed directions for pruning, manuring, planting and digging, and welcomed the newly invented lawnmower with alacrity. Whereas the allusive garden of the eighteenth century excluded women denied a classical education, once the garden was understood as essentially decorative, women could claim it as part of the domestic sphere. And what little education women had usually encompassed botany – ideal now gardens were all about plants rather than poetry. Many women in the nineteenth century became notable plant collectors, and even Jane packed her modest London plot with over 2,000 different varieties.

The Gardener's Magazine had blazed the trail for dozens more gardening periodicals. When Loudon dropped dead in mid-sentence in 1843, it ceased publication, leaving the field clear for its nearest rival, *The Gardener's Chronicle*. Founded in 1841 by Joseph Paxton and edited by John Lindley, this would become essential reading for gardeners for the next hundred years.

After her husband died, Jane Loudon continued to support herself by her pen, writing books and editing a magazine expressly for women.

Mrs. LOUDON'S GARDENING FOR LADIES.

LONDON:
JOHN MURRAY, ALBEMARLE STREET.
1843.

'I would have liked that man for one of my generals'

Plantsman, inventor, engineer, businessman – Joseph Paxton (1803–65) succeeded in everything he turned his hand to. Indeed the Duke of Wellington declared, 'I would have liked that man for one of my generals.' Having lied about his age to get a job at the Horticultural Society's garden at Chiswick, he was lucky enough to make an impression on the garden's next-door neighbour and landlord, the 6th Duke of Devonshire. Thus as dawn rose one May morning in 1826, he found himself outside the gates at Chatsworth, aged just 23, about to take up his new post as Head Gardener. There being no one about, he climbed in over the greenhouse gate.

[I] explored the pleasure grounds and looked round the outside of the house. I then went down to the kitchen gardens, scaled the outside wall and saw the whole of the place, set the men to work there at six o'clock; then returned to Chatsworth and got Thomas Weldon to play me the water works and afterwards went to breakfast with poor dear Mrs Gregory and her niece. The latter fell in love with me and I with her and thus completed my first morning's work at Chatsworth before nine o'clock.

His marriage proved as successful as all his other ventures, Sarah Paxton holding the business and domestic reins while her husband embarked on ever more ambitious enterprises. Paxton remained at Chatsworth for the next 30 years, becoming the Duke's friend and confidant, travelling with him on visits abroad and sharing his limitless passion for new plants. Together, they made the great double act of nineteenth-century horticulture, the Duke as enlightened patron and insatiable collector, and the gardener's boy who would rise above his humble station to end his days as a successful publisher, purveyor of pre-fabricated greenhouses, millionaire railway magnate, MP and Knight of the Realm.

Joseph Paxton (above) stayed with his employer (left) until the Duke's death in 1858, vainly attempting to rein in the Duke's reckless spending on plants.

172

Chatsworth, when Paxton arrived, had been somewhat neglected since the last great overhaul of the landscape by Capability Brown, and Paxton was charged with bringing the gardens back up to speed in a more fashionable formal style. He added ponds and parterres, rebuilt the great seventeenth-century cascade and famous weeping willow fountain and designed a new orangery for the tender plants. The Duke fell in love with orchids, so Paxton built three orchid houses for him: there were 22 glasshouses at Chatsworth before he was finished. The year 1835 saw a new arboretum of 1,670 different species. In 1842 he began work on a monumental rock garden, including the 40ft (12.2m) high Wellington rock and a great boulder that swung gently back at the touch of a finger to reveal a secret path. More engineering triumphs came with the construction of the Emperor fountain   the highest in Europe – and the Great Conservatory, a glasshouse so colossal it took seven miles of hot water pipe to heat it and there was room for two carriages to pass in its ¾ acre interior. Queen Victoria visited in the darkest days of December, was entranced by the tropical scene, and demanded something similar at Kew.

Paxton was also a superlative grower, and in 1849, in another glasshouse of his own devising, was the first to coax the gargantuan water lily *Victoria amazonica* into flower. Fourteen years on, its complex leaf structure would famously inspire his Crystal Palace. This monumental greenhouse, built to house the Great Exhibition of 1851, was three times the size of St Paul's Cathedral, and took

The giant water lily now known as *Victoria amazonica* was first discovered in British Guiana in 1837, and plants had been raised at Kew, but no one could coax it to flower until Paxton built a special glasshouse for it with a tank that simulated the water flow of the Amazon. This image of his daughter Annie standing on one of the leaves was very widely circulated.

173

about a third of the country's annual glass output to glaze it (900,000 square feet [83,613 square metres]). It had its detractors – Ruskin called it 'a cucumber frame between two chimneys', but the public adored it. For Paxton's Crystal Palace was the glittering embodiment of the very forces that were shaping their own gardens – prosperity, economic confidence, the fruits of both expansion of Empire and technological advance, not least the benefits of the world's first railway service, which made both plants and building materials much more cheaply available.

Until the nineteenth century, the function of a greenhouse, hothouse or conservatory was to 'conserve' or overwinter precious tender 'greens'. Heated 'stoves' or 'orangeries' were built in Britain from the sixteenth century, but it was not until well into the eighteenth century that it was realised that light as well as heat was important or that fumes were noxious to plants. Steam heating was developed in Liverpool in 1788, and it was observed that heated water would circulate as early as 1818. The earliest surviving heated glasshouse was built at Bicton in Devon around 1820, and the Great Conservatory at Syon seven years later. They were horrifyingly expensive, not least because glass was heavily taxed. It was not until Lucas Chance produced sheet glass in 1832, followed by James Hartley's improved plate glass in 1844, that large-scale construction in glass really

'On New Year's Day in the year 1837, a traveller was proceeding, in a native boat, on a difficult exploration up the river Berbice in Demerara' … wrote Charles Dickens in 1851, recounting how the discovery of the 'Titanic Water-plant' was to give rise, 14 years later, to another 'Great Giant' appearing in Hyde Park, the Crystal Palace. 'For by a curious apposition, the first parent of the most extensive building in Europe was the largest floral structure in the world.'

became viable. This year saw the birth of probably the world's most famous greenhouse: the Palm House at Kew. Then in 1845 the tax was repealed, with the result that the price of glass fell by 80 per cent over the next 20 years. At the same time, rapid advances in iron and steel technology presented a whole new category of building materials for engineers, architects and designers. The new railways made these readily available, and they were relatively cheap. The final barrier to building in iron and glass was resolved with the invention of a flexible glass putty containing linseed oil, which held the glass safely as metal glazing bars expanded and contracted. Suddenly, such airy constructions were no longer the province of the super-rich, but an affordable and fashionable adjunct to every upper- and middle-class home. Here could be displayed the glorious novelties brought home by the plant hunters from far-distant outposts of Empire – orchids, palms and every kind of tender exotic. In country estates, glasshouses proliferated, in designs variously adapted for the culture of melons, pineapples, peaches and vines (see page 269). But the greatest impact of this new building technology (helped by a convenient fall in the price of coal) was to permit the propagation of colossal quantities of colourful tender and half-hardy annuals, newly introduced from South Africa and South America, to furnish the new fashion of bedding out.

Bedding out

The first experiments in bedding took place in the 1830s at a handful of aristocratic gardens – Bedford Lodge in Kensington, Trentham in Staffordshire, and Shrubland Park in Suffolk. The social conditions were ideal: Britain's central position at the heart of a growing empire and global network of trade both facilitated an influx of new plants and created a prosperous new public to buy them, while there was a copious supply of cheap labour. It was, moreover, a form of planting that suited the more architectural garden styles which were gaining in popularity. Victorian art was preoccupied with strong colour, and here was a whole new arena in which to deploy it, clearly demonstrating the triumph of artistic and horticultural skills over nature. Indeed, bedding out was a garden form that appealed precisely to the Zeitgeist: it was a very self-improving age, and bedding seemed like something you could learn from a manual. Magazines published lists of suitable plants, pattern books were published full of ornate designs for beds, while ready-to-plant garden kits were offered mail order, with a pattern and the plants to make it up. (The penny post, introduced in 1840, seems to have been cheaper and more efficient than our postal services today.) Favoured plants were pelargoniums, petunias, salvias, lobelias, verbenas and calceolarias, planted for dramatic contrasts of colour, arranged in beds of geometric or teardrop shape, which were seen to best advantage set in smooth green lawns kept trim by the newly invented lawnmower.

As the practice became more popular, more and more elaborate forms of bedding were devised. Ribbon borders ran alongside paths, with plants arranged in long parallel stripes of colour. There was a brief vogue for 'dial beds' featuring flowers which opened and closed at successive hours. There were 'rustic baskets' and beds requiring flowers to be grouped by height in a perfect cone. But the most inventive practitioners of this resplendent floral display were the superintendents of the new public parks springing up in our towns and cities. As with glasshouse technology, Paxton led the way. When his Crystal Palace was moved from Hyde Park to Sydenham, it became the centrepiece of a new park, arranged in a series of terraces adorned with a formal pattern of flower beds. The Royal Parks were quick to copy the idea, and colourful bedding rapidly became a feature of every municipal park.

At first brilliance was the thing – the brightest, most sharply contrasting colours. But gradually, the gardening elite began to pine for less strident effects. The 1860s saw the emergence first

Heated debates took place in the fledgling garden press over the most effective use of colour. Here, summer bedding at Lyme Park in Cheshire uses blocks of contrasting colour.

of subtropical, then of carpet bedding, which, relying on foliage plants rather than flowers, were claimed by their supporters to be more subtle.

Subtropical bedding was introduced to Britain by John Gibson at Battersea Park, and relied on dramatic contrasts of large-leaved and brightly variegated foliage plants. He used much the same plants as hot-shot late twentieth-century urban designers – tree ferns and bananas, yuccas and phormiums, cannas and dracaenas – placing them among low-growing plants or singly in grass.

Carpet bedding
on a grand scale
at Cragside in
Northumberland.

Carpet bedding, by comparison, was a work of the utmost restraint. In this style, the surface of the bed, which could be flat or rounded, was planted with a close carpet of dwarf or creeping foliage plants, kept clipped to a uniform height to resemble a piece of tapestry or embroidery. Small succulents such as grey-tinted sedums and sempervivums were ideal for this intricate planting, as were the alternantheras and iresines newly introduced from South America. The style was introduced by John Fleming at Cliveden in Buckinghamshire, spelling out the monogram 'HS' (for Harriet, Duchess of Sutherland), and was rapidly taken up by both householders and parks, where it proved invaluable for geometric designs, coats of arms and other manifestations of civic pride. Something of a competitive sport, it was won outright by Crystal Palace, where in 1875 there appeared six beds in the shape of giant butterflies, each a different species, their wing colours carefully reproduced in foliage. Predictably, a menagerie of animal-themed beds soon sprang up across the country.

Towards the end of the century, three-dimensional planting using galvanised wire frames packed with peat came into vogue. Crowns were a common theme;

Bradford had a floral piano, and the wags of Bridlington produced a rolled-up carpet of carpet bedding. But however ornate the bedding became, there was an inherent flaw – the long months of empty beds before and after planting. Once again, Cliveden's John Fleming took the lead. Dismayed by the contrast between the burgeoning spring hedgerows and his dismally empty beds, he hastily filled them up with forget-me-nots and 'Cliveden Blue' pansies. Soon it became commonplace to have three seasons of bedding: spring bulbs, followed by tender exotics, followed by chrysanthemums and dahlias in autumn. In winter, pots of evergreens were plunged into the beds, while during the 1860s some gardeners planted dark-leaved beets and cavolo nero in a manner that would now seem cutting-edge.

Naturally, all this added considerably to the cost of gardening. Ernest Field, Head Gardener to millionaire banker Alfred de Rothschild, 'once heard it said that rich people used to show their wealth by the size of their bedding plant list: ten thousand for a squire, twenty for a baronet, thirty for an earl and fifty for a duke'. Rothschild had a solid 41,418, and over 60 gardeners to grow them.

To the eco-minded twenty-first century, it all seems scandalously profligate. And in the country seats of the wealthy, it probably was. But in the inner-city parks of Britain's industrial heartland, it was another story. Here, the use of massed bedding, even three or four times over, was a sensible use of resources – simply because the air pollution was so bad that virtually nothing else would grow. In the streets of Manchester in the 1880s not even plane trees could survive. Trees and shrubs in the city's Phillips Park had a life expectancy of only two to three years. To keep the park stocked, 2,500 rhododendrons, the same number of poplars, 1,000 willows, 750 elders and 300 assorted flowering shrubs were planted every single year. By comparison, changing displays of bedding were a snip. Similarly, these cheap and very cheerful ornaments were ideal for the newly built seaside resorts like Eastbourne (a speculative development by Paxton's employer) where wind and salt would spoil more permanent plantings.

Bedding began to fall out of favour towards the end of the century. Arts and Crafts guru William Morris dismissed it as 'an aberration of the human mind'. But bedding has never entirely gone out of fashion, and today's annual displays at Waddesdon Manor show that the production of bedding remains very much at the forefront of technology, and that painting with plants need not necessarily be strident, but can aspire to the condition of art.

THE PERFECT LAWN

The word 'lawn' first appears in English in 1548, as 'a place voyde of trees, as in a parke or forret'. Before that, and after, there were 'grass plats', which didn't have flowers, and 'meads' in which flowers were cherished. Lawn care seems to have been a source of national pride for centuries: Samuel Pepys confidently asserted that the 'green of our bowling alleys' was better than anything to be found in Italy or France.

Smooth turf was an essential part of the landscape garden, and Charles Hamilton put considerable effort into achieving it at Painshill, ploughing the ground 'sometimes five but at least four times' and sowing each acre with 'six English bushels of the cleanest hayseed I could get and ten pounds of fresh Dutch clover seed'. For smaller areas, lawns were usually obtained by cutting sheep-cropped turf.

Eighteenth-century paintings show gardeners hard at work with rollers, brooms and scythes on velvety lawns, and until 1830, all grass was cut by scythe. This was skilled and physically demanding work, best done early in the morning when the grass was still wet with dew. Large gardens employed teams of grass-cutters, with labourers following behind the scythers, sweeping up the cuttings into baskets.

When Edwin Budding invented the lawnmower, adapting a technology in use in the cloth mills of Stroud, he totally changed the nature of work in the garden. His mower worked best when the grass was dry, so it was no longer necessary for workers to rise before dawn. Loudon was thrilled: Budding's mower promised, he wrote in 1831, 'to be one of the greatest boons that science has conferred upon the working gardener in our time'. Budding promised his mower would deliver a better finish. And better still, 'Country gentlemen may find in using my machine themselves an amusing, useful and healthy exercise.'

The mower did not make Budding's fortune: by the time he died, no more than 1,200 machines had been sold. These first mowers, made of cast iron, were extremely heavy and required some force to drive them. However, substantial design improvements were made during the following decades, so that by 1870 the editor of The Gardeners' Chronicle could write:

Twenty years ago mowing machines were but coming into notice and but little believed in. Now they are all but universal, and the time-honoured scythe … is rapidly disappearing. What a revolution! What a saving of time! And how much more healthy are our lawns kept under the new than the old system.

Horse-drawn models were also widely used. The ponies that pulled them wore soft leather booties so as not to damage the turf.

Shirley Hibberd considered a lawn indispensable to every garden, 'whatever its size or situation'. While weeds, especially plantains, were to be eliminated, moss was as 'deliciously soft as a down bed' and 'absolutely essential to the beauty and enjoyment of a lawn'.

Robinson, predictably, was no fan of manicured turf: 'Think of the labour involved in the ridiculous work of cutting the heads off flowers and grass …' On this subject, his words went unheeded (and indeed he changed his mind in time).

In 1893 a Lancashire blacksmith patented a steam-powered mower, and in 1902 came the first petrol-driven mower. The cricketer W.G. Grace was so impressed that he promptly ordered one for the pitch at Crystal Palace.

The die was cast. Henceforth an unkempt lawn would become tantamount to moral bankruptcy, and perfecting the lawn would become a national obsession.

The **ATCO** MOTOR MOWER
solves the lawn upkeep problem.

Running under its own power the "Atco" Motor
Lawn Mower needs only guidance, no pushing or
other labour. In 20 minutes it efficiently cuts 1,000
square yards of turf at an operating cost of less than 2d.
for Petroil, which provides fuel and lubricant at once.

**The "ATCO" needs but ONE attendant
—an intelligent lad will do.**

The adoption of the "Atco" means an immediate saving
of time, trouble and expense to all concerned with Lawn
upkeep. Country Houses, Golf, Cricket, Tennis and
Bowling Clubs, Hotel keepers, &c., should immediately
send for the FREE Booklet, "The 'Atco' Motor Lawn
Mower," which gives particulars of non-committal
demonstration in your own locality.

Price,
Carriage
Paid :   **£75**

*Applications are invited from the Trade for
Local Agencies throughout the United Kingdom.*

CHARLES H. PUGH, Ltd.,
Width of cutters, 22"   Whitworth Works   18, Tilton Road, Birmingham.

Clockwise from top: Scything the lawns at Hartwell House
in Buckinghamshire in 1738. A 1920s advertisement for
a motor mower in *Homes and Gardens*. A flawless lawn at
Sissinghurst in Kent shows how ideas of perfection have
changed: for Shirley Hibberd, moss in the lawn was a good
thing. Edwin Budding patented his new 'grass cutting
machine' in October 1830, promising it would give cleaner
results, no longer offending the eyes with 'those circular
scars, inequalities and bare places, so commonly made by
the best mowers with the scythe'.

Gardens of the super-rich

The Industrial Revolution and burgeoning of international trade had brought prosperity to the middling sorts – merchants, factory managers, purveyors of legal and financial services. But it had also enriched the wealthiest in the land beyond measure – the great landowners who profited from canals, railways and urban expansion, and who now made more money from the coal beneath their lands than the farms upon them. The Duke of Devonshire's gardening was paid for by coal (though he always spent far more than he could earn); the Duke of Westminster made a fortune from speculative building in Belgravia, while the Duke of Sutherland made a killing in canals. As ever, this wealth was poured into doing up houses and laying out ostentatious new gardens. Nothing is more old-fashioned than the fashion just departed, so the super-rich sought a new garden style that would be the antithesis of the naturalistic landscape park. They found it in the grandiose Italianate schemes of architect Charles Barry (1795–1860).

Barry based his gardens on what remained of the great Renaissance gardens he had seen on repeated trips to Italy, but authenticity was of no concern to his clients. What they were after was grandeur, and also a sense of connection with the past, with the English formal garden that they understood to have pre-dated Brown. Barry worked at Kingston Lacy in Dorset in the late 1830s, but the commission that made his name was for the Sutherlands at Trentham. Here he remodelled the

The terrace garden (above) and the lake (opposite), complete with gondola, at Trentham Park in Staffordshire, from Edward Adveno Brooke's *The Gardens of England* (1857). Brooke spent several summers touring 19 country houses, capturing the luxuriant splendour of the Italianate gardens of the super-rich.

ground leading down to Capability Brown's lake into two immense shallow terraces (the site was virtually flat), peppered them with fountains, bordered them with balustrades, built *faux* containers round Portugal laurels to pass them off as orange trees, and placed a cast of Benvenuto Cellini's *Perseus* as the focal point of the garden. Just in case a site in the Potteries still didn't feel sufficiently Italian, he also hired a gondola and gondolier for the lake. These terraces provided the ideal canvas for Head Gardener George Fleming, one of the key innovators in bedding, to display his skills, laying out borders in ribbons and rainbows of colour, experimenting with shading and foliage effects, and creating the delightful innovation of a rivulet of blue and white forget-me-nots meandering like a stream down to the lake.

Trentham became the most fashionable garden in England, and countless Italianate gardens followed. New methods of manufacture had made terracotta cheap, so villa gardens filled up with 'Roman' urns and vases. At Renishaw, Sir George Sitwell attempted to recreate the Roman campagna on the outskirts of Sheffield. Even Prince Albert got the bug, designing Osborne House as an Italian holiday villa. Meanwhile Barry followed Trentham with more grand architectural gardens at Harewood in Yorkshire and Shrubland Park in Suffolk before returning to the Sutherlands at Cliveden in Berkshire, to rebuild the fire-damaged house with an elegant paved terrace that made the most of the enormous views, not least the colossal grass terrace below. A plain 'Quaker parter' in Bridgeman's

Charles Barry had originally hoped to create a version of Lake Maggiore's Isola Bella on the lake at Trentham, but even the Sutherlands' deep pockets would not stretch so far.

day, this was taken in hand by John Fleming (it seems likely Barry poached him from Harewood), who created two parallel lines of hedged triangles leading to a vast circular bed, all bedded out in brilliant colours. Trentham's parterres are now planted with perennials in a twenty-first-century take on cutting-edge horticultural showmanship, but at Cliveden, the bedding tradition continues in full glory. Spring displays combine 11,000 bulbs with over 20,000 bedding plants, succeeded by a further 31,000 plants in summer, all contained within two and half miles of hedging. Happily, the property is blessed with many willing volunteers.

'Italian' was a word loosely applied. When William Andrews Nesfield (1783–1881) took over from Barry as chief purveyor of Italian style, his trademark became intricate parterres based on seventeenth-century French scrollwork. His designs grew ever more complex, with elaborate tracery patterns, monograms and heraldic devices – designs far too complicated to be entrusted to fickle flowers, so they were generally marked out in box with an infill of variously coloured minerals or even painted gravel. This style reached its zenith in 1861 at the new Kensington garden of the Royal Horticultural Society. The irony of making a garden that consisted mainly of stones was not lost on the garden's many critics, and by the time of his death in 1881, Nesfield was very much yesterday's man. But his designs can still be seen in London's Regent's Park and at Kew, while the parterre at Oxburgh Hall in Norfolk is absolutely in the Nesfield mould. Although not designed by him but by a 'clever Scotch gardener called Anderson', the pattern is copied from one of Nesfield's favourite French sources. Traces of coal and cement have been found in the parterre, suggesting that it too was once coloured with minerals in the Nesfield manner.

Also French, and with no aspiration to be Italian, was Waddesdon Manor, nothing less than a fully fledged Loire chateau transplanted to a windy Buckinghamshire hilltop for financier Baron Ferdinand de Rothschild during the 1870s and '80s. All building projects, especially ones that last 22 years, are apt to get out of hand, and we do not know how much Waddesdon cost, as the Baron prudently destroyed all the relevant papers. But he did write a short account of the work (his 'Red Book') which begins 'I took Waddesdon with its defects and drawbacks … perhaps a little too rashly … [but] it had a bracing and salubrious air, pleasant scenery, excellent hunting, and was untainted by factories and villadom.'

The first task was to lay on a water supply, which required 11 miles (17.7km) of pipework back to the local town of Aylesbury. Work then began on the foundations of the house. The old proverb about building on sand proved correct: the foundations gave way, 30ft (9.1m) of sand had to be removed and the building started again on 'a firm bottom of clay'. However, 'the difficulty of building a house is insignificant compared with the labour of transforming a bare wilderness

Opposite: Charles Barry's new terrace at Cliveden in Berkshire still provides the ideal vantage point to look down on colourful displays of bedding. The circular area round the statue would once have been planted too.

Overleaf: Waddesdon Manor in Buckinghamshire remains to this day a showcase for bedding, using innovative computer-aided techniques to create both traditional Victorian and exciting contemporary schemes. It was here that three-dimensional bedding was invented, for Ferdinand de Rothschild's sister Alice, by her Head Gardener, George Frederick Johnson.

into a park', not least since his plan entailed removing the entire top of the hill on which his house stood and levelling the ground around it. Cutting into the hill interfered with the natural drainage, constantly washing away the new-laid soil, so that 'like Sisyphus, we had repeatedly to take up the same task'. A two-mile steam tramway was built to carry bricks and stones from the nearest railway line. Sixteen Percheron mares were imported from Normandy to haul in mature oaks 'brought from all parts of the neighbourhood, and for the moving of which on the highways the telegraph wires had to be temporarily displaced'.

In today's money, it probably cost over £250 million. (It is likely that Cragside in Northumberland cost even more.) But this was the price of social acceptance. Despite their colossal wealth, the Rothschilds had to overcome the social stigma of being moneylenders and Jews. Similarly, although Benjamin Disraeli became a highly successful reforming prime minister (he described his ascent as climbing 'the greasy pole'), there were sections of society that could never quite forgive him for being a Jewish-Italian upstart, or for unseemly habits like writing satirical novels. Though he never became rich, his garden at Hughenden in Buckinghamshire was a declaration of his hard-won social status, much aided by his close friendship with the Queen. It was adorned 'in the Italian style' by his wife, with the brightest

Left: Showy Italianate urns, brightly planted, were the ultimate fashion statement in the modish Victorian garden.

Left: Benjamin Disraeli may have preferred quieter effects: his letters speak of his enjoyment of spring blossom and autumn foliage.

of bedding and 'a beautiful series of Vases', which sparkled in the sun. Disraeli claimed his favourite flowers were primroses, and Queen Victoria sent him a posy every spring. He liked them, he wrote, 'so much better for their being wild: they seem an offering from the fauns and dryads of the woods'. (He knew how to flatter a small, stout, lonely lady.) But somehow truer to the man seems his dictum that 'You cannot have a terrace without peacocks'.

Hughenden was a Gothic pile – another popular style for the mega-rich (as at Tyntesfield in Somerset and Knightshayes in Devon) for it was seen to embody some quintessential quality of Englishness, just as in the garden buildings of the eighteenth century. Similar sentiments fuelled a new fad for all things Elizabethan. Rapacious piratical hustlers like Drake and Raleigh were reborn as national heroes. And the few gardens that had survived from this time became objects of reverence, which did not mean leaving them alone (that understanding of conservation did not become current till the twentieth century), but 'improving' them. Thus Montacute's mount was replaced with a fountain, Lancashire's Gawthorpe Hall received both a new frontage and a new parterre by Barry, and the overgrown topiary garden at Levens was substantially replanted, bulking up so fast that now the nineteenth-century yews are indistinguishable from the old.

At Packwood, another garden of yew, believed to date back to the 1650s, acquired a mystical reputation as celebrating the Sermon on the Mount – the mighty yew atop the Tudor mount representing Christ, with the Twelve Apostles at his feet and the four largest trees denoting the Four Evangelists, while beyond stood the listening Multitude. The story first appears in 1892, and in reality only the Apostles are likely to be original, the 'multitude' probably planted in the 1850s as small topiary specimens marking out a newly planted orchard.

There's something rather inspiriting about the gleeful way the Victorian super-rich raided history for their own delight, thinking nothing of commissioning a Tudor palace (Mentmore) or even a full-scale Norman castle (Penrhyn), or all too often an unholy mixture of styles – so different from the high-minded Arts and Crafts (see Chapter 7). This same mad magpie tendency went to work in the garden, such that Edward Kemp, in his manual *How to Lay Out A Garden* (1850), felt moved to include a whole section on 'What to Avoid', warning against 'Too great a mixture of Styles', 'Unsuitable Decorations', 'Tricks for Surprising People' and 'All kinds of Eccentricity' including 'every sort of 'Sham'. Two gardens, however, seized joyfully on this eclectic spirit and proved that variety could, if done well enough, be indeed the spice of life.

The myth of an ancient garden at Packwood in Warwickshire representing the Sermon of the Mount first appears in 1892 in Reginald Blomfield's *The Formal Garden in England*, attributed to a gardener engaged in 'pleaching the pinnacle of the temple.'

Biddulph and Elvaston
– curiouser and curiouser

In the 1830s, the 4th Earl Harrington scandalised polite society by marrying his long-standing mistress, the actress Maria Foote. The couple retreated to Elvaston in Derbyshire, where the Earl set about making his bride 'the biggest wedding present in the world', a garden made on a theme of chivalric love. Charged with this mission was Head Gardener William Barron, who perfected the art of moving enormous trees and shrubs to achieve, within only 20 years, a mature landscape of formal gardens with secret walks, gilded bowers, picturesque rockwork and an elaborate architecture of yew, enclosed by 11 miles (17.7km) of evergreen hedges clipped 'close as an Axminster carpet'. Entry was barred to all but the Queen (who never came). It was the ultimate stage set for their drama of love, with all the poetic, courtly settings it deserved – an Italian garden, a garden roguishly entitled 'Mon Plaisir', or the 'Islamic' Alhambra Garden, graced with a statue of the adoring Earl kneeling at his wife's feet. When, after his death in 1852, visitors were finally admitted, the garden caused a sensation.

The star now was William Barron, who had made this marvel on a swampy site so devoid of capabilities that Lancelot Brown had declined to work there. (Barron spent his first four years just digging drains.) Unmoved by medieval

The 'Mon Plaisir' garden at Elvaston Castle in Derbyshire, where the reclusive Earl of Harrington created a fantasy world in which even the servants were made to dress up in medieval costume, and plants were coaxed into bizarre and dreamlike forms.

romance, Barron saw the whole exercise as laying out one enormous decorative pinetum: he was devoted to conifers for their year-round value and variety of form and colour. Needing instant impact, he pushed the art of topiary beyond all previously known bounds and grafted trees in ingenious ways to make surprising new forms. He laid out vast avenues with multiple rows of planting, and with a tree-moving machine of his own invention, successfully transplanted thousands of trees, including oaks as high as 70ft (21.3m) and yews 600–800 years old.

Barron's impact on the Victorian garden was instant and colossal. Among those who went home from Elvaston buzzing with ideas was James Bateman (1811–97), a knowledgeable botanist and amateur scientist, an authority on orchids and a man of lively imagination.

Whether a High Victorian garden called itself Elizabethan, Italian or Dutch, in practice it varied very little from the Repton model: a terrace by the house, a parterre below, and views out to parkland beyond. Elvaston was different – authentically medieval in that it was enclosed, inward-looking and divided into

Biddulph Grange in Staffordshire is skilfully designed to make you lose your bearings, so you never know whether your next step will lead you to ancient Egypt or Imperial China, to a stately lime avenue in gardenesque style or a wild Scottish glen. It was designed to be a Cook's tour of plants as well as places. Writing in 1856, Edward Kemp praised 'the marvellous diversity of surface throughout the place' and the way in which James Bateman had found a 'congenial home' for 'nearly all the hardy members of the great plant family which the curiosity or taste of man has discovered and cultivated'.

compartments. (It was simultaneously forward-looking: that structure of hedged enclosures, each one distinctively themed or planted and unseen from the next, would be repeated, albeit in a very different way, in gardens like Rodmarton, Hidcote and Sissinghurst.) This structure of concealment, along with Elvaston's looming conifer avenues and monumental rockwork, was borrowed by Bateman to create his own fantastical journey through time and space, leading the visitor from Scottish glen to Cheshire cottage, from ancient Egypt to the Great Wall of China, all in 22 windy Staffordshire acres.

Biddulph Grange has been extensively restored over the last decade, on the basis of a series of rapturous accounts by Edward Kemp in *The Gardeners' Chronicle*. The charm of the place lies in how each garden is quite separate from the next, cunningly hidden by planting or rockwork, and how ingeniously they are linked, delivering a constant salvo of surprises. A bucolic half-timbered cottage morphs abruptly into an Egyptian tomb, towering avenues of *Wellingtonia* give way to sunny glades and limpid lakes, a tunnel opens suddenly to a fairytale vision of China (page 160).

But spectacle was not all. For each area was planted to offer shelter and appropriate growing conditions for an ever-increasing collection of rare plants, including Far Eastern treasures collected by Robert Fortune, many new rhododendrons from the Himalayas and one of the most extensive collections of conifers in mid-Victorian Britain. The centrepiece of the garden was a geological gallery, in which Bateman, a believer in the Biblical account of creation, sought to reconcile his religious convictions with his own scientific knowledge and to challenge the evolutionary theory of fellow orchid-fancier Charles Darwin. 'To the believer, the problem is not hard to solve,' insisted Bateman. 'Ferns and flowerless plants came early in the divine programme, because the coal into which they were ultimately to be converted, had need to be long accumulating for the future comfort and civilisation of our race; while the genesis of Orchids was postponed until the time drew near when Man, who was to be soothed by the gentle influence of their beauty, was about to appear on the scene.'

Bateman's lovingly tended orchid houses, the colourful terraces of Cliveden and Waddesdon, the pinetums at Elvaston and Cragside, the flower-filled conservatories of innumerable suburban villas – none of these would have been possible without the derring-do of the great Victorian plant hunters. It's time to find out who they were.

The plant hunters

When Joseph Banks died in 1820, the Horticultural Society (which he had helped to found in 1804) took over from Kew as the main centre for plant collecting in Britain. Funds were put up by wealthy subscribers, who in return received seeds of the plants found on expeditions. One of their earliest and most adventurous plant hunters was a young self-taught Scot, David Douglas (1799–1834), who made a series of journeys in North America, travelling thousands of miles on foot or in rough canoes though unexplored forest and mountain. Wherever he went, trouble wasn't far behind. But in spite of runaway horses, snowstorms and starvation, violent attacks by man and beast and repeated gruesome injuries, Douglas managed to collect some 200 new plants before finally being gored to death by a bull in Hawaii. (And that's not counting all the plants he lost when his canoe was swept away by rapids.) His finds included the Oregon grape (*Mahonia aquifolium*) and the silky *Garrya elliptica*; the car park stalwart berberis and ever-popular flowering currant (*Ribes sanguineum*); evening primroses, penstemons and the ancestor of our modern lupin. But the discoveries that had the biggest impact on the garden were undoubtedly his ornamental conifers: the pines, the spruces and the lofty Douglas fir (*Pseudotsuga menziesii*). Nothing could have been more suitable for gardenesque display than these graphic forms, planted singly in smooth lawns to be admired from every angle. And so it was that conifers, in all their variety of shapes and sizes, came to dominate the nineteenth-century garden.

The fernery at Greenway, Devon. Plant-hunting was not confined to Boys' Own adventurers. Back home, plant collectors descended in droves on the danker parts of Devon, as a craze for ferns swept through Britain from the 1840s to the 1890s. Many of the 'pteridomaniacs' (*pterido* is Latin for fern) were young women, for 'fern forays' were deemed a suitable activity for ladies. Ferns were displayed in Wardian cases in the drawing room or in a special indoor or outdoor 'fernery', while fern motifs appeared on wallpaper and textiles, tea-sets and garden gates – even on custard cream biscuits.

Their appeal was clear enough: they were new, and they were, as Barron pointed out, hard-working and handsome throughout the year. 'Winter gardens' planted with conifers and the new *Garrya* (soon to be followed by mahonias, forsythias and winter jasmine) added a season of interest to a previously dull garden. The nursery trade couldn't get enough of them: as early as 1840 Chelsea nurserymen Knight and Perry offered 140 species and varieties of conifers, including variegated and weeping sports. This, of course, offered ample scope for collectors, and before long, many larger gardens made space for pinetums (conifers only) or arboretums (mixed collections of trees). Magnificent examples include Westonbirt in Gloucestershire, founded in 1829 by Robert Stayner Holford, Tatton Park in Cheshire and Killerton near Exeter, original site of and showcase for Veitch, the leading nursery of the day. Douglas's introductions also proved important in the development of the exotic garden – *Pinus radiata* was to prove an invaluable shelter belt plant. They were also economically significant: his fast-growing conifers transformed British forestry.

Douglas had brought home his treasures in the form of seed. So bulking up stocks remained a slow business, necessarily limiting supply. Then, in 1833, Nathaniel Ward invented the Wardian case, essentially a sealed glass box which acted as a closed ecosystem. Ward had hoped the poor would use his invention to grow nutritious salads on their sooty window-sills. Instead, it was seized on by Victorian ladies to grow ferns in their drawing rooms, and by enterprising nurserymen, who saw, for the first time, a way in which living plants might survive long journeys at sea. This made the search for new plants commercially viable – and the 1840s saw an unprecedented level of plant exploration.

The first to use this new technology was Robert Fortune (1812–80), sent out to the newly opened ports of China in 1842. His journey would have made a fine action movie, featuring attack by a mob in a cemetery, assault by pirates and near-decapitation by a monster fish crashing through a skylight during a storm. Complaining continually of the deceitfulness of the Chinese, he was not above sneaking in disguise into forbidden territory to obtain plants by trickery or plain theft. In five journeys to China and Japan, Fortune acquired over 120 new species. He introduced the graceful Japanese anemone, *Viburnum plicatum* 'Sterile', *Weigela florida* and the rhododendron that bears his name (*R. fortunei*). The winter garden owes him three mahonias, two forsythias, winter jasmine and sweet-scented *Lonicera fragrantissima*. But our greatest debt to Robert Fortune is for the 23,892 young tea plants he pirated from China to form the basis of the Indian tea industry – an act of gross imperialism which undermined the Chinese tea industry, but without which life in Britain would be unimaginable.

Meanwhile, the firm of Veitch engaged a pair of Cornish brothers to go collecting on their behalf. While Thomas Lobb scoured the Far East for the pitcher plants and orchids beloved in Victorian conservatories, his brother William was dispatched to the forests of Chile, whence he returned with 3,000 seeds of that quintessentially Victorian plant, the monkey puzzle (*Araucaria araucana*). By 1843, Veitch was offering seedlings at £10 per hundred. Lobb was then sent back to obtain commercial quantities of Douglas's conifers, which couldn't be propagated fast enough. He returned in 1853 with an even greater prize – the tallest tree anyone had ever seen, the gigantic redwood now known as *Sequoiadendron giganteum*, but which was then named *Wellingtonia gigantea* in honour of the Duke of Wellington. A *Wellingtonia* avenue soon became a status symbol, as at Biddulph, Ashridge, and even a modest villa such as Sunnycroft.

The monkey puzzle was introduced to Britain in 1785 by Archibald Menzies, botanist and ship's doctor aboard the survey vessel *Discovery*. Intrigued by some nuts he was served during an official dinner in Chile, he pocketed a handful and sowed them once back on ship. He succeeded in raising five seedlings. But it was not until 1844 that seed was obtained in quantity, and the tree became a Victorian favourite.

Sir Joseph Dalton Hooker was Director of Kew from 1865–85, and one of the greatest botanists of the nineteenth century. He was a close friend and stalwart supporter of Charles Darwin, to whom he dedicated his *Himalayan Journals* of 1854.

DR. HOOKER COLLECTING PLANTS IN THE SIKKIM HIMALAYAS.

From a picture by the late Frank Stone, A.R.A.

These pioneers were succeeded by many more great plant hunters: 'Chinese' Wilson, who travelled 13,000 miles in search of the handkerchief tree (*Davidia involucrata*), only to find it chopped down for timber; George Forrest, who spent 28 years foraging in Western China; Himalayan explorer Frank Kingdon-Ward, who brought back the blue poppy, *Meconopsis betonicifolia*. All made their mark on the late nineteenth-century and early twentieth-century garden, but none with such profound and lasting impact as Sir Joseph Dalton Hooker (1817–1911) confidant of Charles Darwin and later Director of Kew. It is thanks to his finds in the Himalayas (chivalrously named after his colonial hostesses) that the parks and gardens of England have become eternally infested with rhododendrons.

It is difficult to think of a plant more perfectly adapted to nineteenth-century taste. It was fashionably evergreen. Its flowers were large, bright and copious. And its novelty, expense and remote and exotic origins were all attributes that contributed to the status of the possessor. As Hooker's introductions, from 1851 onwards, were added to by the finds of Forrest and Kingdon-Ward, and the breeding programmes of both commercial nurseries and impassioned amateurs offered more and more novel varieties, landowners began to vie with each other for the most exotic and varied collection. Once in the grip of rhododendronmania, expense was immaterial; garden commentator Shirley Hibberd remarked 'The money spent on rhododendrons during twenty years in this country would nearly suffice to pay off the National Debt.'

At Biddulph, Bateman planted rhododendrons round the lake, and a 'rainbow' of rhododendrons and azaleas in concentric bands of colour. At Cragside, a torrent of rhododendrons soon flowed over the fells, 'blooming so profusely as to light up the whole hillside with their varied colours'. Rhododendrons would soon prove the defining ingredient in a new style of wild woodland gardening. The first step on the way was taken deep in southern Cornwall where, from the 1820s, a sequence of deep, sheltered valleys running down to the Helford estuary were miraculously reborn as outposts of the Himalayas.

The brilliance of the rhododendrons at Cragside was praised in *The Gardener's Magazine* of 1872. They were plants perfectly adapted to Victorian taste.

The Cornish Quakers

Glendurgan began as the weekend retreat of Alfred Fox, a Quaker merchant who moved to Falmouth, at that time one of the busiest ports in the country, and grew prosperous in Cornwall's Industrial Revolution. The garden grew piecemeal over the years, the finest trees (like the great tulip trees that now dominate the head of the valley), mostly planted to celebrate birthdays or anniversaries.

The Fox family became one of Britain's great gardening dynasties: Alfred's brothers Robert and Charles made no less adventurous gardens at nearby Penjerrick and Trebah respectively. As partners in a highly successful global shipping business, it was easy enough for the Fox brothers to obtain new specimens, and the thin, acidic soil and mild, moist microclimate proved ideal for a wide range of enthralling new Himalayan and North American plants. Yet the brothers were no stereotypical magnates cramming their gardens with rarities as a form of conspicuous consumption: rather they were honouring God's Creation in the seventeenth-century manner, creating little bits of heaven on earth. Nor were they armchair gardeners. Against the fashion of the times, there was no terrace

Trebah, the domain of Quaker plant collector Charles Fox. The sheltered valleys around Falmouth proved ideal for growing rare and tender exotic plants that made their way back to Cornwall on the ships of the Fox brothers.

at Glendurgan: sitting around in the garden would have been sinfully slothful when there was work to be done. There was, however, no lack of fun – a maze to get lost in, a beach to swim from, and, later, a giant maypole known as the Giant's Stride.

Naturalistic planting never entirely disappeared from the nineteenth-century garden: many gardeners maintained a shrubbery or area of 'wilderness' as a contrast to the immaculate formal areas, but in the Fox gardens, this became the overall plan. Placings were not random: Charles Fox dictated the position of trees from the top of the valley with a megaphone, getting his gardeners to build scaffolding towers to mimic the height of the mature specimen. But for all that they were avid collectors, they were using plants for their landscape effect (in Sylvia Crowe's words, as the materials for garden-making), creating at Glendurgan and Penjerrick an illusion of some lost Himalayan kingdom, while present-day Trebah, with its groves of tree-ferns and vast stands of gunnera, produces a more lush and tropical effect. Although no less artificial, it was the polar opposite of the rigid, high-gloss, richly patterned High Victorian garden, and one that would provide a model for later generations of plant collectors in the great woodland gardens of the late nineteenth and early twentieth centuries such as Abbotsbury, Bodnant, Knightshayes, Exbury and another Cornish showstopper, Caerhays.

The rock garden

Many of the new plants flooding into Britain came from mountainous regions. And soon enough serious growers like Bateman realised that these plants would need special conditions if they were to thrive. But for most gardeners, it was not the plants so much as the picturesque quality of rockwork that counted. At Chatsworth in the 1840s, Paxton imported towering tors and built a grotto inside the Great Conservatory, illuminated with fairy-lights and planted round with bananas and palms. In the 1820s, Samuel Trist, vicar of Veryan in Cornwall, dug out a lake and surrounded it with a dozen 'rockeries' of glittering quartzite boulders; the following decade, at Hoole House in Cheshire, an entire alpine valley was recreated in the garden, with peaks and glaciers sparkling with marble snow. In 1847 Sir Charles Isham made another at Lamport Hall, Northamptonshire and peopled it with a workforce of small ceramic miners – the first garden gnomes in Britain. This spectacle was not surpassed until the 1890s, when Sir Frank Crisp of Friar Park created three acres of mountains and valleys in Henley-on-Thames, including a 30ft (9.1m) replica of the Matterhorn, exactly to scale, with miniature tin chamois leaping from crag to crag. This monumental rock garden (later restored by Beatle George Harrison) was created by the Yorkshire firm of Backhouse, who as early as 1875 were growing alpines in the manner now deemed best by today's leading alpine growers, in deep vertical fissures rather than shallow grit.

At Biddulph, Bateman engaged the help of his friend Edward Cooke, a distinguished painter with an interest in both botany and geology, and one of the first to make use of Pulhamite in successive London gardens. A composite of clinker and Portland cement, it could convincingly be made in any shape or colour: Pulhamite rockwork can still be seen in London's Battersea Park. Cooke and Bateman laboured on the rockwork for 20 years at Biddulph, combining theatrical effect with geological accuracy and plant-friendly habitats, so that the stone became realistically clothed in bilberries, junipers, ferns and dwarf bulbs – plants that had previously been grown only in pots. Notable rock gardens were also made for plantswomen Ellen Willmott in the 1880s and later for Margaret Beale at Standen (page 223).

But for sheer grandeur, nothing quite compares with Cragside – a great brooding house straight out of the Brothers Grimm, perched on the edge of a precipice and teetering atop a titanic cascade of tumbled rock that covers the whole hill from foot to crest with huge grey boulders – the biggest rock garden of this kind in Europe.

The Newcastle industrialist William Armstrong had been a sickly child, who was regularly shipped out from the smoggy city to recuperate in the bracing air of nearby Rothbury. Returning in 1863 for a holiday (his first in 15 years), he found he loved the wild scenery as much

Opposite: Surrounding three sides of the house, the rock garden at Cragside in Northumberland is one of the largest in Europe.

Below: William Armstrong was a very considerable engineer, who made his money selling arms indiscriminately and worldwide, but who also turned Newcastle into Britain's most modern port with his hydraulic cranes, and designed the swing bridge that still graces the city.

Armstrong's descriptions of the ridges, lakes, woods and streams in his Himalayan fantasy are markedly similar to features at Cragside. A fairy-tale house looming above a 'Himalayan' valley, Cragside is essentially a dreamscape.

as ever, and bought a small lodge with 20 acres (8.1ha) as a fishing retreat. It was a barren place – a bleak, bare hillside – but over the next decade the house grew and grew, and the rock garden surrounding it grew also, made with the aid of dynamite, skilful hydraulic engineering and the sheer power of Armstrong's fantasy – achievable when pockets are sufficiently deep. (He had 150 gardeners at work for over a decade.) Years before, he had written a story in which his hero set off on a journey through the Himalayas, exploring the forests, lakes and ravines. Now he brought his story to life. Rock blasted out from the hilltop was shaped into steps and paths and ledges. More rock was hauled in from the fells. He dammed the Debdon Burn to create pools and waterfalls, dug out lakes, and planted the naked hillside with 7 million trees, supplementing native Scots pine with all the fashionable new conifers from North America, including many hundreds of Douglas firs. Beneath them he planted huge drifts of hybrid rhododendrons *Gaultheria* and

Rubus spectabilis – all good cover for game birds – (also, regrettably, the handsome Japanese knotweed) while Lady Armstrong scoured the fells for attractive heathers and ferns. By 1880 the estate extended to some 1,700 acres (688ha), with 40 miles (64.4km) of paths meandering through Armstrong's new 'Himalayan' forest.

As the house continued to expand, the original rock garden was joined by another to the south, with the rock arranged in natural strata as opposed to artistic heaps. A terraced formal garden was also made, carved out of the hill half a mile from the house, with an Italian loggia, carpet bedding, dahlias (a hugely fashionable plant in the late nineteenth-century garden) and ranges of glasshouses. Armstrong took a particular interest in the orchard house, adapting the design of a gun turret to make hydraulically powered turntables on which his potted trees were turned each day to ensure the fruit ripened evenly.

Rock gardens fitted easily into the fashion that would follow for wild gardens, and gardening with alpines received another boost at the turn of the century, thanks to plant hunter Reginald Farrer. 'Nothing', he asserted, 'could possibly fill the small garden plot with perennial delight, so adequately, cheaply and appropriately as a constellation of rock-plants'; by the 1930s, no suburban garden was complete without a rockery.

By 1900, the naked hillside was clothed in conifers, just as imagined in his Himalayan adventure, in which a 'rich mantle of foliage … covered all.'

Rustic adornment

In many ways Cragside is the ultimate Victorian garden, in its ambition, its swagger and its bold embrace of new technology – Cragside not only had flushing water closets, lifts and central heating, but was the first house in Britain to be lit by hydroelectricity. Yet, paradoxically in a house so huge, there is a visible desire for homeliness. Armstrong's architect, Richard Norman Shaw, was strongly associated with a chocolate-box school of painting that celebrated bucolic cottage life.

Rusticity was a major theme in the late Victorian garden, in crazy paving, pine pole summer-houses, thatched alcoves and 'rustic baskets'. Loudon considered a thatched folly or even a rough-and-ready Doric temple an appropriate addition to a third-rate garden – Peckover House in Cambridgeshire has both. And in 1856, Shirley Hibberd, who took over from Loudon as style guru to the middle classes, published a book entitled *Rustic Adornments for Homes of Taste*. Hibberd lived in Stoke Newington, and wrote with his suburban neighbours in mind, cheerfully reassuring every socially anxious lady that even a person of moderate means could demonstrate impeccable taste. While he did not eschew bedding – indeed he rejoiced in conical towers of pelargoniums and 'pincushion' beds round the feet of standard roses – he advised using it in moderation, without too many primary colours, and tempered with foliage to soften the effect. 'During the past twenty years,' he sighed, 'there has been a constantly increasing tendency to superficial glare and glitter in garden embellishment, to the neglect of more solid features that make a garden more interesting and attractive, not only today and tomorrow' but 'all the year round'. Gardeners would be better advised to stick with hardy trees and shrubs, ivies and ferns to provide interest through the winter, and in particular the hardy herbaceous border:

> When well made, well stocked and well managed, it presents us with flowers in abundance during ten months out of twelve. It is the best feature of the flower garden … while the bedding system is an embellishment the herbaceous border is a necessary fundamental feature.

Hibberd's ideal garden started with a 'truly Italian' paved terrace by the house, descending to a lower terrace, 'laid out as an elaborate flower garden on a ground of turf'. 'Here in the summer, your gaudy parrots will chuckle on their poles, your fountains will splash and sparkle in the sun, above glowing parterres of flowers laid out in Italian patterns, and a few of the choicest shrubs, with perhaps a monster vase or two, loaded with gorgeous flowers …' From here paths led off over 'lawns sprinkled with evergreens' to walks and shrubberies, past greenhouses and bee-houses to

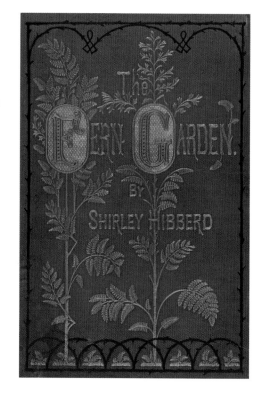

a kitchen garden, and perhaps a rose garden, a rustic summer-house and pond.

Something very like this can be seen at Peckover House in Wisbech, Cambridgeshire, where Quaker banker Jonathan Peckover made a two-acre garden behind his solid Georgian town house. 'Air-inviting lawns' are punctuated with groups of shrubs and some outstanding specimen trees, including a gingko and a tulip tree dating back to the 1790s, fashionable Victorian conifers, and one of the earliest Chusan palms to be planted in Britain. Like the Cornish Foxes, the Peckovers were keen plant collectors, for all that they gardened in more showy gardenesque style. There are island beds, deploying the more restrained plant palette suggested by Hibberd, and ribbon borders, using both annual and perennial plants in long strips of colour. He would also have approved all the ferns and the hollies, the ivy-clad walls, the pretty circular rose garden (recently reconstructed from early photographs) and the serpentine paths which lead, as they should, to successive points of interest, rather than 'winding upon themselves like eels in misery'.

While poking gentle fun at the more gaudy excesses of the High Victorian garden, Hibberd did not believe that a garden should resemble in any way 'a patch of wild nature'. The garden of the Butters family in Hackney was perhaps a little strident, but he commended it warmly for its 'refinement and finish '. 'True nature,' he maintained, 'is not to be shut out of the scene, but nature is to be robed, dressed, and beautified, and made to conform to our own ideas of form and colour …'

It could be Pope talking. It was a view that was about to be vigorously challenged.

Left: A garden made by the Butters family in Hackney in the 1870s, exhibiting all Hibberd's favourite features.

Right: Ribbon borders at Peckover House. Plants were placed in lines of contrasting colour running the length of the border, a style that became very popular in parks.

THE FLORISTS

'NONE but the most sordid and abandoned,' wrote Shirley Hibberd, 'are utterly without either a garden, or the best substitute that can be had for one.' This was certainly true of the Florists, working men in Britain's industrial cities who lavished their love on a very select group of flowers: the anemone, auricula, hyacinth, carnation, polyanthus, ranunculus and tulip, and later the pansy and sweet william. Why they chose these is unclear. Perhaps it was just the challenge. For as Sir Thomas Hanmer remarked of carnations in 1659, 'There is no flower more subject to dye … for many will dye every yeare, let the care of them be never so greate'.

The (disputed) tradition is that the first florists were Huguenot weavers fleeing religious persecution who brought their favourite plants with them to Britain, but by the 1820s, Loudon could report that 'a florists' society is established in almost every town and village in the northern districts', and clear regional favourites had been established. In Sheffield, polyanthus was king. The Lancashire textile workers favoured auriculas. Paisley became famous for exquisite laced pinks. And despite appalling air pollution, miners managed to grow outstanding pansies throughout the Black Country. Tulips were cherished in Wakefield, Stockport and Leeds – the Wakefield and North of England Tulip Society is still going strong today.

At first florists seemed more interested in feasting than flowers. They would meet at a local pub, in which a handsome dinner was followed by a display of flowers. These 'feasts' evolved into cut-throat competitions with prizes of silver spoons, ladles or copper kettles. The Holy Grail was the perfect flower – and what constituted beauty could be argued over in the minutest detail.

Each flower had its own ideal. For auriculas, it was the green edge; for polyanthus, silver and gold lacing. Eighteenth-century gardeners had innocently divided carnations into two categories, Bursters, which split their calyx, and Whole Blowers, which did not; but the Florists dismissed the whole slovenly class of Bursters out of hand. Nowhere was the pattern of perfection more hotly debated than among the tulip fanciers. For centuries, tulip growers had prized the mysterious process, known as breaking, which causes a monochrome tulip to be spontaneously marked with feathers and flames of a new colour. (This is now known to be caused by a virus, but was a mystery to the Florists.) These markings could occur in endless variations, but just three colour combinations were eventually deemed pre-eminent. But here, all agreement ended, southern growers attaching the highest importance to the purity of colour in the base, while northern growers were prepared to overlook a 'dirty bottom' in pursuit of fine feather and flame. Throughout the 1840s, furious dissent rent the tulip world asunder.

No sacrifice was too great to procure a winner. The family might be cold and hungry, but their flowers were sheltered in elaborate 'theatres', and fed with juicy pieces of meat since 'a good part of its bloom is actually owing, like an alderman's, to this consumption of flesh'. The choice blooms of Nottingham were shielded from the sun by awnings of fine lace, while the *Horticultural Magazine* of June 1847 tells of a Dulwich florist who, rather than see his flowers spoiled by frost, gave up the blankets from his own bed, and promptly died of a chill.

Only a handful of the original florists' societies survive. But their legacy lives on in the vastly complex rulebooks that still govern horticultural competition, and the ferocious rivalry still to be seen at every village show.

Clockwise from top: Modern-day florists still compete at the annual Wakefield tulip show. Plants on display in the auricula theatre at Calke Abbey in Derbyshire. Yet commentators at the time observed that 'the auricula is to be found in the highest perfection in the gardens of the manufacturing class'. The gentry, dependent on 'the exertions of hired servants' could not hope to tend their blooms so well. This seventeenth-century still life now at Coleton Fishacre in Devon depicts the flowers that came to be prized by the Florists, including tulip, pink and carnation.

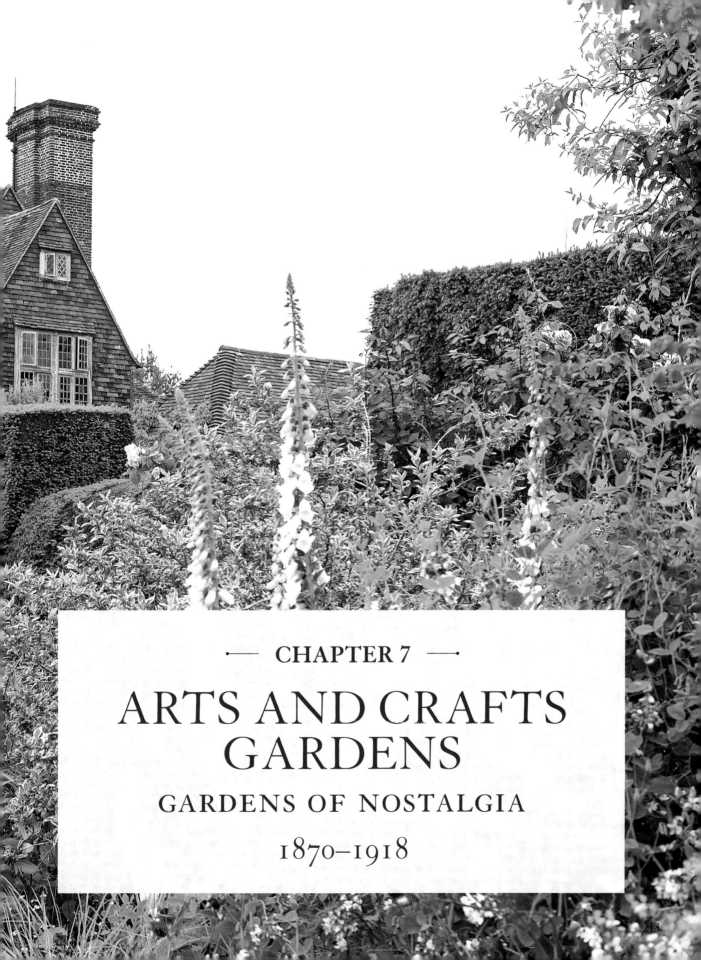

— CHAPTER 7 —

ARTS AND CRAFTS GARDENS

GARDENS OF NOSTALGIA

1870–1918

'Forget six counties overhung with smoke,
Forget the snorting steam and piston's stroke,
Forget the spreading of the hideous town ...'

WILLIAM MORRIS, THE EARTHLY PARADISE

BY the 1870s, Britain had become the most industrialised country in the world. Industrialisation had increased prosperity, and raised Britain to the status of the greatest world power: by 1890 Queen Victoria's rule extended over one-fifth of the globe. Before the nineteenth century, the wealth and population of England had dwelt in the countryside. Now that was no longer so. Economic power had shifted to the towns: industry and commerce were now the principal engines of wealth. The expansion of Empire and global trade links that created such propitious conditions for a new mercantile class had the opposite effect on the landowners, as from 1880 a tide of cheap grain came rolling in from the Canadian prairies and meat from Australia and South America, undercutting the domestic market. Twenty years of deep agricultural depression followed. Between 1870 and 1914, land values fell by two thirds – and families that still depended on farm rents rather than the fruits of industrialisation found themselves at a loss. There was bound to be a backlash.

It came in various forms, all subtly intertwined. It came, from the 1860s, from the Arts and Crafts movement, which drew its inspiration – in houses, gardens, and the wider social sphere – from a pre-industrial age. It came in the nostalgic longings of a now overwhelmingly urban society for a mythical rural past. And it came in the furious bellow of a roaring Irishman, who declared war on the High Victorian garden as the ugliest ever made.

He was not the first to fall out of love with bedding. The mild-mannered rosarian, Dean Hole, came to look on it as an attack of 'scarlet and yellow fever' from which he had been blessedly delivered. Plantsman E. A. Bowles, whose garden at Myddelton House in North London became a treasure house of rare and peculiar plants, deplored the gardening ostentation that 'relies upon Bank of England notes for manure'. But no one was quite as vitriolic as William Robinson (1838–1935).

> *The genius of cretinism could hardly delight in anything more tasteless or ignoble than the absurd daubs of colour that every summer flare in the neighbourhood of every country house in Western Europe.*

Robinson was a man of trenchant opinions who liked nothing better than a spat. Little is known of his early life, but by his early twenties he was working in the garden of a wealthy Irish landowner, caring for a large and valuable collection of tender exotics. The story goes that following a row with his employer, Robinson decided to quit. So, on a night of cruel frost in the freezing winter of 1861, he put out all the hot-house fires, opened the windows wide, and hopped over the wall to Dublin. He fled to a former employer, who recommended him to the Curator at the

Robinson was 47 before he could put his ideas into practice in a garden of his own. In 1884 he bought Gravetye Manor, near East Grinstead in West Sussex. Ironically, he began by installing a formal terrace.

new garden in Regent's Park in London. Wisely, perhaps, he was given an outdoor job, in charge of the herbaceous section.

One of his jobs was to seek out native plants for the park, which took him out to 'the woods and lanes and the lovely cottage gardens in the country round London'. Here he found his inspiration: 'Nothing is prettier than an English cottage garden, and they often teach lessons that great gardens should learn.'

Robinson now taught himself botanical Latin, reinvented himself as a journalist and embarked on a publishing career, producing a series of popular titles for the amateur market. They featured starry contributors such as Gertrude Jekyll, whose ideas he plundered without shame. In 1870, he published a book that took a radical new approach to gardening, *The Wild Garden*. By 'wild gardening' he meant planting that was permanent and informal – bulbs massed in grass, climbers scrambling into trees, natural-looking water and rock, mixed borders of native and exotic plants and, above all, 'the placing of perfectly exotic plants in places they will take care of themselves'. The style, he wrote, was 'best explained by the winter Aconite flowering under a grove of naked trees in February; by the Snowflake growing abundantly in meadows by the Thames side … and by the Apennine

Anemone staining an English wood blue before the blooming of our blue bells'.

Further progressive thoughts followed in *The English Flower Garden* in 1883, probably the best-selling gardening book ever, going through 15 editions in Robinson's lifetime. Much that he recommends still seems startlingly modern: he thinks about attracting birds, covering the soil ('Have no patience with bare ground') and water conservation. He advises planting 'in naturally disposed groups' which merge with each other, and mixing rather than graduating heights in the border. His loathing of stiffness and love of native and species plants sounds remarkably like Beth Chatto. He even recommends ornamental grasses for winter interest. A garden, he explains, should 'arise out of its site and conditions as happily as a primrose out of a cool bank'. He is the first, in other words, to introduce the concept of 'right plant, right place'.

Never one to mince his words, he fulminates against 'pastrycook gardening' (geometric beds set into lawns) and 'railway embankment gardening' (elaborate terracing); pours scorn on fountains ('gigantic water squirts'), mazes ('monstrosities') and sunken gardens ('the most frequent of garden delusions'). He denounces conifers (especially wellingtonias), standard roses and, of course, tender bedding plants: 'the wretched alternantheras and other pinched plant rubbish'. Indeed, a whole chapter is devoted to 'The Evils of Bedding and Carpet Gardening'. Topiary moves him to fury: 'No cramming of Chinese feet into impossible shoes is half so foolish as the wilful and brutal distortion of the beautiful forms of Nature.' Particular venom is reserved for Charles Barry's Italianate garden at Shrubland, whose gravel parterres and naked walls are denounced as death in life.

The very public war of words that followed between Robinson and two champions of formal gardening, J. D. Stedding and Sir Reginald Blomfield (though Stedding was dead and not in a position to answer back) has become known as the 'Battle of Styles', and presented as a battle between formal and naturalistic gardening. In reality, it was something of a phoney war. (Robinson knew full well that there is nothing like controversy to boost sales.) The argument was not really much different from the one that pertains today, namely whether the starting point of the garden should be the arrangement of space (as most garden designers claim) or the planting (as all horticulturists do). Blomfield, as President of RIBA, naturally championed architects; Robinson spoke up for gardeners. But Robinson perfectly understood the need for structure in the garden, and as soon as he finally got a garden of his own, at Gravetye Manor in West Sussex, the first thing he did was to create a formal flower terrace by the house. His friend Gertrude Jekyll found it vastly amusing, remarking on the irony that 'Robinson designed himself a garden all squares', while formalist Reginald Blomfield had 'a garden on a cliff with not a straight line in it'.

Robinson's concept of 'Wild Gardening', he was at pains to point out, was not about letting the garden run wild, nor displacing garden features 'in which good culture and good taste may produce many happy effects'. In larger gardens, however, 'where, on the outer fringes of the lawn, in grove, park, copse, or by woodland walks or drives, there is often ample room, fair gardens and wholly new and beautiful aspects of vegetation may be created by its means'.

The heather garden at Nymans in West Sussex is one of the earliest made in England. The garden was packed with new plants, many brought back from southern continents by Harold Comber, son of the Head Gardener, James Comber.

The idea of woodland and copse embellished by the plant riches brought by the plant hunters was to prove hugely influential, and many gardens were made after this fashion, from the final decades of the nineteenth century right through to the 1920s, and indeed beyond. It had particular appeal for those afflicted with rhododendronmania. From the 1880s, the friends and relations of the Loder family bedecked the slopes of Sussex with a blaze of rhododendrons, many of which they had bred themselves, at Leonardslee, Borde Hill, High Beeches and Wakehurst Place. In 1890, Ludwig Messel, a German immigrant who had done well in the City, acquired nearby Nymans, and established his social credentials with his snootier neighbours by acquiring not only the latest rhododendrons and conifers, but many astounding new plants from Australasia and South America including embothriums, escallonias, styrax and eucryphias. He added one more novelty – possibly Britain's first heather garden, laid out on undulating hillocks with dwarf rhododendrons and other shrubs grown from seed newly collected from the Himalayas. Down the road at Sheffield Park, a Capability Brown landscape progressively wooded since the 1880s, a new burst of planting added resplendent autumn colour. From 1919, Leonard de Rothschild, who described himself as 'a banker by hobby, but a gardener by profession' made the apogee of rhododendron gardens at Exbury in Hampshire. Highly coloured, labour-intensive and concentrated on a single season, it was the absolute antithesis of what Robinson had intended – Wild Gardening had come full circle. Gardens that remained truer to the Robinsonian spirit were Emmetts in Kent, where Robinson advised on the design and planting, and Knightshayes in Devon, where The Garden in the Wood was laid out from 1950. Some 25 acres (10.1ha) of walks and glades, with carpets of bulbs, flowering shrubs, and patches of herbaceous planting, the garden is packed with rarities but presented without fanfare, in a way that would have gladdened the old man's quarrelsome heart.

Arts and Crafts

Robinson's abhorrence of the High Victorian garden was wholeheartedly shared by William Morris (1834–96), artist, designer, printer, typographer, bookbinder, writer and leading light of the Arts and Crafts Movement. Morris, however, felt that a garden 'should by no means imitate either the wilfulness or wildness of nature', but 'should look both orderly and rich' and be 'well fenced' against the outside world. In fact it should resemble as far as possible the jewelled enclosed garden of the medieval manuscripts.

Morris was obsessed with all things medieval from childhood. He had, he claimed, read all of Walter Scott by the age of seven (presumably reading in the pram) and would ride through Epping Forest on his pony, dressed in a diminutive suit of armour. Inspired by the Pre-Raphaelites and the hugely influential philosopher-critic John Ruskin, he became a political radical, attacking the capitalist industrial system and arguing that mass production not only produced

Opposite above: When Morris built Red House, it was set among Kentish orchards and offered bucolic rural views.

Left: *The Tale of Sir Degrevaunt: The Wedding Procession*, one of three frescoes (from an intended series of seven) made for Red House by Morris's lifelong friend Edward Burne-Jones.

shoddy goods without artistic merit, but debased the people who made them. His solution was to return to the values of the Middle Ages, when artists and craftsmen had worked together to a common purpose, to glorify God through their care and skill. He proposed a revival of the medieval crafts guilds, which he saw as a type of socialist brotherhood in which workers could rediscover the creativity and dignity of labour. Their inspiration would be 'first, diligent study of Nature and secondly, study of the work of the ages of Art'.

In 1859, Morris commissioned his friend Philip Webb to build him a new house, set in an idyllic Kentish orchard (the site at Bexleyheath was still countryside then). The garden of Red House was imagined as a Chaucerian 'pleasaunce', with jasmine and honeysuckle clambering neo-Gothic red-brick walls, spaces enclosed with wattle hurdles and rose-covered trellis (the inspiration for his first and most famous wallpaper design), flowery meads and an inner courtyard

'Trellis' was one of Morris's favourite designs: he chose it for his bedroom at Kelmscott House in Hammersmith where he spent his final years.

ornamented with a pixie-hat well that echoed the pointy lines of the roof. The house was filled up with furniture, textiles, embroideries, stained glass, ceramics and paintings by his friends, and in 1861 he started the firm of Morris, Marshall, Faulkner & Co to bring these new designs to the masses. It was a Victorian version of the 1990s 'chucking out the chintz' – getting rid of specious ornament in favour of simplicity and functionality; embracing a new, classless life of handmade pottery and honest oak furniture. Only the price points were different: because all was handmade, only the wealthiest could afford Morris's products. Many of the patterns he employed, in wallpapers and textiles, were derived from his garden: 'Acanthus' and 'Sunflower', 'Jasmine' and 'Chrysanthemum'.

As the city advanced towards Bexleyheath, Morris started spending his summers at Kelmscott Manor in the Cotswolds, and in 1891 set up the The Kelmscott Press, producing hand-printed books to be cherished as works of art. In one of these, *News from Nowhere* (1892), Kelmscott is depicted on the frontispiece – a modest Elizabethan stone house with standard roses lining the path to the door. Kelmscott typified the love affair of the Arts and Crafts movement with the past. Whereas at the start of the century, any man of means with some crumbling manor house at his disposal would have knocked it down and started again, these dilapidated remnants now acquired an air of romance. In 1877 Morris founded the Society for the Preservation of Ancient Buildings, starting a fashion for restoration that endures to this day. Alfred Cart de Lafontaine set the bar with Athelhampton House in Dorset, engaging Arts and Crafts architect Inigo Thomas to restore the 'mutilated' Elizabethan manor house and to transform a forest of larches into a garden that would 'curtsey' to the house. Painter Alfred Parsons designed a new garden for the medieval manor of Great Chalfield in Wiltshire, while the Jenner family rescued Lytes Cary in Somerset, restored the house to seventeenth-century style and made a garden to flatter it – a sequence of crisp yew hedges and quirky topiary, of billowing borders and pergolas dripping with roses. There were countless gardens made in this poetic manner that became known as the 'Old English' or 'Manor House' style.

At the same time, new houses were built to look old. Architect Richard Norman Shaw was the master of this, as at Cragside, for which he borrowed the look of ancient cottages in the Kentish Weald. At Wightwick Manor, West Midlands, a half-timbered 'Old English' exterior dressed up a new house equipped with all mod cons. And at Standen in West Sussex, Philip Webb planned his design to incorporate an existing medieval cottage. As at Red House, interior and exterior were conceived as one, to the point where even the wallpaper

Opposite: *Kelmscott Manor* by Charles March Gere, engraved by W. H. Hooper in 1892. Situated on the banks of the Thames near Lechlade in Gloucestershire, Kelmscott was romance realised in Cotswold stone.

Left: Lytes Cary in Somerset. Doing up old manor houses became something of a fad around the turn of the century. As a neighbouring squire put it in 1907, 'An Old Manor House is, as it were, a dewdrop from the past – pure, pellucid, peaceful.'

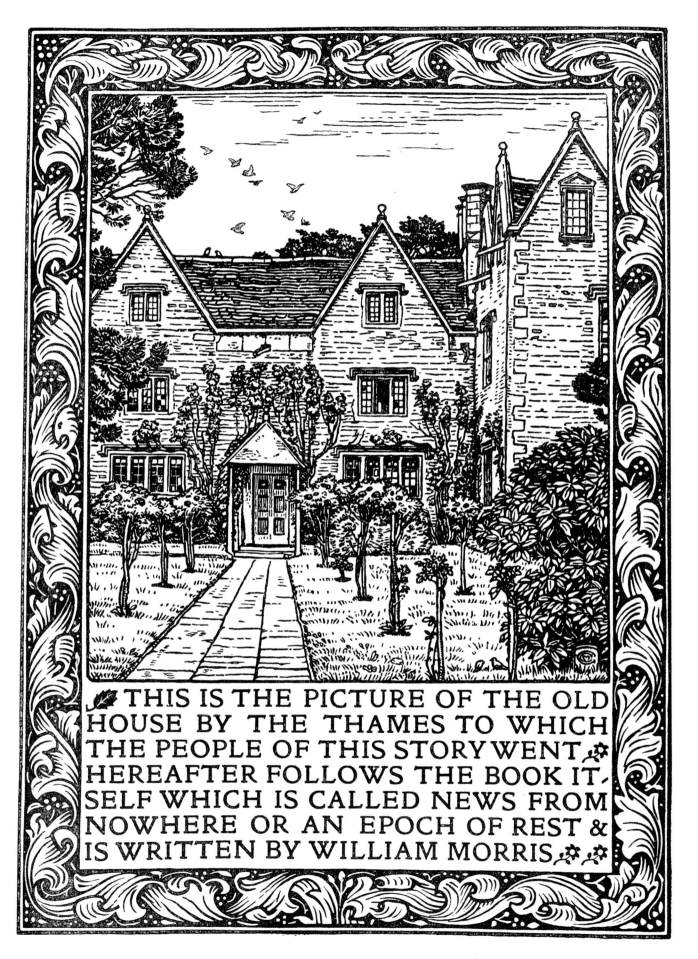

THIS IS THE PICTURE OF THE OLD
HOUSE BY THE THAMES TO WHICH
THE PEOPLE OF THIS STORY WENT
HEREAFTER FOLLOWS THE BOOK IT-
SELF WHICH IS CALLED NEWS FROM
NOWHERE OR AN EPOCH OF REST &
IS WRITTEN BY WILLIAM MORRIS

and curtains (William Morris, of course) should harmonise with the climbers peeping in at the windows.

The first garden plans for Standen had been drawn up in Gardenesque style. Webb started again, setting the house further back into the hillside and opening up spacious lawns with views over the High Kent Weald, creating terraces from the same sandstone that was used for the house, and building hefty oak trellises that his clients, James and Margaret Beale, smothered in roses. It was the exposed sandstone cliff that now flanks the entrance drive that persuaded the Beales to build here – transformed by Margaret into a rock garden. Another followed later in the quarry dug out behind the house, furnished with rare ferns and Japanese exotics. During a round-the-world trip in 1906, Margaret had fallen head over heels for Japan: the acers she ordered on her travels are believed to be some of the oldest varieties in England.

With no previous gardening experience beyond a tiny plot in Notting Hill, Margaret sought the advice of William Robinson, at nearby Gravetye. She proved an apt pupil and became a highly respected plantswoman, her 12 acre (4.9ha) garden something of a laboratory for trialling new plants, especially from Veitch and the Oriental specialists V. N. Gauntlett. At the same time, Standen remained very much a family garden, with croquet lawn and swimming pond, and when, by 1910, James Beale became too frail to reach the upper areas of the garden, a flat, shaded path, 'Grandfather's Walk', was cut into the slope to reach a new summer-house where he could enjoy the views. Standen also, in true Arts and Crafts style, clung resolutely to its earlier agricultural character, with a cattle path running through the centre of the garden, beehives and chickens in the orchard and an

Opposite: When Margaret Beale was planting her acers and camellias from Japan, these were still plants that were little known in Britain.

Below: Margaret's planting of 13 lime trees and tulips, recently reinstated along Grandfather's Walk.

approach to the main entrance resembling a village green. Margaret Beale kept a garden diary from 1890 until 1934, which, along with an archive of catalogues and letters, has recently formed the basis of a major restoration. Her planting has been reinstated as far as possible (though re-establishing her rose garden is proving a challenge), showing that the Arts and Crafts garden, unlike the pastel creations of the late twentieth-century imagination, was awash with exuberant colour.

While the wealthy did up manor houses, or built their own country retreats, the middle classes contented themselves with dreaming of a country cottage. Life in the country has always been tinged with romance by those who don't live there, and as the towns spread inexorably outwards, the myth of the cottage garden grew ever more seductive, providing a new theme for the suburban garden. By the late nineteenth century, it had become an obsession, fuelled by watercolourists such as Myles Birket Foster (whose work did indeed appear on Cadbury's chocolate boxes from the 1860s), Helen Allingham and Beatrice Parsons, who depicted luxuriant borders nodding with lupins and hollyhocks, roses and honeysuckle clambering to the eaves and smiling rustics of immaculate cleanliness going about their none-too-taxing chores. The reality, after 30 years of agricultural depression, was more likely to be holes in the thatch, sickly children and the garden given over to potatoes.

So the gardener in that period from the last years of Victoria until the First World War was faced with a bewildering array of choices – whether to seek out the new or to cherish the old (people were starting to collect antiques for the first time), whether to go for Dutch or Italian or Old English style, whether to make a formal garden or a wild garden or a cottage garden, or any combination of the above. Happily, a duo was on its way that would weave this tangle of disparate strands into one harmonious whole.

A Cottage near Brook, Witley, Surrey, by Helen Allingham. Paintings like these did much to nurture the urban myth of bucolic rural life.

'A Lutyens house in a Jekyll garden'

Philip Webb was revered as 'the father of Arts and Crafts architecture', but died in 1915 in poverty and obscurity. Not so Edwin Lutyens (1869–1944) who became architect of choice to the both the fashionable *Country Life* set and the Great British Establishment. That he did so is largely down to the influence of his friend and working partner, Gertrude Jekyll: 'A Lutyens house in a Jekyll garden' became the Edwardian equivalent of penthouse and Porsche.

The two met over tea in the garden of rhododendron-breeder Henry Mangles. Jekyll (1843–1932) had made a garden of 15 acres (6.1ha) across the road from her mother's house in Surrey, and was looking for an architect to build a home of her own. It seems, perhaps, an unlikely friendship, between the untried young architect, just in his twenties, and the clever, cultured and somewhat formidable middle-aged spinster. But the two hit it off straight away, and were soon rattling round rural Surrey together gathering ideas.

Brought up in artistic circles and unusually well travelled, Miss Jekyll defied the conventions of her times. She was one of the first women in Britain to train as an art student (from 1861, aged just 17). She was on visiting terms with the Pre-Raphaelites and a devotee of Turner. She famously claimed to be a painter *manqué* who turned to gardening only when her eyesight failed. But this is to neglect her accomplishments as a photographer, textile artist, decorator, metalworker and furniture designer. She even made her own bespoke garden tools, and she had gardened enthusiastically since childhood.

To Lutyens she became a kindly mentor, known affectionately as 'Aunt Bumps'. Together, they made over a hundred gardens – less than one-third of Jekyll's prodigious output, but justly legendary. For from the tangle of conflicting ideas that enmeshed the turn-of-the century garden, they wove a supremely satisfying synthesis in which the loose, informal planting beloved of Robinson was displayed within a tight geometric framework. A profound understanding of the needs and possibilities of plants; a new appreciation of rhythm, harmony and colour; respect for place both in anchoring

Gertrude Jekyll surveying her work in the garden of The Deanery, in Berkshire. The house was built by Lutyens in 1901 for Edward Hudson, the founder of *Country Life* magazine.

the garden in the landscape and the use of local vernacular materials, combined to make gardens which many believe have never been surpassed.

Much was already familiar. Repton had recommended a gradual transition from formality near the house to a relaxed wildness in the outer reaches of the garden; Jekyll believed a garden should melt imperceptibly into its surroundings and used native trees and shrubs to link her gardens with the surrounding countryside. Loudon and Robinson had both championed cottage gardens, which Jekyll raided as a source of both plants and ideas. 'They have a simple and tender charm,' she wrote, 'that one may look for in vain in gardens of greater pretension.' The leading practitioners of bedding had, like Jekyll, studied colour theory, noting the effects of both harmonies and contrasts of colour, observing how no colour stands alone, but can only be perceived in relation to the others around it. What Jekyll brought to the party was her myopic exactness of observation, a fine appreciation not just of nuances of colour, but of texture and form. This was mirrored in Lutyens' subtle manipulation of spaces – orderly and proportionate but rarely symmetrical, broken up by terracing and pools, and characterised by exquisite attention to materials.

Immaculate stonework softened by planting characterises the Jekyll–Lutyens garden. At Hestercombe in Somerset, Jekyll encouraged *Erigeron karvinskianus* to self-seed into steps, walls and even fountains.

Lutyens was a master at manipulating levels. Steps lead down to the Great Plat at Hestercombe, and up again to the pergola in the background, closing off the views over the Vale of Taunton below.

'Formerly a border was planted according to the heights of plants only,' wrote Jekyll, 'and they were placed, not only without any regard to colour combination, but in single plants, so that the whole effect was like a patchwork of small pieces indiscriminately dotted about.' Jekyll, instead, planted in large, loose drifts where colours blended into each other, carefully placed 'to follow each other in season of blooming' so that the border would change through the seasons. She grouped plants to offer satisfying vignettes within the borders, and gave close attention to form and foliage – favouring the silvery, aromatic foliage of Mediterranean plants and the bold forms of hostas, bergenias and yuccas. There was nothing wishy-washy about her schemes. Indeed, she retained a certain fondness for the brightly

coloured annuals commonly used in bedding displays. It was not their fault if they were horribly used by Victorian park keepers: in her hands they could be things of beauty. She would often drop in tender plants in pots for the summer, such as scarlet pelargoniums or vivid blue *Salvia patens*. Plantings inspired by original Jekyll designs at Barrington Court in Somerset show just how zestful her palette could be.

As a student, Jekyll had spent long hours copying Turners, learning how the artist could use colour to manipulate not only perceptions of space, but atmosphere and emotion. She learned how to use hot reds for focus and drama, yellow fading to white to evoke an aerial quality, while purples, silvers and blues suggested distance. Writing about her summer border at her home, Munstead Wood, she described how one colour flowed into another, from cool to hot and back again, and how juxtapositions of colour could create delicious optical illusions: 'The brilliant orange African marigold has leaves of a rather dull green colour. But look steadily at the flowers for thirty seconds in sunshine and then look at the leaves. The leaves appear to be bright blue!'

Jekyll, then, approached the garden as a painter: her plants were 'paints set out upon a palette', and the job of the gardener was 'so to use the plants that they shall form beautiful pictures'. These pictures did not begin and end in the border. A keen advocate of woodland gardening, she was no less delighted by birch stems gleaming pale against dark rhododendrons, or light filtering through the trees to illumine a patch of white foxgloves.

Almost nothing remains of these gardens today. What we know of them is gleaned principally from photographs, many of them Jekyll's own, and her vivid and practical writings. There is a small formal garden at Hatchlands in Surrey; at Folly Farm in Berkshire the Lutyens layout is being repaired and reanimated with new plantings by Dan Pearson, and at Upton Grey in Hampshire Jekyll's plantings have been meticulously reconstructed, using original plans. Most celebrated is Hestercombe in Somerset, where from 1903, Lutyens and Jekyll demonstrated how planting and architecture could work together to be more than the sum of their parts. It is true of the large effects – the great sunken 'Plat' with its confident diagonal axes accentuated by hefty clumps of bergenias, and the massive pergola, swathed with roses, closing the vast views across the plain below. But it is also true of the fine detail: intricate silvery planting enhancing a delicately fenestrated orangery, slender pencils of iris balancing the long, narrow rill, or a scattering of daisies lending lightness to Lutyens' graceful steps.

Above: Helen Allingham's painting of Munstead Wood, Jekyll's home in Surrey, accurately records her method of planting in drifts of colour.

Opposite: Lutyens' rill at Hestercombe, brilliantly exploiting the drama of changing levels as it races towards nothingness.

As her sight weakened, Jekyll became increasingly reclusive, and most of her later designs were done at home, working from photographs. Lutyens went on to ever greater things, not least designing imperial New Delhi. He also designed several gardens without her, of which the most famous must be Great Dixter in East Sussex. Here he worked with Nathaniel Lloyd, laying out a complex framework of walled courtyards and tightly hedged rooms, punctuated by pools, steps and elaborate topiary, which would later be so splendidly exploited by Nathaniel's son Christopher. At around the same time, he started work on Castle Drogo for Julius Drewe. This enterprising grocer had made so much money from his Home and Colonial stores, selling tea to the masses (effectively the first branded grocery chain, with 500 stores by 1903) that he was able to retire at 33 and employ the country's most prestigious architect to realise his fantasy of a full-scale medieval castle, hewn out of granite, perched on a spur overlooking Dartmoor.

While Lutyens laid out gardens, he never called himself a garden designer. No more did Ernest Barnsley, at work from 1909 at Rodmarton in Gloucestershire; both were architects, conceiving house and garden as one. Here Barnsley's garden of intimate 'rooms' seems the natural extension of the house, in which every tiny detail from a window catch to an alpine trough is a carefully considered work

The timeless beauty of Rodmarton in Gloucestershire, where the commitment, craftsmanship and love that went into creating the house extends seamlessly into the garden.

of art. Planted by owner Margaret Biddulph, one of the first women to receive a professional horticultural training, it still somehow carries the fingerprints of the idealistic community of Cotswold craftsmen who made it.

The first to make the distinction, and to call himself a 'landscape architect', was Thomas Mawson (1861–1933). He saw his job as making peace between the conflicting demands of architect, engineer and gardener, and creating a harmonious setting for the house. He had his work cut out at Wightwick Manor, the high-octane Arts and Crafts confection built for Wolverhampton paint magnate Theodore Mander, complete with pele tower, minstrels' gallery, acres of stained glass and interiors by Morris and William de Morgan. Faced with this intensive decoration and jumble of architectural styles, Mawson's priority was to create some kind of breathing space: the two broad grass terraces he dug out in front of the house are oases of calm. A simple corridor of cylindrical yews draws the eye firmly down the lawn, balancing the width of the house; high hedges conceal the drive and an earlier flower garden and divide the sloping site into large, clear 'apartments', here a croquet lawn, there an orchard or kitchen garden. A Yew and Holly Walk leads to a rustic summer-house thatched with heather, a formal Long Walk unrolls between high yew walls; beyond them the land falls away 'by easy gradation' to

Faced with the farrago of architectural styles at Wightwick Manor in Wolverhampton, Thomas Mawson sought to make a calming garden that would give some visual coherence to the scene.

woodland and ponds. While not all Mawson's plans were implemented, Mawson was sufficiently pleased with Wightwick to include it in later editions of his 1901 book, *The Art and Craft of Garden Making* – a book that would influence Lawrence Johnston at Hidcote. From modest beginnings (he left school to work for his builder uncle at the age of 12), Mawson built up an international practice, and made a number of high-profile gardens, often in a monumental Italianate style. By the turn of the century, the Italian garden was once again all the rage. But in this style poor Mawson was just the Salieri to the Mozart of Harold Peto.

The perfection of Peto

When financier Alexander Henderson (later first Lord Faringdon) bought Buscot Park in Oxfordshire, he inherited an arboretum to the east of the house, through which a walk led down to a boathouse on the lake. Yet despite being only a quarter of a mile apart, house and lake remained strangely dissociated. The task he gave to Harold Ainsworth Peto (1854–1933) was to forge a link between them. Peto devised a long and narrow water garden, enclosed by box hedges and tall elms (since lost), running downhill to the sheet of water below and luring the eye across to a mysterious domed pavilion on the farther shore. The elements he used were few – just grass, hedge, stone and water, but this spareness only enhances the garden's power. A stone-edged canal descends the hill, opening into a succession of rills and pools, flanked by quiet, austerely ornamented lawns. In the highest pool, a gambolling fountain sends water tumbling down the slope in a narrow cascade, and slipping on through another pool to dive under a Venetian bridge into a glassy canal. Here a line of water lilies leads the eye finally, calmly, to the lake. Despite the optical trickery (the lake seems first nearer, then farther, than you think, and the grandly balustraded bridge turns out to be tiny), and despite a clutch of fat-faced little figures frolicking among the cypresses and herms, the garden has a chaste and dreamy dignity – gravitas without pomposity.

Peto spent many years on the Italian Riviera, where he designed both villas and gardens, and was profoundly influenced by the Italian Renaissance. His genius was to integrate the architecture of the formal Renaissance garden – terraces, colonnades, statuary and fountains – into the softer landscapes of Britain. Nowhere did he do this more perfectly than at his own garden at Iford Manor, a vision of Arcadia magically translated to a steep Wiltshire hillside. Whereas Barry and Mawson's version of Italian was heavyweight and imperial, Peto's was all lightness and grace – even under grey English skies he could capture the sunny spirit of the Renaissance garden. Wiltshire does not resemble Italy: the garden he made was romantically, quintessentially English. Yet even today, hearing the sound of a flute threading through the trees (Iford hosts an annual music festival), you would not be surprised to come upon the goat-footed god playing upon his pan pipes, or to see a wood-nymph flitting among the trees.

Peto had spent a decade searching for his 'ideal of a country house' before in 1899 he chanced on Iford. Its primary purpose was to house a collection of artefacts

Opposite: Harold Ainsworth Peto's exquisite Cloister sums up Iford's Italianate enchantment.

Overleaf: Harold Peto's water garden at Buscot Park in Oxfordshire, fusing elements of the classical, the Venetian, the Mughal and the mythic – the most powerful and poetic of spaces.

collected on his travels. Thus the pigsties were demolished to furnish stone for the 'Casita' and decorated with twelfth-century marble columns from Verona – possibly the world's most beautiful toolshed. An exquisite Cloister was built round a Venetian well-head and the Great Terrace running across the top of the garden was lined with statues and sarcophagi, a Roman colonnade framing views of the valley below. 'Old buildings or fragments of masonry carry one's mind back to the past in a way that a garden of flowers only cannot do,' wrote Peto, in a very eighteenth-century way. 'Gardens that are too stony are equally unsatisfactory; it is the combination of the two in just proportion which is the most satisfactory.' At Iford he got it just right.

The first impact of the war

Work on the Cloister began in 1914. It seems astonishing now, almost crass, but no one saw what was coming. In the first heady days of war, gardeners and bosses alike rushed to enlist. Between August 1914 and January 1916, when conscription was introduced, 2,467,000 men volunteered to fight for their country, and went on volunteering even when it became apparent what horrors lay in store. Wounded servicemen were shipped back to hospitals in England, and one of these was established at Cliveden by the Canadian Red Cross in 1915. Inevitably, many died. Lord Astor had designed a sunken Italian garden, dug into the hillside and planted with cypresses, as an atmospheric setting for fragments of Roman sculpture. Now the mosaic floor was dug up, and the garden became a cemetery. Forty combatants were buried there, alongside two Canadian nursing sisters.

With so many away at the front, gardens were consigned to the care of old men and boys – or, in the Dorchester area in late 1914, to prisoners of war: Thomas Hardy had one working at Max Gate. *In extremis*, some even turned to women. Some 2,000 members of the Women's Land Army were put to work as gardeners, though once the war was over, nearly all returned to their 'proper duties at home'. However, there were by this time at least a handful of professionally trained women.

As long ago as 1796, the Quaker philanthropist Priscilla Wakefield had suggested that gardening might offer an 'eligible maintenance' to women of the 'noble and merchant classes': she did not see gardening as something for the lower orders. Exactly a century later, the first women were taken on at Kew, prompting cheeky music hall songs about their uniform bloomers. They had been trained at Swanley, the first horticultural college to admit women, which became all-female in 1902. The first horticultural college expressly for women was set up a few years earlier by the scandalous Daisy, Countess of Warwick, who managed to be simultaneously a committed socialist and mistress to the Prince of Wales. There were, she noted 'one million surplus women' who must be equipped with the means to support themselves. This was followed by The Glynde School, which aimed to prepare women for careers as head gardeners, botany teachers and market gardeners. Interestingly, Swanley developed a colonial branch, which by

1916 had trained over 250 women to work as superintendents of farms, orchards and gardens in various parts of Empire.

The irony is that women finally succeeded in becoming professional gardeners just as the profession lost its status. With the demise of the country house, there was less and less need for highly trained head gardeners, fewer and fewer places to ply their trade. As gardening became increasingly 'deskilled' over the course of the following century, the brawn to tote a heavy strimmer became more marketable than brain. That still needs to be put right.

Until Annie Gulvin and Alice Hutchings joined the staff at Kew in 1896, the only women there had been pot-washers. They were joined soon after by classmate Eleanor Moreland, and by 1898, Alice had been promoted to the dizzy heights of sub-foreman.

THE JAPANESE GARDEN

WHEN, after two centuries of isolation, Japan opened up to foreigners in 1853, the West couldn't get enough of it. Fashionable ladies took to wearing kimonos, and no drawing room was complete without an Imari teapot. The first wildly exotic Japanese acers and azaleas started to arrive on our shores in the 1860s. However, it was not until the 1890s, following the publication of Josiah Conder's *Landscape Gardening in Japan*, that the first Japanese gardens began to appear in Britain.

While Conder gave layouts to follow, and lists of essential features such as lanterns, rocks and miniature hills, at Heale House in Wiltshire, Louis Greville took no chances, and imported a team of Japanese gardeners to create and maintain his new garden. But by the turn of the century, anyone could buy a 'Japanese' garden complete from a specialist nursery. V. N. Gauntlett and Co. Ltd, a favourite of Standen's Margaret Beale, offered a 400-page catalogue covering lanterns, cranes and all 'authentic' features as well as Japanese plants. Or if space was a problem, Liberty's could supply a miniature garden for just 26 shillings and sixpence.

The craze for all things Japanese culminated with the Japan-British Exhibition of 1910. No one knows for sure whether Henrietta Bankes of Kingston Lacy paid a visit, but between 1910 and 1915 she created a garden in an old quarry in the woods – in no way an authentic Japanese garden, but an Edwardian fantasy of Japan. Alan de Tatton certainly did attend, and returned to Cheshire determined to build his own Japanese garden. Like Greville, he employed Japanese craftsmen, and included traditional features such as stepping stone bridges, a Shinto temple, stone lanterns of different forms (some designed to trap snow, to enhance the beauty of the winter garden), and a mound capped with white stones, to represent the snow-capped peak of sacred Mount Fuji. The symbolism of Japanese gardens is deep and complex, and strict rules concerning the layout of gardens had been codified from the eleventh century. Transgression was believed to bring the direst consequences: death, disease and the invasion of your garden by demons. So a garden must be laid out not only to please the eye, but to be propitious. The placing of stones was particularly delicate, with no fewer than 17 taboos to be negotiated. Tatton Park's garden, while far from the genuine article, became (and remains, since its restoration in 2000–1) the most widely admired Japanese garden in Europe.

It was the tranquil aesthetic rather than the spiritual dimension of the garden that caught the European imagination. Peto was entranced by his visit to Japan and worked Japanese elements into a number of his gardens. In the 1930s, the spareness and asymmetry of Japanese art was a major influence on the Modernists, while the brilliant twenty-first-century garden-maker Christopher Bradley-Hole has acknowledged Japan as the greatest influence on his style.

Clockwise from top left: The focus of the Japanese garden at Cliveden in Berkshire is, curiously, a Chinese pagoda. A garden scene by the Japanese master print-maker Kuniyoshi, brought home to Standen as a souvenir of Japan. Catalogues from the Yokohama Nursery Company, one of the largest suppliers of Japanese plants to the Western nursery trade. The Japanese garden at Tatton Park in Cheshire.

239

TOPIARY

Topiary was introduced to this country by the Romans (indeed *topiarius* was the Latin word for a gardener); and apart from a lull in the eighteenth century, topiary has rarely been absent from the English garden, whether in hedges, in regular geometric forms such as cones, cylinders and balls, or in more fanciful shapes. Seventeenth-century writer William Lawson, for example, recommended trimming 'small trees into the shapes of men at arms, or swift running grey hounds to chase the deare, or hunt the hare'. Almost exactly 300 years later, at Knightshayes in Devon, a hedge was made with a fox running along the top and hounds in hot pursuit.

It was this kind of whimsy that moved poet Alexander Pope to scorn. In a satirical article in 1713, he drew up a catalogue of evergreens for sale, beginning with 'Adam and Eve in yew; Adam a little shattered by the fall of the Tree of Knowledge in the great storm' and 'St George in box; his arm scarce long enough, but will be in a condition to stick the Dragon by next April …' Topiary went out of fashion for the next hundred years.

The return of formality in the nineteenth century brought a revival of topiary in both sculptural forms and intricate box parterres. Towards the end of the century, there was a move to recreate the romance of gardens like Levens Hall, where seventeenth-century yews grown into enormous wobbly shapes – chess pieces and crowns, a 'Judge's Wig' and a 'Jug of Morocco Ale' – were supplemented with new plantings. Overgrown topiary casts a similar spell at Packwood (see page 190) and at Athelhampton, where the child-size yew obelisks planted in the rose garden in the 1890s have grown to a phalanx of giant pyramids, over 30ft (9.1m) high. The roses disappeared long ago, but grass and topiary alone can make a very satisfying garden, as at Lytes Cary, Great Dixter (Christopher Lloyd's father, Nathaniel, was an expert topiarist) or at Ascott in Buckinghamshire, where a minimalist garden by Jacques and Peter Wirtz has joined an earlier love-letter in golden yew.

Nowhere realised romance in topiary quite like Elvaston in Derbyshire (see page 191), a Disneyland of living architecture which introduced new forms and colours to the High Victorian garden, including variegated holly and golden yew. Topiary became a key element in the Arts and Crafts garden – dividing up the space with living walls of green and peopling it with all kinds of complicated shapes and quaint creatures (a habit borrowed from cottage gardens) – hens and peacocks being favourites. Hidcote took topiary to new heights in the Stilt Garden – essentially a pair of airborne hedges.

This clean style has proved popular with modern garden designers, notably Jacques and Peter Wirtz, best known in England for their majestic landscape of topiary and water at The Alnwick Garden in Northumberland. Clipped topiary masses counterpoint fluid perennial planting in the gardens of Christopher Bradley-Hole, Piet Oudolf, Andy Sturgeon and Tom Stuart-Smith, and it remains an invaluable structural element in gardens big and small.

Topiary gives form to the garden, whether directing movement through the space (top left, at Hidcote; top right at Lytes Cary); creating rhythm (centre right, Montacute); enlivening the scene with humorous fantasy (centre left, Knightshayes) or just enclosing the space with a bit more panache, as the crenellated walls at Knightshayes (bottom).

· CHAPTER 8 ·

INTERWAR GARDENS

HIDING FROM HISTORY

1918–1940

'It isn't that I don't like sweet disorder,
but it has to be judiciously arranged.'

VITA SACKVILLE-WEST

A cataclysm of the magnitude of the First World War was bound to have an effect on gardening. The gardeners, it is often said, marched off to war, never to return, spelling the end of the great Edwardian gardens. In reality it wasn't like that. At Caerhays in Cornwall, for example, J. C. Williams declined to be deflected from the serious business of collecting camellias. The terraces at Bodnant, in development from 1904 to 1914, were finally finished in 1919. To a large extent, the country house and the gardening tradition that went with it limped on until the Second World War: the leisured but often cash-strapped world of P. G. Wodehouse is not so very far from the truth. There was no grand and poignant finale for the aristocratic garden, but rather a slow and messy death by a thousand cuts.

Of course gardeners died in the trenches – when 6 per cent of British men aged between 18 and 41 were killed, they were bound to be among them – but, proportionately, not nearly as many as their masters. Then the flu epidemic of 1918–19, perversely targeting the young and healthy, saw off as many again. Yet more estates were left without heirs to tackle a killer combination of rising taxes, fuel shortages and a workforce demanding shorter hours and higher wages. The years 1918–21 saw the greatest shift in land ownership since the Dissolution of the Monasteries 400 years before – but problems of succession were really only the latest instalment in a chapter of woe that had begun with the great agricultural depression of the 1880s. (The war, in fact, proved rather a boost, since many landowners received subsidies to grow food.) Throughout the nineteenth century, except in times of war, the wealthy landowning classes had lived largely untroubled by taxation, but from 1907 they found themselves specifically targeted by a series of new taxes; death duties, introduced in 1894, had reached 40 per cent by 1919.

For centuries, the great country house with its fashionable garden had been a symbol of political clout. Now it was a millstone, and aristocratic families on their uppers hastened to be rid of them. Finding that none of her children wished to inherit Cliveden, the widowed Duchess of Sutherland sold it off to William Waldorf Astor, heir to a vast fortune in American real estate. But in general the new buying class were people like the Beales at Standen, the Manders at Wightwick and the Lloyds at Great Dixter – lawyers, industrialists, entrepreneurs – and they wanted charm and nostalgia rather than magnificence, and preferably a location handy for the railway. For many of this new moneyed class continued to work – unthinkable in the 1850s when any aspiring gentleman would have instantly turned his back on commerce.

Sometimes the problem could be solved by marrying money, and many a garden (not least Blenheim Palace) was saved by the 'dollar princesses,' American heiresses who traded their millions for an ancient British title. But there just weren't enough rich Americans to go round. The first trickle of demolitions began – Trentham, for example, was demolished in 1912.

Opposite: From 1921, the Edwardian architecture of The Courts Garden in Wiltshire was given a rich overlay of planting by Lady Cecilie Goff, and remains a plantsman's dream.

After the war

In Europe, the effect of the war appeared to be a wholesale rejection of history. Modernist architects imagined new ways of living, in clean white boxes, bathed in sunlight. In Britain, by contrast, the first response to the war was a rapid retreat into the safety of the past. Work continued at Rodmarton in the same hand-crafted way. Charles Paget Wade had served in the trenches, dreaming of a ruinous Cotswold manor house he had glimpsed in *Country Life*. He bought Snowshill Manor in 1919 and turned it into a living museum, with a no less eccentric and intriguing garden. Lutyens and Jekyll collaborated once more, designing cemeteries for the fallen, which Jekyll planted to evoke the cottage gardens of home. In Wiltshire, Lady Cecilie Goff studied Jekyll's *Colour in the Flower Garden*, and applied her ideas at The Courts; gardeners would follow suit for the next hundred years. Lutyens picked up the pieces at Castle Drogo, albeit on a slightly reduced scale. The garden he made here was proof against not the winds of change, but the winds of Dartmoor, enclosed by high hedges and a belt of beeches, with a sunken garden at the centre.

St George slays the dragon in the courtyard of Snowshill Manor in Gloucestershire.

The garden stands apart from the castle, arranged over three levels. The lowest is the most formal, with a sunken rose garden flanked by broad herbaceous borders, through which thread geometric paths strongly resembling the Mughal patterns Lutyens was working with in India. At each corner stands a yew pavilion, originally roofed with pleached elms. Steps lead up to the next level, where a terrace of fragrant planting gives way to an informal wilderness. At the topmost level stands a vast circular wall of yew. Within is nothing but an expanse of flawless lawn – made for tennis or croquet out of the wind, but also a superbly dramatic counterbalance to the complex patterning below.

Lutyens specified wistaria and yucca as focal points, but otherwise the planting was left to George Dillistone. (He also planted Goddards, the Arts and Crafts

Left: Self-styled 'Garden architect' George Dillistone tended to work for less exalted clients than Gertrude Jekyll, but in his planting at Castle Drogo in Devon proved himself entirely her equal.

house of the chocolate-making Terry family in York.) Early photographs show just what a challenge this was, on the thin, shaley soil, blasted by winds, 1,000ft (305m) above sea level; yet Dillistone managed to produce a luxuriantly colourful and richly textured planting, balancing the sumptuousness of the main herbaceous borders with a cool all-blue terrace planting in Jekyll style. (She had introduced the notion of single-colour borders.) So far, so Edwardian. But there are also elements, like the chequerboard layout of single-colour rose beds in the sunken garden, that have a whiff of European modernism about them, looking towards the bright colours and angular shapes of the Jazz Age.

Devon in the 1920s was a little hotspot of Art Deco, though Coleton Fishacre, on the outside, just looks like an oversized cottage. It was built as a seaside holiday

Above: In contrast to the elegance of the Lutyens and Dillistone garden, the Wendy House hidden in the woods behind the hedge resembles a typical 1920s suburban plot.

home for Rupert D'Oyly Carte, son of the D'Oyly Carte who had so profitably brought together Gilbert and Sullivan. His business empire included the Savoy Hotel and Claridges, both icons of Art Deco, and the interiors at Coleton Fishacre were designed in similar style. The garden, too, had a theatrical quality, making fullest use of the mild microclimate and high light levels to grow a wide range of tender exotics. From the paved terrace and loggia, used as outdoor dining rooms, a series of Lutyens-style walled terraces sheltered tender, sun-loving divas both human and vegetal, giving way eventually to a jungly landscape of streams, bamboos and exotic flowering trees in the Cornish manner. It would be a while yet before Modernism crept cautiously out into the garden. The Arts and Crafts style of garden rooms, of high hedges and topiary and overflowing herbaceous borders, was still very much in the ascendant. And nowhere was it achieved more gloriously than Hidcote – which despite its site on a cold and windswept hillside is widely regarded as the greatest English garden of the twentieth century.

The D'Oyly Cartes first spotted the site for Coleton Fishacre from their yacht, and the house and garden were constructed to make the most of the sea views.

Left: Coleton Fishacre's comfortable cottagey exterior gives no clue to the snazzy Jazz Age decor within.

Left: A map hanging over the fireplace in the library, painted by George Spencer Hoffman, shows the enviable situation of the house. In the foreground is D'Oyly Carte with his dog.

American beauty

The pretty Cotswold town of Broadway was frequented at the turn of the century by a coterie of American arty types, which may have recommended it to wealthy New York socialite Gertrude Winthrop in her search for an English home for herself and her eldest son. In 1907 she bought 267 bleak and windy acres (108ha) on a nearby hilltop at Hidcote Bartrim, with the plan that her son, Lawrence Johnston (1871–1958), should become an eligible gentleman farmer. Instead, he lavished his love on a tribe of dachshunds and set about turning the fields into a garden.

His starting point was a small walled garden adjoining the farmhouse, shaded by a single lofty cedar. From here he ran an axis east–west across the garden, then added another longer one at right angles. Around this basic T-shape he assembled a network of garden rooms, possibly encouraged by his reading of Mawson, who recommended making 'a series of apartments rather than a panorama which can be grasped in one view'. This would arouse curiosity, 'always inviting further exploration', and this is certainly the case at Hidcote, where every room reveals some new delight, anticipation increased by the height of the hedges and the

The Pillar Garden in early summer shows the extraordinary density and complexity of the planting attempted at Hidcote: the garden changes colour as the season progresses, the exuberant froth of the borders balanced by the austere pillars of yew.

narrowness of the doorways between them. Indeed, he picked up a number of tips
from Mawson – the delight of looking along a 'smooth-shaven green alley' to a
glimpse of countryside, how to integrate different levels into the lie of the land, the
need to give a satisfying end to a vista, and not least the usefulness of gates for this
purpose: the view up to a gate that seems to open to the sky has become one of the
abiding images of Hidcote.

Johnston thought of himself primarily as a plantsman, and joined several
plant-hunting expeditions to Kenya, to the Victoria Falls and to China, seeking
out rarities both for Hidcote and for Serre de la Madone, his other garden on
the French Riviera. His enclosures, then, were primarily intended to shelter an
extraordinarily diverse collection of plants, supplemented over time by other
specialised habitats including stream gardens, a rock bank and an alpine border
bristling with puyas and aloes. But the great benefit of the garden room structure
(apart from the sheer beauty of the hedges), and the reason Hidcote proved so
influential, was the scope it gave to play with numerous ideas, colour schemes,
atmospheres – all the best bits of an English cottage garden, Italian palazzo or
Mediterranean retreat rolled headily into one. It could feel all too much, but

There is a
strongly Italianate
feel to Hidcote,
in its formality,
powerful axes
and masterful
manipulation of
space. We see
(clockwise) an
entire garden
room taken
up by a pool,
a tight space
transformed by
enclosure in
mid-air, and an
axis that leads
dramatically to
the sky.

the supreme achievement of Hidcote is its balance: just as the incredible concentration of planting threatens to become overwhelming, a doorway beckons to an empty green space, the wilderness offers a sylvan retreat from the intensity of the inner gardens or the severity of clipped hornbeam in the Stilt Garden provides a cool corrective to the prettiness and profusion preceding it.

Johnston worked at his garden for over 30 years, and the garden as it exists now tries to capture its appearance in the 1930s. For much of this time he was aided and abetted by his good friend Norah Lindsay (1866–1948). It was his intention to leave Hidcote to her, and it was only because of her sudden death that it came to the National Trust in 1948 – the first property to be acquired solely for its garden. Prior to the war, Lindsay had developed a frothy, romantic planting style at her garden at Sutton Courtenay in Oxfordshire, encouraging serendipity and self-seeding in a way that dismayed her more tidy-minded visitors, with giant thistly cardoons or inebriate columns of Irish yews rising dream-like from a riot of swoony colour. Following the collapse of her marriage soon after the war Lindsay scratched a living going from house party to house party, advising society hostesses (and hosts) on their plantings in return for a modest annual retainer. She worked for Nancy Astor (daughter-in-law of William Waldorf) at Cliveden, for Nancy Tree at Kelmarsh and Ditchley Park, for the future Edward VIII at Fort Belvedere and, bravely, for the notoriously tasteless Philip Sassoon at Port Lympne. At Blickling in Norfolk, where Philip Kerr was sweeping away the cluttered Victorian interiors, he employed Lindsay to do the same outdoors. Sadly, only her parterre remains, where she simplified a 'pastrycook' pattern of 80 fiddly beds into four large, painterly squares, animated by bold and rhythmic topiary. Her genius, garden designer Russell Page observed, lay in the seasonal ebb and flow of her plantings. 'She captured the essence of midsummer … or gave the pith of autumn … She lifted herbaceous planting into a poetic category and gave it an air of rapture and spontaneity.'

For the rest of the century, gardeners took inspiration from the Hidcote formula of tight formal structure with abundant and informal planting. Outstanding gardens were made by Ralph Dutton at Hinton Ampner in Hampshire and Phyllis Reiss at Tintinhull in Somerset. Perhaps unfairly, these have been somewhat eclipsed by another garden in which the makers of the garden exert as strong a fascination as the garden itself. Sissinghurst Castle, the romantic, idiosyncratic and deeply inconvenient home of Harold Nicolson and Vita Sackville-West, has acquired an almost mythical resonance as the nonpareil of English gardening, adored, revered and copied all over the world.

Beautiful, witty and vivacious, Norah Lindsay scraped a precarious living by designing gardens for her rich friends, developing Jekyll's painterly approach in a looser, livelier manner.

Left: At Blickling Hall in Norfolk, Lindsay cleared away all the Victorian frippery, retaining only the topiary and seventeenth-century fountain and replanting in her own dreamy style.

Below: In 1933 Phyllis Reiss made a garden of extraordinary balance and serenity at Tintinhull in Somerset, which was further enhanced by Penelope Hobhouse during the 1980s and early 1990s.

THE HERBACEOUS BORDER

The herbaceous border is the most expressive feature in the garden, romantic, tranquil, exhilarating or bold. Strictly speaking, it should consist only of herbaceous perennials, but in practice, has nearly always contained a mixture of shrubs, bulbs and annuals to give backbone and variety to the scheme. Borders like these appeared, in a simpler form, in the seventeenth century, and are only just now being displaced by looser, more naturalistic modes of planting.

While vibrant bedding schemes were the hot new thing in the Victorian garden, perennial planting was never entirely abandoned. J C Loudon recommended a 'mingled' style in the flower garden, combining plants so as to 'present a gay assemblage of flowers of different colours during the whole season'. These could be chosen 'without much regard to variety of form or diversity of character' as long as they offered masses of flower. Being Loudon, he worked it all out mathematically, concluding that a minimum of 36 different plants would be needed to produce a decent show from February to October, this pattern to be repeated as required. For a really swanky border, however, employing four rows of plants in four colours, a lavish 96 were prescribed. 'Every approach to irregularity and a wild, confused, crowded or natural-like appearance' was to be avoided: irregular side shoots or straggling stalks must be trimmed off to keep plants neat, with plenty of earth showing between them.

This, then, was the taste that Gertrude Jekyll turned upside down, with her soft surges of colour and careful attention to foliage and form. Moreover, she suggested that different borders might be made in different colours, some even in one colour, rather than all looking the same.

Others before her had attempted a subtler approach – the great double borders at Arley Hall in Cheshire, which she praised as the best planting in England, had been in place since the 1840s. But her writings reached a wide and eager audience, and for over a century a fine herbaceous border (and preferably a double border, with a path bisecting two deep banks of planting) was the highlight of almost every serious garden. It made the garden softer and more romantic, it widened the palette of plants that could be used, and it somehow set the tone for the garden, especially in the skilful hands of practitioners like Norah Lindsay and Penelope Hobhouse.

While low-maintenance ground cover gardening became popular mid-century, by the 1970s and '80s, the herbaceous border made a genteel comeback as the pinnacle of Country House style, edged in dwarf box and draped in old roses. Planting was exclusively in polite, pastel shades – hot colours, and especially orange, were now seen as horribly vulgar. Magenta induced visible shudders, though, curiously, deep 'garnet' reds were permissible among the dusty pinks, lilacs, silvers and blues.

Inevitably, adventurous gardeners rebelled. At Great Dixter, the Long Border became a riot of clashing colour, as Christopher Lloyd joyously challenged the dead hand of Good Taste. At Hadspen in Somerset, Nori and Sandra Pope created a floral colour wheel, exploring nuances of colour with minute exactness. Spectacularly, at Packwood, Head Gardener Mick Evans reinvented mingled borders for the twenty-first century, as dynamic hot borders exploding with exotic forms. He also reinstated the double borders done away with in the 1930s, planting them in smudgy moody colours, but with a looseness that gestures towards the New Perennials style.

Great herbaceous borders remain the high point of innumerable gardens – at Nymans and Hidcote, at Tintinhull and Forde Abbey, at Felley Priory, Blickling and The Courts. There is no greater test of the gardener's skill.

Clockwise from top: Resplendent double borders at Nymans in Sussex. Mick Evans's triumphant reinvention of the nineteenth-century mingled style particularly associated with Packwood House near Solihull, featuring sunflowers, phormiums and mounds of *Euphorbia mellifera*, punctuated with the shiny mahogany rosettes of *Aeonium* 'Zwartkop'. A fulsome Norah Lindsay border reinstated at Cliveden in Buckinghamshire. A traditional herbaceous border at Lytes Cary in Somerset, including roses and other flowering shrubs as well as herbaceous plants.

'Lady Chatterley above the waist and the gamekeeper below'

Vita Sackville-West (1892–1962) was a commanding presence – tall, manly, aristocratic, alarming unwary visitors as she strode about her garden in top boots, breeches and pearls. She lived and breathed poetry, wrote turgid novels and riveting histories, and hoped to be remembered as a poet; instead she is celebrated as a flamboyant figure on the fringes of the Bloomsbury set, as the muse and lover of Virginia Woolf, for her unconventional marriage to writer and diplomat Harold Nicolson (who also had numerous lovers of both genders), but principally for the garden that she and Harold made together – a shared passion that became an unshakeable bond.

Vita was brought up at the great Tudor palace of Knole in Kent, which she loved with a visceral fervour. As a woman, she was debarred from inheriting, and her sense of loss and injustice never left her. Sissinghurst, created around a remnant of Elizabethan castle deep in the Kent countryside, became her consolation – more than a garden, it was a fitting context for her sense of self, connecting her with her ancestral past. Her first sight of it, in 1930, is recalled in her novel *Family History*: 'The hard winter starlight revealed an untidy courtyard, enclosed by ruined walls, and opposite, an arrowy tower springing up to a lovely height with glinting windows.' She fell 'flat in love' within a minute, and undeterred by ruin, rubble and bramble, determined to make it her home.

Her husband, Harold Nicolson, was less starry-eyed. But he gamely entered into the spirit, and scaling the tower, shouted down his instructions to his sons below, as they marked out with canes and string the confident geometry of enclosures, walks and vistas that Vita would fill with her fulsome planting. Like Hidcote, Sissinghurst is a garden of rooms, with ten different areas providing vivid contrasts in atmosphere and planting. But unlike Hidcote, Sissinghurst came together as needs must, its form dictated by the detritus of former centuries too expensive to remove, and without the benefit of a limitless chequebook.

To finance the garden, Vita turned to journalism, and her weekly columns in the *Observer* made her one of the first modern media gardeners. She was no expert, she insisted, but she wrote from her own experience, in a commonsensical, confiding tone: 'I have very little hope that you will be able to follow my advice. I proffer it only knowing that it is right, which does not mean that I follow it myself.' She was forthright in her prejudices, declining to have rhododendrons in her garden ('fat stockbrokers, who we do not want to have to dinner') or the bright pink roses 'American Pillar' and 'Dorothy Perkins'. 'I know this attack on two popular roses will infuriate many people,' she declared unrepentantly, 'but if one writes gardening articles one must have the courage of one's opinion.' She preferred old roses, choosing them as much for their romantic names as their fragile beauty, imagining Zéphirine Drouhin as a character in a novel by Flaubert. Although Sissinghurst was never named, her columns traced its evolution, including, in 1949, her first thoughts about her White Garden.

The defining quality of Sissinghurst Castle in Kent is its sheer romance, with its fairy-tale Elizabethan tower, its fulsome planting and everywhere tangles of gorgeous old roses. It has become England's best-loved garden.

I am trying to make a grey, green and white garden. This is an experiment which I ardently hope may be successful, though I doubt it … I cannot help hoping that the great ghostly barn owl will sweep silently across a pale garden, next summer, in the twilight – the pale garden that I am now planting, under the first flakes of snow.

No garden, before or since, has ever been so widely copied: there are White Gardens today on every continent.

Vita was full of admiration for Lawrence Johnston, in awe of both his use of hedges to create a feeling of secrecy, and his abundant, naturalistic planting: 'a kind of haphazard luxuriance, which of course comes neither by hap nor hazard at all'. This she tried to reproduce at Sissinghurst. It was largely down to her that Hidcote was acquired by the National Trust, yet she would not hear of doing likewise. 'Never, never, never,' she stormed, ten years before she died. 'Not that hard little metal plaque at my door … as long as I live no Nat. Trust or any other foreign body shall have my darling. No, no.' Sissinghurst was transferred to the Trust five years after her death and rapidly became its most popular garden.

Vita and Harold outside the South Cottage, which housed their bedroom and a study for Harold. The Priest's House across the garden provided a bedroom for their two sons and a kitchen and dining room, while Vita wrote in the tower.

Machines for living

At the same time as Vita and Harold started digging through the old bedsteads and general detritus surrounding Sissinghurst, a few brave souls were attempting to introduce a very different vision of house and garden. Throughout the 1920s and '30s, a handful of radical architects were briefly active in the Home Counties, building country houses in the International Modern style – houses characterised by asymmetry, plain flat surfaces unrelieved by decoration (often rendered white), and huge picture windows, designed to frame the view and forge a sense of connection between inside and out. There was no consensus over what the garden of such a house should be like. At Joldwynds in Surrey, in 1925, both house and

Simple, sculptural planting at The Homewood in Surrey, where the garden takes its cue from the surrounding woods and heathland.

garden were designed for sun-bathing, but the house proved so uncomfortable, it was soon pulled down. At High and Over in Buckinghamshire (which still survives) the geometry of the house was set off by formal triangular rose beds and a circular swimming pool. Most often the houses floated like white liners among a sprinkling of silver birches. In France, the granddaddy of Modernism, Le Corbusier, designed his Villa Savoye floating on legs over an Arcadian pasture. Not being a gardener, he imagined the benefits of fresh air, views and sunshine, without the bother of maintenance.

This villa was the primary influence for The Homewood, built in Surrey by Patrick Gwynne in 1938. Gwynne had built the house for his parents, knocking down their original house but retaining the woodland garden that surrounded it. Over time he began to blur the distinction between the garden and the neighbouring heathland and to introduce new features such as reflecting pools and heather banks, but the garden still retains elements of the Modernist garden, as defined by Britain's leading practitioner, Christopher Tunnard. Tunnard believed that the purpose of the modern garden was to provide rest, recreation and beauty. Anything further was spurious, and should be eliminated. There was much to be learned from Japanese gardens, from their asymmetry and sense of spaciousness. (The Homewood went a step further in enthusiastic use of Japanese plants, with numerous acers and azaleas.) Beauty could be added by framing a view, or by introducing works of art. His most successful garden, Bentley Wood in East Sussex (1934–8), combined both: a figure by Henry Moore lay to one side of a huge, house-height frame, enclosing a view of the South Downs. Similarly, at The Homewood, the garden is laid out to offer pleasing prospects from the picture windows, with two large sculptures at focal points. The house stands on stilts, echoed in the pillars of tree trunks, and a small formal terrace merges into a wild garden of birch, pine and weeping willow. There is also a notably late-century feature: the patio with built-in barbecue.

Modernists like Gwynne sought to lose the separation between inside and outside.

Gardens for people

The mantra of the Modernists was that gardens should fulfil the needs of the people who used them. Following the war, more new gardens were made, for more people, than ever before. David Lloyd George had promised 'homes fit for heroes': men who had survived the horrors of the trenches could scarcely be expected to return to Victorian slums. And so between 1919 and 1939 nearly 4 million homes were built in England and Wales, amounting to one-third of the country's total housing stock. A million of these were rented to ordinary working families, who now experienced the luxury of their own garden (and an indoor lavatory) for the very first time. The London County Council, in particular, built huge estates on the fringes of the city, following the model of the pre-war Garden Cities with just 12 houses to the acre. (Except for a few brief years after the Second World War, no housing has been built at such low density before or since.) The largest was the Becontree Estate in Dagenham: 300 acres (121ha) of land, generously provided with parks and green spaces, offering 27,000 houses all with front and back gardens.

Further homes were built by the fast-expanding underground rail companies: now people no longer lived where they worked, it was necessary to commute. The Metropolitan Railway built ten sprawling estates along their new line to Uxbridge and Amersham, promising commuters a semi-rural idyll among open fields and wild flowers. The chosen style of 'Metro-land' harked back to the Arts and Crafts: mock-Tudor dwellings with more than a whiff of Helen Allingham. These sturdy semi-detached houses, with their steep roofs and half-timbered gables, naturally called for cottage gardens. With the help of penny seeds and sixpenny roses from Woolworth's, and a reassuring word from that nice Mr Middleton on the wireless, anyone and everyone could be a gardener now.

Metro-land offered an escape from the city to a suburban Arcadia offering a front and back garden.

METRO-LAND

PRICE TWO-PENCE

THE ROSE GARDEN

According to rose lore, the first garden devoted entirely to roses was made by the Empress Joséphine at Malmaison, where she grew every rose known to man. This is not, alas, true – though she certainly had many, many roses scattered across her estate. The Germans had got there first.

The first dedicated rose gardens in England were probably designed by Humphry Repton, as early as 1800. His Red Book for Ashridge shows an especially ambitious 'rosary' with ten beds radiating from a central fountain like the petals of a daisy, surrounded by trellis panels, arches and hoops, all liberally festooned with pink roses. It involved a good deal of artistic licence, as the roses required to realise this plan did not then exist. Nonetheless, it spawned a fashion for circular rose gardens that persisted for over a hundred years. There are versions at Wightwick Manor, where roses grow along chains to a central seat; at Peckover House, where a typically Victorian layout is planted up with Victorian and Edwardian favourites; and in the 1902s rose garden at Nymans. A stupendous modern variant is the Rose Labyrinth at Coughton Court in Warwickshire, planted with over 200 varieties and honoured by the World Federation of Rose Societies as one of the very best rose gardens in the world.

For centuries, roses flowered just once in the season for a few magical weeks, so it made sense to group them together, concealed behind walls or hedges, where they need not be seen outside their season of glory. Then, in the 1750s, the first handful of perpetual-flowering roses arrived from China, bringing with them not only this game-changing mutation, but bright, shiny foliage and exciting new colours (pure reds and yellows) outside the white-to-pink-to-crimson spectrum known to date. These would be the ancestors of both repeat-flowering Old Roses and Modern Roses. The first Hybrid Perpetuals (a misleading description) appeared in the 1830s, the first Hybrid Tea in 1867. (Roses are broadly divided into Old Roses known before that date, and Modern Roses introduced thereafter.) The first standards arrived from France in 1818: J. C. Loudon decreed that a 160ft (48.8m) suburban garden should include at least sixteen, plus up to 96 bush roses and a further 80 varieties trained on trellis.

Gertrude Jekyll was another who liked to see a garden amply stocked with roses, clambering up pillars, scrambling into trees and sprawling over pergolas, a situation that suited ramblers, in particular, very well. Rose-covered pergolas rapidly became a fixture in the Edwardian garden. If you must have a garden reserved for roses, said Jekyll, it should be a surprise, 'embowered in native woodland'. This was attempted by Geoffrey Jellicoe at Cliveden, where a rose garden was laid out in the midst of a wood in an amoebic shape inspired by the paintings of Paul Klee, the colour shading dramatically from red to yellow across the garden. The original 1960s plantings proved unequal to the shade and were later dug up, but the garden has recently been restored.

By the 1950s the Hybrid Tea was king, and no suburban garden was complete without a row of bony bushes lined up along the path. By far the most popular was 'Peace', introduced to Britain by the irrepressible Harry Wheatcroft, famed for his loud clothes, mutton-chop whiskers and

Clockwise from top left: Repton's circular 'rosary' provided a template for rose gardens for the next 100 years. Rose-covered pergolas rapidly became a fixture in the Edwardian garden – most resplendently at Polesden Lacey in Surrey, where society hostess Mrs Ronnie Greville converted a former kitchen garden into the most romantic of rose gardens. *Rosa* Graham Thomas, who installed his collection of old roses at Mottisfont Abbey in Hampshire.

Communist sympathies. This rose came out in Europe during the war years in three countries under three different names, but hit the jackpot when it was launched in America as 'Peace' on the day that Berlin fell in 1945. By this time the old shrub roses had all but vanished from English nurseries – yet some clung stubbornly to the romance of old roses, notably Vita Sackville-West at Sissinghurst and Graham Stuart Thomas, who installed his peerless collection of pre-1900 shrub roses at Mottisfont Abbey in Hampshire (now a National Collection), underplanting with swathes of perennials to create one of the most ravishing spectacles in the English garden.

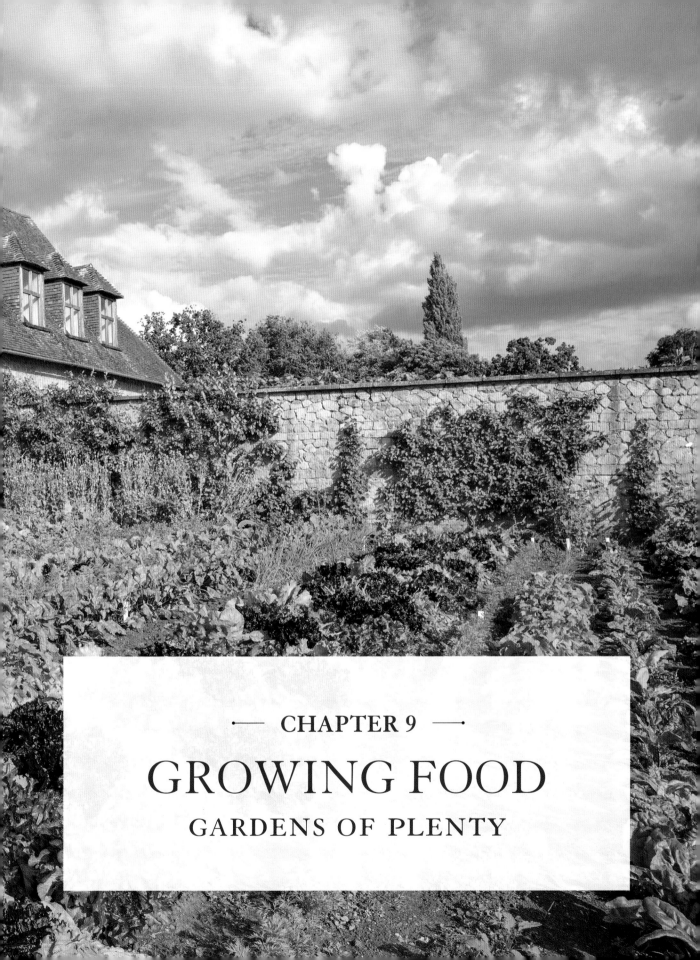

— CHAPTER 9 —

GROWING FOOD

GARDENS OF PLENTY

'Have millons at Mihelmas, parsneps in Lent;
In June, buttred beans, saveth fish to be spent.'

THOMAS TUSSER, *FIVE HUNDREDTH POINTS OF GOOD HUSBANDRIE* (1573)

S O far, we have explored mainly ornamental gardening, but of course, for the vast majority of people, gardens were primarily for food rather than flowers. The Romans introduced to a dull island diet of sea kale, beans and wild carrots the unimaginable luxury of figs and walnuts, mulberries and medlars, parsley, beetroots and peas. Less happily, they also brought a popular salad vegetable, ground elder, and a small meaty snack, the rabbit. Many of their vegetables were lost when the Roman Empire fell, to be slowly reintroduced over succeeding centuries, first to the gardens of the rich, then to the subsistence plots of the poor.

By Tudor times, the growing of herbs and vegetables was considered the province of the housewife – despite a widespread belief that even a glance from a menstruating woman would cause gourds and cucumbers to wither and die. A well-stocked garden, advised Thomas Tusser in 1573, was the sure-fire way to the heart of the labouring man. Growing fruit, however was man's work, and gardeners both humble and great took enormous pride in their orchards. For the eleven years that Catholic protester Thomas Tresham was in and out of prison, nothing seems to have worried him more than the state of his fruit. Four years after his death, his widow found it politic to sell off his precious trees to the all-powerful Robert Cecil.

During the Commonwealth, fruit offered spiritual as well as physical nourishment. Herefordshire grower John Beale, believing the Day of Judgement was nigh, wrote on 'how to plant an orchard that may last till the world's end'. In France, by contrast, growing fruit was a high-fashion art form, and the Sun King himself would lead his guests round his potager, admiring the apples, pears and peach trees trained into columns and fans, arches and crowns, goblets, tridents and boats. Sophisticated pruning techniques came back to England with the Restoration, although generally simpler forms such as espaliers, cordons and fans were preferred. Fruit became an important decorative feature in the seventeenth-century garden, trained on walls or flanking paths with espaliers of pears and apples. Vegetables, too, were planted in formal patterns of beds, edged with box, hyssop or lavender, often with a row of strawberries or gillyflowers behind: even an unostentatious gentleman's kitchen garden, such as that recreated at Packwood, could be highly decorative.

It was during the seventeenth century that it became customary to separate the kitchen garden from the ornamental or 'best' garden – sometimes as a distinct part of the walled garden, as at Canons Ashby, but increasingly in its own walled area. There was a keen appetite for new crops, such as cauliflowers, first grown in England in the 1590s, and broccoli, which arrived in the late seventeenth century. Tomatoes and potatoes were still a novelty; carrots were generally purple or white (the first orange ones were just coming in from Holland); radishes were grown for their pods rather than their roots. Artichokes were so highly prized they were often given their own walled garden – which of course created space for more fruit. Walls became

steadily higher, allowing a greater range of fruit to be tried – apricots and peaches on south-facing walls, morello cherries on north-facing ones, as well as apples, pears, plums and sweet cherries.

More exotic fruits were tried too. Oranges had been grown in England since Elizabethan times: Robert Cecil built a shelter for his oranges, lemons and pomegranates as early as 1562, and by the seventeenth century, elegant orangeries were overwintering the pots of oranges and lemons that were a standard feature in the formal garden. Oranges were more than merely decorative, however – they were thought to ward off the plague.

Peaches at Barrington Court in Somerset. Peaches were grown from the seventeenth century, and by the 1750s no gentleman would be 'without his peaches and nectarines'.

These orangeries were warmed by pans of burning charcoal, but other crops were raised with the heat of fermenting dung – 'hot-beds' proved an excellent technique for growing melons. But the piles of fresh manure detracted from the beauty of the garden, so by mid-century the 'melon ground' occupied a space of its own. As time went on, gardeners became increasingly adventurous: in 1767 a visitor to Gawthorpe Hall in Lancashire reported that the bananas were disappointing, but that passion fruit was produced 'in high perfection', along with aubergines, figs and sugar cane. But the ultimate test of the gardener's skill was the pineapple – cosseted in its own 'Pinery' at vast expense, but so desirable that the ambitious hostess could rent them for her dinner table. The fruits were grown in pots, sunk into troughs of fermenting bark, with hot water pipes running beneath for bottom heat. Further heat came from manure pits on either side. Not any old manure would do, but horse manure with plenty of well-soaked straw to work up a good heat – the test was whether it was hot enough to cook a carrot. A painting hanging at Ham House shows Charles II being presented with a pineapple, probably imported from the West Indies, in around 1677. (Sailors at this time would celebrate their safe return from the tropics by hanging a pineapple on their front door.) What is certain is that it was not grown by his Head Gardener, John Rose, also in the picture: the first pineapples did not fruit in England for another 40 years.

During the eighteenth century, gardeners who no longer had formal gardens to maintain had more time to spend on fruit and vegetables, and this was the time that the first great walled gardens began to be built, such as Blenheim and Beningbrough in Yorkshire. These were now placed at some distance from the house, ideally on an open, southerly slope. They were usually near-rectangular (the

Above left: There are several versions of this painting, which may have been commissioned by George London to honour John Rose, who died in 1677. The first pineapple was not raised in Britain until around 1715, in Sir Matthew Decker's garden in Richmond.

southerly wall a bit longer than the northerly one), with the longest walls running east–west to make the best of the sun. The growing space was divided into four 'quarters' with a dipping pond at the centre, with perennial crops like rhubarb and asparagus generally grown in beds round the perimeter walls. Vines were widely grown, great strides were made in the breeding of apples and pears (the apples Blenheim Orange, Ribston Pippin and the pear 'Williams' Bon Chrétien' all date from this period), and gardeners employed increasing ingenuity in cheating the seasons. This was not new – when Elizabeth I visited Sir Francis Carew, he was able to present her with fresh cherries well over a month 'after all cherries had taken their farewell of England.' (He had kept his cherry tree for months in a cool, wet tent.) But now it became an art. From around 1750, fruit was grown on hollow walls, heated by internal pipes and flues: at Tatton Park, the Greek urns ranged on top of the wall are actually disguising chimney pots. After brick tax was introduced in 1784, 'crinkle-crankle' walls, built just one brick thick, were briefly popular, the curves helping to hold the heat. Walls were fitted with blinds and shutters, to be lowered at the first hint of frost. Hot-beds became increasingly sophisticated, forcing sea kale, rhubarb and new potatoes and growing strawberries, asparagus, beans and peas out of season.

The place to see all the latest technology, from 1805, was Thomas Anson's great walled garden at Shugborough, hailed as 'a kind of Academy for the study of Horticulture, in which young men enter themselves to assist without pay, for the purpose of improving themselves and gaining knowledge in the art'. There was a hot wall, 'well-stocked with the choicest fruit-trees' and 'very extensive ranges of hot-houses, in which the pineapple, the grape, the peach, the fig, and other varieties

The one-and-a-half-acre walled garden at Beningborough in Yorkshire boasted cutting-edge technology. Fireplaces set in the other side of the wall powered hot-air flues to heat the walls, and Britain's first (and only remaining) coal-fired propagation bench

of hot-house fruits, flowers and plants are cultivated in the highest of protection. One of the hot houses is heated with steam, in which melons and cucumbers are produced in perfection at all seasons'. This perfection came at a cost. The Head Gardener's house was conveniently situated between the hothouses, and during the day, all the smoke from their boilers was channelled into the upstairs bedrooms, to be released at night when it would not disturb Lord Anson. What Mr Nicol, the Head Gardener, made of it is not recorded …

In the days before supermarkets, every country estate aimed to be, as far as possible, self-sufficient, feeding not only the family but a substantial household of indoor servants. (Estate workers were expected to feed themselves from their cottage gardens.) One acre of intensively cropped kitchen garden was reckoned to feed about a dozen, so smaller families would generally require a plot of one to one and a half acres (0.4–0.6ha); a larger family around 5 acres (2ha), while a large aristocratic establishment might command as much as 25 acres (10.1ha). Even then, the bulk of the fruit trees would be grown in separate orchards, and potatoes, cabbages and roots out in the fields. Once glass tax was repealed in 1845, followed by brick tax the following year, there was no holding back the army of enterprising

Growing citrus fruit had been a status symbol since the Renaissance, but in the nineteenth century perfect grapes vied with pineapples as the high point of the table.

gardeners. Specialised glasshouses were built for cucumbers, peaches, pineapples and vines (the vines liked to have their feet outside), while a vast range of produce was grown under glass to be ready long before or after its normal season: our ingenious forebears thought nothing of producing asparagus in February, or bringing cherries to the Christmas table. The season was further extended by the skilful use of early and late varieties: by the turn of the century, gardeners could call on over 1,400 different sorts of apples, 140 varieties of peaches and nectarines, about 100 kinds of plums and over 40 varieties of cherry. Every vegetable we know today was grown – and many we have since forgotten, such as rocambole (a kind of garlic), or couve tronchuda (Portugal cabbage), along with purple and green striped carrots, prickly cucumbers and the blue coco bean.

Some of this was sheer one-upmanship. The house party at the country estate played a crucial role in Victorian and Edwardian society, and to offer your guests delicacies that no one else could lay their hands on was a clear way of demonstrating your social superiority. Fruit had particular cachet: the climax of the meal was the 'dessert' – not a pudding, but a spectacular display of fruit arranged with all the sumptuousness of a Dutch old master painting. So a head gardener

A magnificent display of fresh fruit demonstrated both the skill of the gardener and the largesse of the host – the more expensive and exclusive the better. Bone-bladed knives would be supplied lest the fruit be tainted by metal, and the finest dessert wines would be served.

who could deliver a reliable supply of fragrant pineapples, and grapes and peaches with perfect bloom, was key to his employer's social standing. He would also have to produce the flowers on the table, the floral decorations for the house and a parade of exotics to fill the conservatories that became fashionable from the 1850s onwards. And he would often have not just one, but several houses to keep supplied with produce, which would be packed up in baskets and sent up to London on the train. To add to his burdens, the kitchen garden must at all times be immaculate, for the high sheltering walls and heated glasshouses made it a popular place for guests to visit, especially when the weather turned chilly. Knightshayes in Devon is typically designed as a show garden, with its broad flower-lined paths, its fairy-tale turrets and handsome stepped walls.

The other side of the wall

The sunless frame yard on the other side of the wall, however, was not a thing of beauty. Here were the smelly hot-beds and dank mushroom house, the sheds and boiler rooms where the gardeners worked. This is where plants were propagated, composts and chemical potions were mixed (ready-made mixtures arrived only in the 1940s) and where fruit and vegetables were carefully stored for the winter. Here too were the bothies where most of the gardeners lived, working 12-hour days, six days a week, and often at nights too – someone always had to stoke the glasshouse boilers to keep them going through the night. Teams were large and there was a strict hierarchy: 'indoor' men were considered superior to 'outdoor' men who worked the 'quarters' of open ground. The lowest life form, lower even

Opposite: The kitchen garden was just as much a showpiece as any other part of the grounds. The garden at Knightshayes in Devon was designed of a piece with the house, with turrets and stepped stone walls in similar baronial style.

Left: The gardener's bothy at Calke Abbey in Derbyshire offered unusually light and spacious working conditions – and even a grandfather clock to tell the time.

than the garden boy who washed the pots, was the weeding woman brought in to clean the beds and gravel paths.

When the men marched off to war in 1914, many of these great walled gardens fell rapidly into decline. With neither the manpower nor the fuel to keep glasshouses going, the carefully nurtured plants soon died. Even Paxton's legendary Great Stove at Chatsworth became a graveyard: in 1920 it was blown up.

The first allotments

The combined effect of industrialisation, enclosure, rapid population growth and agricultural reform was to leave a significant part of England's rural population without any means of feeding itself. The first allotments as we would know them were set up in the 1790s, as unemployment, starvation wages, widespread food shortages and a succession of disastrous harvests brought rural society to its knees. The movement gathered force in the 1830s, after agricultural workers rose in protest and broke up the threshing machines that were stealing their jobs. A third wave followed in the 1870s, less concerned with saving families from starvation (though they certainly did that) than moral improvement: keeping men busy kept them out of the alehouse. It was not until 1908 that local authorities were legally obliged to provide land for allotments. But with the outbreak of war, the 1914 Defence of the Realm Act forced landowners to hand over land for growing food. In just four years, over the course of the war, the number of allotments trebled to over 1,400,000.

Allotments assumed national importance during the two world wars. Here, in June 1940, a gardener tends a plot made in the moat of the Tower of London. It was by no means the most unusual site: in London alone there were vegetables growing on the rugby pitch at Twickenham, at the Hurlingham Polo Club and round the Albert Memorial. Even the bomb-damaged roof of Selfridges was turned into a makeshift allotment.

The First World War

Once the war was underway even the King dutifully tended his allotment: potatoes and cabbages replaced the geraniums in the Royal Parks, and even the glasshouse parterres at Kew were all laid down to onions. Prior to the war, England produced only one-fifth of her own food supply, and as the blockades cut off the supply of food from overseas, the shortfall had to be made up somehow. Food was grown on railway embankments and building lots, in parks and palaces – efficiency rather than luxury was now the order of the day.

Social historians have tended to suggest that the great Edwardian flowering of British horticulture, embodied by the estate garden, perished on Flanders fields. Certainly things changed in the aftermath of war. Fuel and labour costs rose, and after 1918 the working week was reduced from 56 to 48 hours. Conservatories went out of fashion – the vogue now was all for fresh air. Post-war, it became possible to buy imported grapes or pineapples of decent quality, so it was no longer worth keeping all those expensive glasshouses going. Nonetheless, many gardens, such as Knightshayes in Devon, soon returned to full production and gardening manuals published in the mid-1920s describe as great a range of vegetables as ever – many more than now.

Officials hoped that gardens and allotments would produce as much as a quarter of non-cereal supplies, and exhorted every citizen to pick up his – or more likely her – spade.

Digging for Victory

In 1939, once again, reliance on cheap food imports left Britain ill prepared for war. Anxious to avoid the shortage of food and medicinal herbs of the 1914–18 conflict, the Ministry of Agriculture sprang into action and the Dig for Victory campaign was born. Nothing was left to chance. Little pamphlets were published showing novice gardeners exactly how to hold a spade, or dig a trench, or sow a seed. There were detailed cropping plans, and tables of the most productive veg. '*Tomato Growing is not Difficult*,' proclaimed one Ministry leaflet encouragingly, while *Root Vegetables for the Small Grower* suggested feeding the freshly squeezed juice from raw swedes to luckless infants in place of orange juice. Advice was dispensed in magazines, on posters, in training films, even on cigarette cards. Growing food became a patriotic duty, the number of allotments almost doubled, and by the end of the war, Britain was feeding more people in proportion to the area of its own soil than any other country in the world.

Your own vegetables all the year round... if you DIG FOR VICTORY NOW

The post-war years

The end of the war left Britain exhausted and impoverished. The Ministry of Agriculture turned its attention to new forms of intensive agriculture, increasingly mechanised and dependent on heavy use of chemicals. This inevitably spilled over into domestic growing, and now notorious pesticides such as Lindane, Captan and DDT found their way into the garden. Rationing continued until 1954, so growing your own remained popular until well into the 1950s. But in 1951, the Festival of Britain seemed to open the door to a different way of living – to a new, labour-saving world of hoovers and refrigerators, wipe-clean Formica and drip-dry Terylene. In came Britain's first supermarkets (Tesco had 35 self-service stores by May 1951) and with them, the first convenience foods. Who would spend long hours labouring over a veg plot when you could have quick, cheap and hygienic frozen peas? The same applied to the estate gardens, where self-sufficiency no longer made economic sense. Walled gardens were turned over to Christmas tree plantations, allotments were built over, and back gardens became 'outdoor rooms'.

The revival

It took decades for the tide to turn. But towards the end of the twentieth century, growing food made a comeback. In 1962, Rachel Carson published *Silent Spring*, and its horrifying account of the effects of DDT on the environment prompted people to start asking what was in their food. This gave a boost to the organic movement, to organisations like the Soil Association and HDRA (now known as Garden Organic) that promoted chemical-free growing. In the 1970s, this

At West Dean in West Sussex, from 1991, Jim Buckland and Sarah Wain brought 16 derelict Victorian glasshouses back to vibrant life.

became conflated with the idea of self-sufficiency, as the manuals of John Seymour showed idealistic townies exactly how to decamp to the countryside and pursue 'The Good Life', undeterred by the popular TV sitcom of that name.

Another TV programme was to prove influential: in 1987 *The Victorian Kitchen Garden* showed the restoration of a run-down walled garden in Wiltshire. This inspired gardeners Jim Buckland and Sarah Wain to restore the crumbling glasshouses at West Dean in West Sussex, reintroducing a beautiful and rigorous regime of kitchen gardening any Victorian head gardener would have been proud of. Meanwhile, salad pioneer Joy Larkcom reminded people just how many delicious vegetables had been forgotten, or remained to be discovered, while garden designer Rosemary Verey, in her photogenic potager at Barnsley House, showed that vegetables could be decorative as well as nutritious. After Verey helped the Prince of Wales to redesign the kitchen garden at Highgrove, the potager became the very height of fashion. The National Trust, which for years had used its kitchen gardens as car parks, began to think how they might be more productively used. At Llanerchaeron, in Wales, volunteers led the way, spending every Thursday for ten years slowly recovering the productive garden, which finally opened to the public in 2002. Restorations commenced at Beningborough and Tatton Park. Experiments began with Victorian methods of growing – although not with the pest controls routinely used in Victorian gardens, which included tobacco smoke, sulphuric acid, phosphorous paste and arsenic. At the time of writing, over 30 of the Trust's 145 kitchen gardens are back in full production, and at Attingham Park and Calke Abbey, Knightshayes and Barrington Court, you can see – and taste – the astonishing range of produce that was once grown in these gardens – heritage rhubarb, rare local apples, icicle radishes or zebra-striped tomatoes.

The health and taste benefits of growing your own have been eagerly seized on in recent years, bringing many long-abandoned kitchen gardens back into use.

SCULPTURE IN THE GARDEN

THE sixteenth century went for heraldic animals, the seventeenth for classical figures, led by the Earl of Arundel, first of the great English art collectors, who made England's earliest sculpture garden to show off his treasures from Italy. (Three centuries later, Lord Fairhaven did much the same at Anglesey Abbey.) Towards the end of the century, garden sculpture became more light-hearted, including Harlequins and Columbines, cheeky cherubs and rustic maids and shepherds, and in one case an alarmingly lifelike gamekeeper about to take a pot-shot at a guest. London and Wise, who had a virtual monopoly of the formal garden, promoted the wares of Jan van Nost, a celebrated Flemish sculptor who had set up shop in London, providing lead vases, baskets of flowers, Cupids and sundry mythological figures. The charming flute-playing boy at Canons Ashby is his work.

In the eighteenth century, a smattering of classical statuary cemented your credentials as a Person of Taste. Sculpture was also used to send coded messages, often of great complexity, and there were strict rules governing its use: heaven forfend there should be 'impropriety in the Gesture and Habiliments' of garden gods.

At the end of the century, Eleanor Coade invented an artificial stone that could be cast rather than carved, making sculpture far more cheaply and more widely available. When she died in 1829, her recipe died with her, but sculptor Stephen Pettifer believes he has recreated her technique, and Coade stone

ornaments are making a comeback, as in the recent restoration of the Temperate House at Kew.

All kinds of famous people are remembered in gardens, from Leonard and Virginia Woolf to Winston Churchill and Prince Albert, as indeed are animals: at Shugborough, the Cat's Monument honours a globe-trotting moggy who sailed round the world with Admiral George Anson – or possibly his brother's pampered Persian, 'Kouli-khan'. Gardens abound with figures of animals, but none more intriguing than the pair of granite baboons at Cliveden, representations of the Ancient Egyptian god Thoth and believed to be over 2,000 years old.

Sculpture can be profoundly moving in the garden, as Ben Nicholson's white wall at Sutton Place, seeming to float on its reflecting pool, or Rosie Musgrave's carved boat at Coughton Court, which honours the dead of the 2004 Boxing Day tsunami. Some of the most beautiful sculpture in the modern garden has been made by William Pye, who works with water and reflective surfaces to produce astonishing effects. At Antony in Cornwall, a gleaming cone echoes the shape of the topiary in the garden, while at Woolbeding in West Sussex, a glistening chalice of steel commemorates a much-loved Cedar of Lebanon. Another doomed tree, a dying standing oak, provided material for David Nash at Kew in 2013, carved in situ over a year-long exhibition. The forms of nature also inspire Peter Randall Page, whose work can be seen both in gardens and in the wild.

Clockwise from top left: William Pye's water sculpture 'Cedra' at Woolbeding in West Sussex commemorates a grand old cedar tree that fell in a storm. An ancient Egyptian baboon god at Cliveden, Berkshire. Slate sculpture by Richard Long, at Ascott in Buckinghamshire. Corten steel bull at Buckland Abbey, Devon. A monument to the victims of the 2014 Boxing Day tsunami, at Coughton Court, Warwickshire. The charming flute boy at Canons Ashby in Northamptonshire.

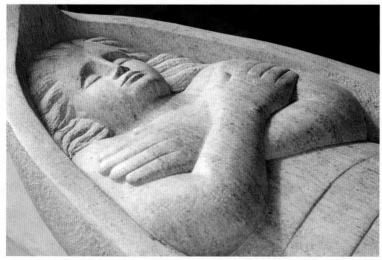

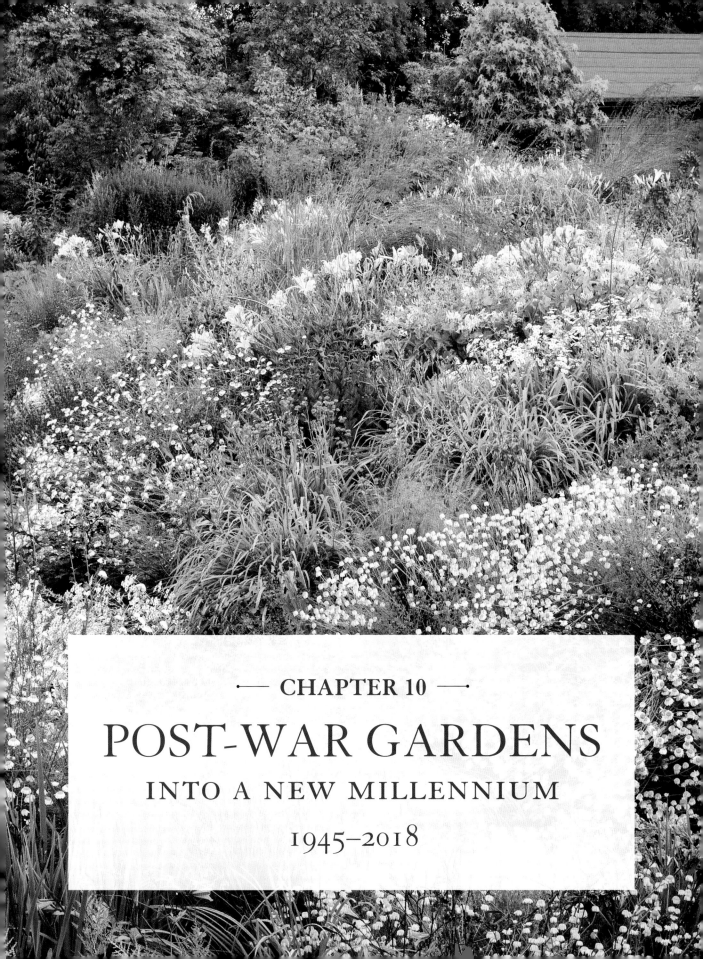

CHAPTER 10

POST-WAR GARDENS

INTO A NEW MILLENNIUM

1945–2018

'The new kind of garden is still supposed to be looked at. But that is no longer its only function. It is designed primarily for living, as an adjunct to the function of house.'

THOMAS CHURCH, *GARDENS ARE FOR PEOPLE* (1955)

Victorious Britain in 1945 was wan, battered and completely broke. Gardens and nurseries, with all their precious stock, had been destroyed by the need to grow food. The great country house, which for centuries had led the way in gardening, was done for: impoverished families, handed back the wreckage of requisitioned houses, lacked the funds or the will to repair them. By 1955, one country house was demolished every ten days. In times of acute austerity, garden-making wasn't high on the agenda, so designers turned their attention to the public sphere and the idealistic task of national renewal. Designers such as Brenda Colvin, Sylvia Crowe, Frederick Gibberd and Geoffrey Jellicoe all became deeply involved with the New Towns, battling to establish landscape values in the architect-led new 'science' of town planning. Crowe, in particular, worked on colossal public schemes, trying to integrate into the landscape buildings far larger than had ever preciously existed – power stations, factories, huge mineral workings – along with new reservoirs and vast tracts of conifer forest.

When the bombed-out families of the inner cities were eventually rehoused in Bracknell or Hemel Hempstead, in Peterlee or East Kilbride, they chose to garden in an entirely new way. The turning point was the Festival of Britain, devised in 1951 as a 'tonic to the nation'. Out went drab drudgery and 'make do and mend': in came everything labour-saving, bright and 'gay' (a very Fifties word). In came low-maintenance flowering shrubs and vast hybrid tea roses, with an arsenal of fearsome garden chemicals on hand to service them. In came practical weed-free concrete – in crazy paving, patios and planters – such a hit in the Festival of Britain's self-consciously 'modern' gardens on London's South Bank. Snazzy new gadgets like electric hedge-trimmers promised to make light of garden work. After long years of toil, the garden would be henceforth a place of leisure.

Television had helped to spark a fundamental shift in the leisure activities of working people

The mid-century garden was to be a place of leisure rather than labour, with the help of new materials, new tools and new chemical herbicides and pesticides, including the notoriously toxic DDT.

Water gardens and fountains, a tree walk, funfair, puppet shows and a performing clock were just some of the attractions of the Festival Gardens in Battersea Park, a short boat ride from the main Festival site.

from being mainly communal (football, the park and the pub) to being centred on home and family. The garden was key to this, and the new mood was caught exactly by John Brookes in his 1969 book *Room Outside*. Various European Modernists who had fled the Nazis had resettled in California, and from here in the 1950s emerged the idea of the garden as an informal outdoor living room. This concept, best expressed by Thomas Church, was reintroduced (it was scarcely new) to Britain by Brookes, and has become more or less scripture. What Brookes also suggested was that anyone could design their own garden – initiating an enthusiasm for garden makeovers that reached a peak around the turn of the century.

'Concrete is perhaps the most useful of all materials in a small garden,' enthused garden sage Richard Sudell in *The Labour Saving Garden* in 1952. Busy in her farmhouse garden in Somerset, Margery Fish did not agree. Indeed, she went to far as to take a crowbar to the concrete paving her husband had laid, in order to create comfortable niches for thymes and other creeping plants. Margery was a Fleet Street secretary who had married her boss, Walter Fish, in her forties. A gardening novice when the couple bought East Lambrook just before the war, she rapidly fell in love with plants, especially old-fashioned cottage-garden

At a time when it was usual to arrange plants in tidy rows with plenty of bare earth in between, Margery Fish covered the ground with mat-forming plants with handsome foliage. 'There is no bare soil in the wild; it is only man who keeps scratching away to keep clean the naked soil he has produced artificially,' she wrote in *Ground Cover Plants* in 1964, arguing that clothing the ground made life easier for both plants and gardener.

plants, and out of love with her husband's very regimented, Victorian style of gardening, provoking a horticultural war of attrition that lasted until his death in 1947. It is hard to exaggerate her importance – as a popular garden writer; for rediscovering so many easy, understated plants so long neglected they were in danger of being lost; and later, following an eye-opening trip to the United States, as a pioneer of ground-cover planting. Anyone could learn to garden, she insisted, and anyone could make a relaxed, informal garden that they could manage themselves. She showed that there was a delightful, dynamic alternative to the dreary plantings of heather and dwarf conifer recommended for easy-care gardening in the 1960s; she sang the praises of snowdrops and hellebores, hardy geraniums and grasses, and handsome shade-lovers like pulmonarias and ferns. Today's pretty, flowery, mussed-up-round-the-edges version of the cottage garden owes its enduring popularity to Margery Fish.

Plants remained the focus throughout the 1960s and '70s, aided by the rise of the garden centre (the first had appeared in the mid-1950s) offering containerised plants: for the first time instant gratification was available to gardeners. During the 1970s, Adrian Bloom revived island beds to show off his brightly coloured conifers, provoking a rash of amoebic blobs cut out of lawns in a thoroughly Victorian manner. (Strips of red, white and blue bedding plants, rockeries and spotty laurel

remained as popular as ever.) And in 1975, an Essex farmer's wife called Beth Chatto took her first stand at an RHS show.

Beth's husband had studied plant ecology, and when they built a new house on a somewhat intractable piece of waste ground, they turned to his research to plant up their new garden, choosing plants that would succeed in the various challenging conditions that faced them. Beth was an expert flower arranger (a skill highly regarded mid-century, made popular by the doughty Constance Spry) and her exquisite eye for selecting and combining plants made her an outstanding nurserywoman. Her first book, *The Dry Garden*, was published in 1978: her part of Essex has lower annual rainfall than parts of Greece. Four years later she published *The Damp Garden*, dealing with boggy conditions. In 2000 came *The Gravel*

Left: Beth Chatto's Gravel Garden was a game-changer, freeing gardeners from Arts and Crafts convention and showing them how to adapt to a changing climate.

Below: Chatto introduced many superlative plants to a wider public, through her legendary stands at the Chelsea Flower Show during the 1970s and 1980s.

Garden, explaining how she turned an old car park into a groundbreaking garden planted with drought-tolerant species that were never watered. Her triumphant demonstration that selecting plants by reference to their natural habitats might be a guiding light rather than a limitation in the garden has had a profound influence over the last half-century, preparing the ground for the ecological movement of the 1990s. At the same time, another great plantsman, her friend Christopher Lloyd, was throwing out the rule book at Great Dixter, combining plants in radical and exciting new ways. Keith Wiley, meanwhile, was making innovative naturalistic plantings, most memorably of South African species, at The Garden House on the fringes of Dartmoor. In 2004 he started work on his own garden, Wildside, embracing naturalistic plantings in thrilling variety, and on an awe-inspiring scale. 'By allowing our observations of natural landscapes to inform our plantings,' he writes, 'I believe that we can loosen the straitjacket that long-established

In her Essex garden, Beth Chatto turned a boggy meadow into a spectacular garden, mixing natives with exotic foliage plants, and shared what she had learned in *The Damp Garden*, now a gardening classic.

horticultural practices impose, allowing the enormous creative potential, latent within most of us, the freedom to express itself.'

It was the new economic climate of the 1980s that ushered in a change in gardening. The age of civic idealism had melted away with hippy flower power: there was now little political interest in public works. The council parks departments that had nurtured great gardeners such as Roy Lancaster were stripped of funding, parks became increasingly degraded, and gardening deskilled. National Trust gardens began to take their place as venues for horticultural display and family recreation. Those still in possession of historic houses and gardens took note and, aided by new Lottery funding, sought to emulate their success. At the same time, favourable tax rates left the wealthy with a good deal more money to spend on gardens. By the 1990s, gardening was deemed to be the 'new rock and roll'.

Though bog gardening is far from easy, 'when it is successful I think it is possibly one of the most beautiful forms of gardening', wrote Chatto. Keith Wiley's stream garden at Wildside in Devon bears this out.

Playing with the past

While the small suburban garden willingly embraced each new trend, from monstrous hybrid begonias in the 1950s to millennial tree ferns and decking, it took a long time for larger gardens to escape the Arts and Crafts ethos, not least because the template was so successful. Also, people had begun to take an interest in the history of plants and gardens: the Garden History Society (now the Gardens Trust) was established in 1965, the Garden Museum in 1977, and in 1983 English Heritage began listing gardens of historic interest. 'Historic' features such as knots and arbours began appearing in manor house gardens; Gertrude Jekyll regained her former status as the Queen Victoria of gardening, giving the herbaceous border a new lease of life.

In 1971 the National Trust undertook its first full-scale garden restoration, at Westbury Court, underpinned by meticulous academic research. Private owners, however, could have fun delving into the bran tub of history to make appealing pieces of garden theatre. At The Menagerie in Northamptonshire, the garden became a playful skit on eighteenth-century themes; West Green in Hampshire was decked out with a water staircase and nymphaeum by Prince Charles's favourite architect, Quinlan Terry; at The Laskett in Herefordshire, Sir Roy Strong and his wife Julia Trevelyan Oman made full use of her skills as a set designer to make a garden that wove a celebration of all things Elizabethan into a narrative of their lives. For sheer bravura though, Woolbeding in West Sussex remains unsurpassed. Formal garden rooms intricately planted by designer Lanning Roper in the 1970s give way to a thrill-a-minute pleasure ground with a ruined abbey, hermit's hut, Chinese bridge, grotto, Gothick summer-house and Italianate secret garden. Developed from the start of the new century by Julian and Isabel Bannerman, it is an exercise in pure fantasy, done with delicious lightness of spirit.

The Gothick summer-house at Woolbeding in West Sussex, presiding over an area of garden theatrically re-imagined as selected highlights of an eighteenth-century pleasure ground.

Utterly different, though in its way equally theatrical, was the garden made by filmmaker Derek Jarman on a shingle beach in the shadow of the Dungeness B nuclear power station. Made of stones, flotsam and jetsam and whatever salt-tolerant plants would survive among the pebbles, it turned the idea of what a garden could be on its head – a dying man's audacious two fingers to centuries of cooing over the pastoral. While it spawned countless cheery beach-themed gardens made without a second's deeper thought, Prospect Cottage was also widely understood as a piece of art, in the eighteenth-century manner. This is true also of the work of Kim Wilkie, best known as a master of land sculpture. Drawing on environmental artists such as Andy Goldsworthy and Richard Long as much as Claremont or Studley Royal, his spare and beautiful landscapes have been described as 'inhabited works of art'.

The late twentieth century saw a satisfying resurgence of the garden as a vehicle for ideas, although the greatest of them, Little Sparta and The Garden of Cosmic Speculation, are both in Scotland and therefore outside the scope of this book. Cosmic speculations, however, have informed gardens in the Cotswolds (Througham Court) and Devon (Plaz Metaxu), while in the 1980s the octogenarian Geoffrey Jellicoe (1900–96) turned his mind to the workings of the subconscious. Trained as an architect, he made his name with a study of Italian Renaissance gardens before turning to Modernism. Later in life, informed by his reading of Jung, he strove to make gardens that would express his sense of man's place in the universe. He is probably best known for his sparkling musical water staircase at Shute House in Dorset, the culmination of an allegorical journey from a woodland

'A garden is a treasure hunt, the plants the paperchase.' In his garden composed of shingle, salt-tolerant plants and combings from the beach, Derek Jarman showed that beauty could be made in the most inhospitable surroundings.

spring, or for his monument to John F. Kennedy at Runnymede. But his most profound work was at Sutton Place in Surrey: a vast allegory of creation, life and aspiration that begins in a foetus-shaped lake and ends at a pure white wall of Carrara marble reflected in a dark mirror pool. Beyond enclosing hedges of yew lies sunny parkland, managed for wildlife. In this poetic vision of death lapped about by teeming life, Jellicoe eloquently presents Jung's conviction of the ultimate unity of all existence.

The simplicity and elegance of this garden showed how the Modernist thinking that failed to take hold in the 1930s might finally find acceptance, if only in furnishing serene interludes in more traditional gardens, as at Knightshayes

The gleaming marble White Wall at Sutton Place in Surrey appears to be floating on the water. Based on a 1938 maquette by Ben Nicholson, it was installed by Jellicoe in 1983.

in Devon or the 1999 water garden at Kiftsgate in Gloucestershire. In small town plots, however, a pared-down urban chic became the norm. It was a garden at the Chelsea Flower Show that ultimately persuaded the great British public that a minimalist modern garden could be a thing of beauty: Christopher Bradley-Hole's Latin Garden in 1997, all gleaming white stone and sparsely planted gravel, finally offered a corrective to the chintzy romanticism that remained the dominant taste. Calm, purely proportioned compositions of luminous clarity, Bradley-Hole's gardens reveal how space and light are as important to the garden as flowers and trees, and how a strict geometry can provide a showcase for nature rather than oppress it.

Twenty-four gilded bronze Philodendron leaves, designed by Simon Alliston, sway gently on their stainless-steel stems in the Water Garden at Kiftsgate Court in Gloucestershire.

New Perennials

In 1994 Christopher Bradley-Hole attended a now legendary symposium at Kew, introducing British gardeners to the very different ways herbaceous perennials were being employed in Europe, particularly in Holland and Germany. The 'New Perennials' movement, as it came to be known, was to transform the planting of the English garden. Its origin could be traced back to 1930s Germany, where pioneering nurseryman Karl Foerster began to promote a naturalistic style, massing grasses and species perennials, replicating the way plant communities grew in the wild. The style was widely adopted by German public parks as it required so little maintenance, and traditional lawn and bedding arrangements gave way to mass-plantings of colourful perennials. It was also taken up in the United States, exploiting that country's rich resource of beautiful native prairie plants.

This non-interventionist approach to planting brought together several strands in the English garden. The organic movement, kick-started by Lady Eve Balfour in 1943, had gained ground in the 1970s with the pioneering work of Dame Miriam Rothschild. Concerned by the impact of intensive agriculture on our flowers and insect life, she clothed her house in ivy, replaced her flower beds with native flowering shrubs and turned her lawns and tennis court over to wild flowers. An organic farmer, she also encouraged wild flowers to thrive in her fields, and eventually marketed a seed-mix called 'Farmer's Nightmare'. Her experiments encouraged designers like Dan Pearson to include both wildflower meadows and

The beauty of the New Perennials style is that it builds seasonality and change into the garden, allowing tidal movements of colour through the loose drifts of planting, as here at Pensthorpe in Norfolk.

Right: Wildflower meadows have become increasingly popular over the last half-century. It does not, however, take long to find out that this is an extremely demanding form of gardening.

Below right: Gardening for wildlife, regarded as slightly batty in the 1970s, has become mainstream, and now forms a major plank in the government's ten-year National Pollinator Strategy, launched in 2014.

native, meadowy planting in their schemes, while landowners from the Prince of Wales to the National Trust hastened to introduce or reinstate flower-rich meadows.

This went hand in hand with the efforts of ecologist Chris Baines to turn our gardens into sanctuaries for increasingly embattled wildlife. In 1979 he created the first wildlife garden on TV, followed six years later by a show garden at Chelsea, with plants lovingly grown by the Weed Research Station at Kidlington. The RHS was baffled, but the public loved it. Now wildlife gardening has become mainstream, it is hard to remember that when Baines began his campaign, any wild thing that appeared in the garden was regarded as either pest, disease or weed.

While not specifically organic, the self-sustaining New Perennials style was designed to require minimal input. It was championed in Britain by writer and nurseryman Noel Kingsbury, who, noting the limitations of native wildflower meadows, looked further afield for inspiration, and found it in Dutch designer and nurseryman Piet Oudolf. Oudolf had set up his nursery expressly to trial new material for his designs, experimenting with plants from as far afield as Siberia and Japan, and introducing new genera that had not previously been considered fit for the garden, such as *Eupatorium*, *Filipendula*, *Sanguisorba* and *Veronicastrum*. A 'Best in Show' (collaborating with Arne Maynard) at Chelsea Flower Show in 2000 introduced his work to a rapturous British public, and was followed by gardens at Bury Court in Hampshire, Scampston Hall in North Yorkshire, at Trentham in Staffordshire and the Hauser and Wirth Gallery in Somerset. While his style is developing all the time, broadly it consists of large irregular blocks or matrices of summer-flowering perennials interspersed with grasses, usually cut through with paths and glades to encourage a very direct and immersive experience of the plants. These are chosen to offer the longest possible season of interest, and left standing after flowering, so that their seed heads can be enjoyed through the winter, especially after frost. The disadvantage of the style is the blank period between cutting them back in February and regrowth in May – which gardeners with deep pockets can make good with bulbs. None the less, it is proving immensely adaptable, used in inventive ways by Christopher Bradley-Hole, Dan Pearson and Tom Stuart-Smith in particular. It also overlaps with the work on sustainable planting done at Sheffield University by James Hitchmough and Nigel Dunnett, the brains (with Sarah Price) behind London's breathtaking 2012 Olympic Park, and with Hitchmough's experimental 'climate change' borders at the Oxford Botanic Garden.

So we leave this book at an exciting time for the history of the English garden. After nigh on two hundred years of obsessing about colour, this new method

The New Perennials movement looked for beauty where gardeners had not previously seen it, promoting genera such as *Veronicastrum* (above), *Filipendula* and *Sanguisorba* for their colour, robustness and enduring winter form.

of planting places far more emphasis on texture and form. We are not leaving formality behind, but finding new ways of expressing it, in grids of planting, or more adventurous use of hedges and topiary, or in deploying new plants, like swathes of grasses, as formal elements. (Scampston Hall, for example, has a ground plan as geometric as anything by London and Wise.) We are learning new ways of measuring time in the garden, finding the beauty in death and decay. And we are learning to respect our fellow travellers on the planet, gardening in ways that won't do them (or us) more harm.

It's much harder work, of course, gardening like this. Rather than treating our plants as merely colours in a paintbox, we must know so much more about them – their origins, their requirements, their relative vigour – in order to combine them successfully. (Many of us are already returning, gratefully, to easy-going shrubs.) And it's hard work finding alternatives to peat, or pesticides, polluting concrete or cheap imported Indian stone in order to make the rest of our gardens equally sustainable. But English gardeners, as Thomas Tusser affirmed 500 years ago, have always been canny and resourceful. Extremes of weather, political isolation, economic depression – we have survived them all before, and we have made gardens out of all we have experienced. Our gardens are the very best of us.

At Scampston Hall in North Yorkshire, Piet Oudolf demonstrated that the new planting style could work perfectly within a formal ground plan, as in this inspired re-imagining of the grass parterre using wavy stripes of *Molinia caerula*.

Select bibliography

Adams, William Howard, *Nature Perfected*, Abbeville Press, 1991

Anderton, Stephen, *Christopher Lloyd: His Life at Great Dixter*, Chatto & Windus, 2010

Batey, Mavis and Lambert, David, *The English Garden Tour: A View into the Past,* John Murray, 1990

Berridge, Vanessa, *The Princess's Garden, Royal Intrigue and the Untold Story of Kew,* Amberley, 2017

Bisgrove, Richard, *The National Trust Book of the English Garden,* Viking, 1990

Bisgrove, Richard, *William Robinson, The Wild Gardener*, Frances Lincoln, 2008

Bradley Hole, Christopher, *The Minimalist Garden*, Mitchell Beazley, 1999

Brown, Jane, *Gardens of a Golden Afternoon,* Allen Lane, 1982

Brown, Jane, *The English Garden through the 20th Century,* Garden Art Press, 1999

Brown, Jane, *The Modern Garden,* Thames & Hudson, 2000

Brown, Jane, *Vita's Other World,* Penguin, 1987

Buchan, Ursula, *The English Garden*, Frances Lincoln, 2006

Buchan, Ursula, *A Green and Pleasant Land,* Hutchinson, 2013

Buchan, Ursula, *Garden People: Valerie Finnis and the Golden Age of Gardening,* Thames & Hudson, 2007

Campbell, Gordon, *The Hermit in the Garden: From Imperial Rome to Garden Gnome,* Oxford University Press, 2013

Campbell, Susan, *A History of Kitchen Gardening*, Frances Lincoln, 2005

Campbell-Culver, Maggie, *The Origin of Plants,* Headline, 2001

Chatto, Beth, *Beth Chatto's Gravel Garden*, Frances Lincoln, 2000

Chatto, Beth, *The Damp Garden,* J M Dent, 1982

Cooper, G & Taylor, G, *Paradise Transformed,* Monacelli, 1997

Davies, J, *The Victorian Kitchen Garden,* BBC Books, 1987

Dixon Hunt, John & Willis, Peter, eds., *The Genius of the Place,* MIT, 1988

Ellacombe, Canon, *In a Gloucestershire Garden,* Edwards Arnold, 1895

Elliott, Brent, *Victorian Gardens,* Batsford, 1986

Farrar, Linda, *Ancient Roman Gardens*, Sutton Publishing, 1998

Farrar, Reginald, *The Rock Garden*, Thomas Nelson, undated

Fearnley-Whittingstall, Jane, *The Garden, An English Love Affair*, Ted Smart, 2002

Felus, Kate, *The Secret Life of the Georgian Garden: Beautiful Objects and Agreeable Retreats,* I.B. Tauris, 2016

Fish, Marjorie, *We Made a Garden,* Collingridge, 1956

Fish, Marjorie, *Ground Cover Plants,* Collingridge, 1964

Fort, Tom, *The Grass is Greener: Our Love Affair with the Lawn,* HarperCollins, 2000

Gardiner, Juliet, *From the Bomb to the Beatles,* Collins & Brown, 1999

Girouard, Mark, *Life in the English Country House,* Yale, 1978

Green, David, *Blenheim Palace,* Jarrold Publishing, 1950 (2000 edition)

Hanmer, Thomas, *The Garden Book of Sir Thomas Hanmer* (1933), Clwyd, 1999

Hayward, Alison, *Norah Lindsay, The Life and Art of a Garden Designer,* Frances Lincoln, 2007

Henderson, Paula, *The Tudor House and Garden*, Yale University Press, 2005

Hibberd, Shirley, *Rustic Adornments for Homes of Taste*, ed Century, 1987

Hobhouse, Penelope, *Plants in Garden History*, Pavilion, 1992

Hobhouse, Penelope, *The Story of Gardening*, Dorling Kindersley, 2002

Horwood, Catherine, *Gardening Women: Their Stories from 1600 to the Present,* Virago, 2010

Hoyles, Martin, *Gardeners' Delight. Gardening Books from 1560–1960,* Pluto Press, 1995

Hoyles, Martin, *Bread and Roses: Gardening Books from 1560–1960,* Pluto Press, 1995

Hoyles, Martin, *The Story of Gardening*, Journeyman Press, 1991

Jacques, David, *Georgian Gardens, The Reign of Nature*, Batsford, 1983

Jekyll, Gertrude, *Colour in the Flower Gzarden*, Bloomsbury, 1896

Jellicoe, Geoffrey and Susan, Goode, Patrick & Lancaster, Michael, eds., *The Oxford Companion to Gardens,* OUP, 1991

Jennings, Anne, *Medieval Gardens*, English Heritage, 2004

Jones, Barbara, *Follies and Grottoes*, Constable, 1974

Lacey, Stephen, *Gardens of the National Trust*, Pavilion, 2016

Laird, Mark, *The Flowering of the Landscape Garden. English Pleasure Grounds 1720–1800,* University of Pennsylvania Press, 1999

Landsberg, Sylvia, *The Medieval Garden*, British Museum Press, 1995

Lasdun, Susan, *The English Park: Royal, Private & Public,* The Vendome Press, 1992

Lloyd, Christopher, *Other People's Gardens,* Viking 1995

Morgan, Joan & Richards, Alison, *A Paradise out of a Common Field,* Harper & Row, 1990

Pavord, Anna, *Landskipping*, Bloomsbury, 2016

Pavord, Anna, *The Naming of Names*, Bloomsbury, 2005

Pearson, Graham, *Lawrence Johnston, The Creator of Hidcote*, Hidcote Books, 2015

Potter, Jennifer, *The Rose,* Callisto, 2010

Quest Ritson, Charles, *The English Garden, A Social History,* Viking, 2001

Richardson, Tim, *The Arcadian Friends: Inventing the English Landscape Garden*, Bantam Press, 2007

Richardson, Tim, *The English Garden in the Twentieth Century,* Aurum Press, 2005

Richardson, Tim & Kingsbury, Noel, *Vista: The Culture and Politics of Gardens,* Frances Lincoln, 2005

Robinson, William, *The English Flower Garden*, Bloomsbury, 1996

Rohde, Eleanour Sinclair, *The Story of the Garden,* Medici Society, 1933

Rutherford, Sarah, *Capability Brown and his Landscape Gardens*, National Trust, 2016

Sackville-West, Vita, *In Your Garden* (2 vols), Oxenwood Press, 1996

Schama, Simon, *A History of Britain (3 vols),* BBC, 2001

Shulman, Nicola, A Rage for Rock Gardening, Short Books, 2002

Spens, Michael, *Gardens of the Mind: The Genius of Geoffrey Jellicoe*, Antique Collectors Club, 1992

Strong, Roy, *The Renaissance Garden in England,* Thames & Hudson, 1984

Strong, Roy, *The Spirit of Britain: A Narrative History of the Arts,* Hutchinson, 1999

Strong, Roy, *The Story of Britain,* Pimlico, 1996

Tankard, J & Wood, M, *Gertrude Jekyll at Munstead Wood*, Pimpernel, 2015

Thacker, Christopher, *The Genius of Gardening,* Weidenfeld and Nicholson, 1994

Thacker, Christopher, *A History of Gardens,* Croom Helm, 1979

Walpole, Horace, *The History of the Modern Taste in Gardening,* Ursus Press edition, 1995

Waterson, Merlin, *The Servants' Hall,* Routledge & Kegan Paul, 1980

Whalley, Robin, *The Great Edwardian Gardens of Harold Peto,* Aurum Press, 2007

Wilkinson, Anne, *The Victorian Gardener,* Sutton Publishing, 2006

Willes, Margaret, *The Gardens of the British Working Class*, Yale University Press, 2014

Willes, Margaret, *The Making of the English Gardener*, Yale University Press, 2011

Williamson, Tom, *Polite Landscapes: Gardens and Society in Eighteenth-century England,* Country House, 1998

Wilkie, Kim, *Led by the Land,* Frances Lincoln, 2012

Wilson, C. Anne, *The Country House Kitchen Garden 1600–1950*, Sutton Publishing, 1998

Plus numerous NT property guides

GARDEN HISTORY JOURNALS

28:2 Crane, Eva and Walker, Penelope, *The History of Beekeeping in English Gardens,* 2000

30:1 Meir, Jennifer M, *Development of a Natural Style in Designed Landscapes between 1730 and 1760: the English Midland and the work of Sanderson Miller and Lancelot Brown,* 2002

31:2 Phibbs, John, *The Englishness of Capability Brown*; Fry, Carole, *Spanning the Political Devide: Neo-Palladianism and the Early 18th Century Landscape,* 2003

33:1 Symes, Michael, *Flintwork, Freedom and Fantasy: The Landscape at West Wycombe Park, Buckinghamshire,* 2005

34:1 Felus, Kate, *Boats and Boating in the designed Landscape, 1720–1820,* 2006*

34:2 Nicky Smith, *Lodge Park and Charles Bridgeman, Master of Incomprehensible Vastness,* 2006

35: Supplement 2 Elliott, Paul, Watkins, Charles & Daniels, Stephen, 'Combining Science with Recreation and Pleasure': Cultural Geographies of 19th century Arboretums; *William Barron and 19th century British Arboriculture: Evergreens in Victorian Industrializing Society;* Elliott, Brent, *From the Arboretum to the Woodland Garden*; Sophie Piebenga and Simon Toomer, *Westonbirt Arboretum: from Private, 19th century estate collection to National Arboretum,* 2007

36:1 Rawcliffe, Carol, *Delectable Sights and Fragrant Smelles: Gardens and Health in late medieval and early modern England,* 2008*

38:2 Bartos, Jim, *The Spiritual Orchard: God, Garden and the Landscape in 17th century England before the Restoration,* 2010

PRINCIPAL ONLINE RESOURCES

Parks and Gardens UK

British History online

Acknowledgements

I should like to thank the many people who have assisted me in the preparation of this book, notably the many incredibly helpful and well informed gardeners, property managers and volunteers at National Trust and other gardens, too numerous to list here, who have been so generous with their time and knowledge. This book is respectfully dedicated to them, to all the gardeners who keep these places beautiful for our delight, and to my faithful dog, who spent so many tedious hours waiting for me in National Trust car parks. I should also like to thank Richard Wheeler for keeping me on the historical straight and narrow, Claire Masset for her prompt and stalwart assistance with every aspect of this book, Jan Kingdom for her helpful reading of the text and constant encouragement, and my children for their patience as domestic life steadily unravelled. I gratefully acknowledge my debt to the UK Parks and Gardens blog – the most entertaining as well as most informative of sources. Above all, I thank Ursula Buchan for bringing me to this project, and for the unfailing support she has given me all the way through it. She has found time when I knew she had none, been unstinting in sharing her wisdom and experience, and brought her customary elegance of mind to bear on my text, to my very great benefit. No one could have had a more kind or generous mentor, and I am profoundly grateful.

Picture credits

Index